SCOUTING
FOR MOYES

SCOUTING FOR MOYES

The Diary of a Football Scout

Les Padfield

SPORTS
BOOKS

Published by SportsBooks Ltd

Copyright: Les Padfield
October 2010

SportsBooks Limited
PO Box 422
Cheltenham
GL50 2YN
United Kingdom
Tel: 01242 256755
Fax: 0560 3108126
email   randall@sportsbooks.ltd.uk
Website   www.sportsbooks.ltd.uk

Cover designed by Alan Hunns.

Cover illustration: Miroslaw Pieprzyk, iStockphoto

A CIP catalogue record for this book is available from the British Library.

ISBN 9781899807 95 6

Printed by Thomson Litho Ltd, East Kilbride, Scotland

About the author

Born and bred in Bethnal Green. Wasted a grammar school education by infatuation with sport. Apart from games excelled only in woodwork and Religious Studies so advised to become an undertaker. Sang at Reggie Kray's wedding. Worked in Truman's Brewery. Played football with Harry Redknapp for East London – I remember him, he can't remember me! – then London, then at Orient and Millwall before getting bored by commitment and going to York to become a PE teacher. Got bored again and taught English. Wrote poems for fun which someone published. Wrote songs which no-one sang. Played, coached and refereed football until too old to run. Whilst waiting to be discovered became a football scout with mighty Stockport County, progressing and regressing until arriving at Bolton in 2007. Have been asked to speak at functions on the topic 'My meteoric rise to mediocrity'. Still waiting to be discovered.

Contents

ACKNOWLEDGEMENTS

Thanks are due to the following people who have helped in various ways in the compilation of this book. No blame for any mistakes, inaccuracies, imaginative embellishments or complete desperate falsifications attaches to any of them.

Justyn Barnes; Keith Burt; Vas and Lisa Christo-doulou; Terry Darracott; Steve Dawson; Sven-Goran Eriksson; Tom Graham; Alan Harper; Colin Harvey; Steve Jenkins; Steve Leatherbarrow; Cliff Portwood; Vince Nacey; Greg Wildigg; Robert Wilson and Livingston FC ; friends and family members.

FOREWORD

Les Padfield has worked as a scout for me at five different clubs over the years, going through highs and lows, promotions and rescue acts, providing team assessments, player reports, suggesting who I might and might not buy. I've told him regularly that if he'd done a better job I might be England manager now. He's told me that if I'd paid him more he would have. Having read this book he'll be lucky to get any payment at all in the future.

Scouting is an aspect of football that gets little coverage, but a knowledgeable, reliable and conscientious scout can be a great asset to a club. I look forward to finding one! Stories in this book illustrate some of the ups and downs of the job as well as giving some insights below the surface of this crazy, compelling, chaotic game called Football. The chapters are short enough to hold the attention of even an Australian and when one doesn't work it's quickly subbed by another. Ideal to pick up when the ITV adverts interrupt the coverage. Enjoy.

Gary Megson

Chapter 1

AUGUST IS APPROACHING

The long, empty, aimless days of late May and June and July are receding. The boring bare-top barbecues, the warm walks by the rippling river, the compensating thrills of Test match cricket are turning tail as the spectre of winter winds rises up on the horizon. The temperature is dropping. A new season is beginning. Meaning and purpose are returning to life.

Bolton have stayed up.

Megson is still in a job, at least for another four or five games. Colin Harvey, an Everton legend, remains the chief scout, though he still refuses to employ an interpreter of Scouse. And the lovely Liz, who organises tickets and I'm certain really runs the club, still brightens up days with her cheery Lancashire twang at the end of the phone.

I've devoured the fixture lists, highlighting my likely match reports. Holidays and trips away for the next nine months need to be planned carefully to coincide with fallow periods. Family weddings, anniversaries, christenings have to be negotiated with tact. Funerals may prove more difficult. The newspapers are gradually tilting the balance back from golf and tennis and cricket to the oncoming season. I relocate my notebooks, my diagrams, my player database, my long-johns, scour the internet for the latest transfers and sackings and gossip. I can feel the tension in my toes already. The sap is rising. The virgin season waits to be disrobed...

Here I come!

Chapter 2

SCHOOL

'Sir, sir, is it true you're a scout for a Premiership team?'

I've only been at this school for three days, my sixth post-retirement job, and suddenly my street-cred is in the ascendancy.

'Mr Evans says that you're a football scout, sir. Is it true?'

I smile and nod. 'That's right Chris, I am.'

'Which team, sir? Man U or Liverpool or Chelsea?'

'Er, no.'

'Arsenal?'

'Actually, it's Bolton. Bolton Wanderers.'

I see the curtain of disappointment slowly descending over the group of faces that have gathered round expectantly.

'Oh,' Chris says politely before turning away with visible indifference.

'But I do get to see some really good matches,' I add quickly, trying to rescue some credibility. Unsuccessfully.

Another voice chimes in. 'Do you support Bolton then, sir?'

'No,' I laugh desperately, 'I wish I did. I support a London team.'

'West Ham?'

'Lower division.'

There's a brief pause for thought. 'Charlton? Millwall?'

'Actually it's Orient. Leyton Orient.' There's a hiatus in proceedings. No point in saying any more. A helpful voice chimes in: 'My mate's dad used to support Leyton Orient.' I am thankful for small mercies. 'But he said they were crap and now he supports West Ham.' My lips are squeezed tightly together to hold back the tears.

'So, you work for Bolton and support Leyton Orient?' I can hear the mixture of contempt and disbelief in Chris's voice.

'Well, you know Chris, win some, lose some, as they say,' as the crowd begins to drift away. A parting voice adds, 'Don't win too many with those two though, sir.'

I'm a marked man.

It could be worse. A few years ago it would have been, 'Er, Stockport County', with attractive fixtures like Barnet v Rochdale to watch and invite a guest to. Spells at Southampton, then Stoke City, West Brom and Nottingham Forest – all beacons on the path to the Reebok.

After a few weeks, when I've taken Billy Gleeson to watch Arsenal play his beloved Chelsea, the kids come round and start talking to me again. It's the magic of the universal game. There must be a few places in the world, like Kashmir or the Shetland Islands or the whole of North America, where the ice can't be broken by a chip to the head or mention of Ronaldinho, but with a few horribly balanced people as exceptions, the Esperanto of sport is an open channel to communication in most continents and certainly most schools.

Even the headmaster of St Olave's tries to get in on the act. He's really a rugby man, though he has boyhood affinities to Oxford United, but talk of Arsenal and Tottenham and the like has made him keen to go to a match. I promise to take him sometime, enduring a few sarcastic staffroom comments about brownie points in the process.

Shortly after, I am invited to the Governors' Garden Party.

Chapter 3

THE LIONS' DEN

2 October 1996

It started with a chance meeting one Wednesday night at Millwall.

My mate Bob, an ex-pro and a feted coach down in Sussex, had managed to get a couple of tickets for the Millwall game against high-flying Stockport. It was a while since I'd been to a game, the mania of the '60s and '70s having been watered down to almost invisibility by the cynicism of Leeds United, the fences that turned grounds into prisons and the pathetic performances of the England side for thirty years with their mediocre players who seemed a million miles away from Hurst, Moore and co. But it was a freebie and Bob was driving.

I was amazed, though I shouldn't have been. I remembered the old Den and its clientele – I'd even played there before going off to college. Since time immemorial the Millwall faithful have been as pleasant and welcoming to visitors as Baghdad would be if George Bush appeared there as a stand-up comic. A new and more luxurious setting seemed not to have impressed many into improving Neanderthal manners one iota, adding to my conviction that Communism is rubbish. I was not surprised to find the same degree of hostility and stupidity that I recalled of old. But tonight we were in the hospitality section, not on the terraces behind the goals. And it was the guys in suits and ties, having just got off the train from the City, who were doing even more effing and blinding

11

– or maybe just using more extensive adjectives to describe everything that moved outside and sometimes inside a blue shirt. These weren't dockers any more. The new breed of Millwall higher thinkers probably worked in solicitors' offices or banks or would have been trading millions up in town in ways that few understood. Including them, I suspect. Which is why they could afford hospitality prices.

It was a good game. Best of all, Stockport scored a late goal to win the match 4-3. I was pleased because they deserved it, having played some really good football. But it was more pleasing to see Dean and Darren and their suited mates gutted. I quietly wished them a bad day at the office in the morning.

In the aftermath of tea and sausage rolls I saw a face from the past. John Sainty was a Tottenham player in the days when I thought about becoming the next Pele and gave me some good and ultimately useless advice. He was now chief scout at Stockport and was sitting with his counterpart from Preston. In ten minutes of chat, he claimed unconvincingly that he remembered me, found out that I had long since given up trying to play and suggested that I offer my services to Preston, who didn't have a scout in the London area. David Moyes was the manager and his chief scout, who never even told me his name, was looking out for one.

I was signed up. As quickly and as simply as that. Without references, recommendations or money changing hands, it was a done deal. I was scouting for Moyes.

My brief, I was told, was to report on teams that Preston would be playing, but more invitingly to go out and 'find the club a few good Roy of the Rovers'. (The Chief Scout and I obviously went back a few years with our taste in comics.) Now I was Scouting for Roys! The incongruity of Roy of the Rovers playing for Preston North End was not one I dwelt on. A foot in the door was enough. No training, no handbook, use your knowledge and common sense, he said, and if you're no good we'll boot you out. Fair enough.

My reward was one and sometimes two tickets to a match, a club coat that he said he'd send me and 30p a mile expenses. And a Preston North End pass. Which was the clincher! Bob had done some occasional work for Newcastle and I'd always secretly coveted the pass that he produced to get tickets, like a copper getting onto a bus with a flick of a warrant card. Now, I'd have my own!

It would actually be my second, but the first that was valid. A few months before I had had a bet with Bob that I could blag my way into a ground as a foreign scout. By chance, I was going to Coventry about that time to visit my brother-in-law and we put a life-changing 50p on the table that I could get in by impersonating a scout from Werder Bremen. Having sent a spoof fax, I made a Werder ID from an old credit card, using bits from a club magazine that my elder son had brought back from a year of studying in Bremen. 'Hans Jurgen Witt' duly turned up at the ground, accompanied by No. 2 son, and, with a stunning German accent, asked for and received two Directors' Box tickets for the game against West Ham. Convinced that we were going to be rumbled and arrested at any second, (my elder solicitor son informing me that we were 'gaining a pecuniary advantage by deception' with frightening vocabulary) or that someone would come up and begin speaking German to me, I informed Nick not to show any emotion if West Ham – his team of course! – scored, and not to speak audibly without turning his Ws into Vs. It didn't occur to me that we might have spoken in our native language if we'd both been from Deutschland, so my two 'Zat vas a gut goal' were ridiculous attempts to sound authentic as he sat on his hands and his team scored twice to draw 2-2.

Reminiscent of a teenager embarking on his first fling I was briefly starry-eyed at the prospect of being involved with a professional club again. But also like a youthful romance it lasted less than a fortnight. Out of the blue John Sainty wrote to me to say that he'd agreed with the Preston people for me to transfer my affections to Stockport, who had just lost their London scout. John would therefore like me to work with him and as Stockport were top of the league he thought I'd have a better and more productive time. Goodbye Moyes: hello Dave Jones. I began to feel like a cork on the sea but in an atmosphere of blissful naiveté I concurred, convinced, if I needed to be, by the fact that he asked me to do a team report the following Tuesday. I was on my way, and what a game to start with: Millwall versus Shrewsbury!

Six weeks later I had my own ID from Stockport, disappointed that Bob was not quite as overwhelmed as me.

Chapter 4

PALACE v TOTTENHAM

22 January 2005

At first, it felt strange, almost unnatural, to be sitting down, watching a game from the Directors' Box, dressed in jacket and tie.

The real place to watch a football match is, of course, standing on a stone terrace, stuck in a corner behind a goal, pressed against a metal crash barrier with Man Mountain and probably his brother in front of you blocking out most of the field. To make it a classic it needs to take place on a cold, rainy Tuesday night in February when your team are bottom of the league and 3-0 down at half-time. Exquisite!

Picking up tickets by simply saying your name and club, then entering an area where there are other jackets and ties, with tea and maybe sandwiches or cakes or biscuits at half-time, took a bit of getting used to.

But not too much.

Now if you ask scouts what they expect from a club, most will probably reply that if they're provided with a decent seat and a team-sheet, then they can do their job. Anything else is a bonus. But the bonus becomes the norm on most occasions. Clubs will vary in their hospitality, from providing a two-course meal with wine, to an array of cakes and sandwiches, to simply tea and coffee and biscuits. And most will offer something in the form of a welcome to visiting scouts.

Though not at Crystal Palace.

The ticket admits you to the Executive Lounge and informs you of a dress code that prohibits jeans and trainers, though quite why isn't clear as the lounge turns out to be a cross between a transport café and a local pub. It's invariably crowded and seats are at a premium. Little red-coated Les is the one cheery face that greets you, if he sees you, with, 'Hello, you back again!' even though you haven't been here for a year. It's Les, though, who will be your only chance of getting a team-sheet. Sweet talk him. Your ticket informs you that you are in Row ZZ, and if this sounds like the back of beyond, it is. Even in the height of summer the temperature in this stand approaches freezing as the wind blows through straight from Siberia. Row ZZ is the very back row and by the time you are seated there the ball becomes virtually impossible to see if anyone hits it over head height. At half-time the world and his dog squeeze down through the one exit back into the lounge and queue for a plastic cup of tea that isn't quite ready. It appears that the makers of the beverage haven't yet fathomed that half-time comes after about 45 minutes, every game, so when the first punters arrive down the steps they jump up in a feverish panic and put the kettle on.

Today Palace were entertaining – in the loosest sense of the word – Spurs. Dragging myself away from the magnetic ambience of the Executive Lounge, I took my seat in Row ZZ to soak up the pre-match atmosphere. It was a quarter to three. By ten to I was shivering. At five minutes to the hour, the cold, plastic, vacant seat next to me was filled.

It's Sven. Come to watch Defoe, no doubt. Sven, sitting in Row ZZ!

I shook him by the hand and greeted him like a long-lost friend and we began to chat, but I couldn't help stating my disbelief that they put the England manager right up here, expecting him of course to queue for his cuppa with the rest of the mob at half-time. I've never worked out if there is such a place as a Directors' Box at this ground, but there had to be something better than this! He was very gracious though and uncritical. He liked going to all grounds, he said, though he let on that Anfield was his favourite. He was also patient and good-humoured when plagued by dozens of irritating people sitting nearby coming up or sending their kids to ask for his autograph or a mobile phone snapshot with Johnny next to him. He refused none, though more time was spent writing his name than writing anything about Jermain. With enormous difficulty and fantastically admirable self-control I refrained from telling him about Defoe, which players he should be looking at, and just how the England team should be organised to play forthcoming matches. I also avoided mentioning the night I phoned Radio 5 expressing my desire to punch his lights out, having heard him state 'I tink ve have learned some useful tings' after our defeat to Australia – Australia!!! – surely our national sporting nadir, worse even than losing to the Yanks. He needed to bleed like an Englishman!

Let bygones be bygones.

Palace trounced Spurs, who were remarkably inept, 3-0. Defoe had a crap game and noticeably wasn't included in Sven's next team. By 70 minutes the Swede had had enough. It was colder here than in Stockholm and he was beginning to slur his words. He wished me good afternoon and made his way home to bed.

Not before he'd signed my team-sheet though, and had a photo with me next to him.

Chapter 5

JULY

For many football addicts a new year doesn't start on January 1st but somewhere around early August. And just as many might take a few sombre and solemn moments, as Big Ben chimes out the old, to wonder what the next twelve months will bring. So, in the occasional summer sunshine, as the first balls are kicked in real earnest, thousands embark upon the nine-month marathon which, without a single doubt, will bring to every supporter its share of madness, exhilaration, anger, despair, surprise, frustration – even occasional enjoyment.

One of the regrets about the modern Premiership, in many people's views, is the predictability of the top echelons of the league. Go back a few decades and there was never a certainty that a dark horse wouldn't spring a surprise and run off with the old Div. 1 Championship: Derby County, Forest, Ipswich in their first ever season in the top flight, QPR very nearly...

This season? Well, we all know it's going to be Man U or Chelsea, with Arsenal or Liverpool on the rails, but apart from Man City, who are trying to buy the world, it's certain that no-one will have a prayer of getting into the top places. What a pity! One of the great things about sport is its unpredictability, so when the race is between five as opposed to 21 teams, something vital is lost. I heard Stan Collymore commentating on Wigan v Liverpool last season say that this was the kind of game that Liverpool should win ten times out of ten. Well Stan, given that commentators and pundits talk rubbish for much of the time, if you're right about that then there's no real point in turning up, especially if you're a Wigan fan. People who are sometimes accused of being 'anti-Man U' or 'anti-Chelsea' are, I suspect, more 'anti-monopoly'. And on the other side of the coin, followers of these teams nowadays think that success is theirs by right, that to finish fourth in the toughest league in the world is a failure and grounds for changing the manager.

What else is sure about the coming season? Life's three certainties – death, taxes and the sacking of managers on a fairly regular basis after a bad run of four or five games. I wonder who will be the first big name to go. Come May, will Gary Megson still be at Bolton? More importantly, will I still be working for them?

By late July Bolton have bought Sean Davis from Portsmouth, a player I flagged up over a year ago. The wheels turn slowly it seems. Robinson has come from West Brom – another solid full-back I saw when he was at Watford – Ricketts from Hull, and now Zat Knight from Villa. Knight's always worried me: an accident waiting to happen. Even when I watched him at Fulham reserves he had all the attributes for a top player, but once or twice a game he'd switch off and do something daft. Do that in the Premiership this season, Zat and you'll be very popular. But Bolton have signed no-one that I can see is going to knock in goals, and that was their biggest problem last season. £11 million Elmander notched up five during the season – not exactly a great return – and a total of forty-one as a final count meant that lots of games were won with low scores.

Can't get them to go for David Bentley, who's still lounging around unwanted at Spurs. He'd be my No. 1 target but Gary doesn't seem to like him – thinks he's a lad. Just after Gary had got West Brom into the Premiership I tried to push him to get Bentley on loan from Arsenal. Unsuccessfully.

'Gary, I don't usually expostulate about reserve team players, but this lad Bentley...' I'm hoping the use of a long word will persuade him.

'Seen him. What's his best position?'

'Right side, left side, play him where you will.'

'Got an attitude though.'

'Got talent, too. Too good for the reserves and Arsenal will let him out on a year's loan.'

'Too dodgy. I need players who are going to keep us in the Premiership.'

'Well you could do a lot worse than...' The line goes dead. Bentley goes to Norwich and then Blackburn and then into the England squad. When I mention our conversation to Gary, which I do as often as possible, he jokes that he didn't like his haircut at the time. So no Bentley for Bolton it seems. I ask why they didn't approach Michael Owen and Colin says he is injured too often. We shall see! A Nigerian player I suggested, Kalu Uche, playing for Almeria, is being chased by Fulham; Peter Odemingie, an impressive winger playing for Moskow Lokomotiv, looks like he's another forgotten recommend. The youngster Jonjo Shelvey remains at Charlton. So where are the goals coming from, folks?

It's pre-season friendly time but as the teams warm up I'm abroad and the only game I take in is the friendly between Orient and Newcastle, a late rearrangement because of a cancelled European match for the Magpies. I'm interested in who might be leaving the north-east in the coming weeks. I feel sure that a few of their players will want to carry on playing Premiership football, and people like Duff and Martins (and maybe Barton?) certainly could still hold their own. I like Martins in particular. He's a real professional, apparently often training in the afternoon when the other stars have left to take their ear-rings round to the girlfriend's for a quick polish.

Newcastle begin with a pretty strong side in the first half – no Newcastle United XI this. And a good few hundred of their fanatical fans have turned up even for this fixture. After three minutes they go a goal down. Then they give away a penalty to make it 0-2 before the referee plays pay-back time and gives them a spot-kick to make it a half-time score of 2-1. The Orient fans are delighted with the first 45 minutes and as one of them I'd happily take the score for a full-time result. The second half, though, starts with the visitors playing some decent passes and controlling the midfield. I comment knowingly to my mate sitting alongside that Newcastle are settling down, looking dangerous and are starting to open Orient up. To prove the point, a minute later Orient score a third. Then a fourth. Then a fifth. And then a sixth. 'Carrying goals to Newcastle,' mutters my mate, as their team seem to fall apart. Even given the substitutions that bring on younger players, by the end of the game they're a shambles. What might this say about their forthcoming season? Well, my prediction is, Nothing. But someone's got to get to grips with the club.

Chapter Six
NORTH END... BAGGIES

My brief encounter with Preston introduced me to the vagaries of the modern game, but I felt grateful to John Sainty for giving me the toe-hold into this world and by the end of the season he and Dave Jones had guided the club to promotion, aided and abetted, I assured myself, by some of the fine team reports that I'd supplied! I waited for an invitation to the party that surely would be held to celebrate the success but it didn't come. Instead both men moved to Southampton. Stabilisers were put on my bike to try to accommodate all these changes.

I spent a few miserable days pondering the end of my short career and dwelling on all the things that are rotten about football, when I got a call from John asking if I'd be happy to work for them now in the Premiership. Happy! I ate half the telephone receiver trying to bite his hand off. Exactly an hour later I got another call from an unknown northern voice who announced himself as Harry McNally. He informed me that he'd moved in as chief scout at Stockport while Gary Megson had come in as the manager. Between them they'd picked up a few of my recent match reports and wanted me to continue scouting for them. Rags to riches in one hour.

I told Harry that I'd call him back and then worked out the logistics of working for both clubs. I could foresee a few potential problems but decided to give it a go. Southampton sent me a pass, a club jacket, a match programme every fortnight and 40p a mile for my journeys. Stockport sent me another welcome letter and spelt my name wrong.

I decided it was politic not to tell either club that I was doubling up and it worked for a while. There were some difficulties when both clubs wanted me to attend the same match – were there really two Les Padfields working in the London area, some clubs asked. But it wasn't the logistics that caused me to put all my eggs in the Stockport basket. Dave Jones was replaced by Glen Hoddle, John Sainty by John Mortimore, a true gent who worried about the club's image incessantly, and I was now asked to do only player reports: the match reports were left to a couple of full-time scouts. Half the fun had disappeared, even though it was half the work. Southampton and I parted company on amicable grounds.

I met up with Harry, Gary Megson and others one uproarious Friday evening in Cheadle Hulme where we drank, ate and laughed our way through stories until four in the morning. Harry was a particularly larger-than-life character who told me privately that he regularly pretended to go to matches when he was actually at home with his feet up. He seemed to feel no compunction about this and encouraged me to do the same. (A little while later .when he was actually sussed, he got the sack and moved to work at Northwich Victoria). Gary came across as a genuine, down-to-earth and hard-working manager, though after our late night he didn't seem to have the wherewithal to save Stockport from a 2-0 defeat next day. But by the end of his second season there he crossed swords – not for the last time – with the club chairman and moved to Stoke. I was invited to join him.

The chief scout here was John Rudge, the long-time and highly respected manager of Port Vale, arbitrarily sacked after donkeys' years of service to the club. I wondered how difficult the trip had been across the city to join the other Potteries team, but John seemed forever cheerful, organised and professional. Alongside Gary they moved Stoke to the top of the third division before a group of invading Norsemen from Iceland laid claim to the club and booted Gary out – surprisingly, given his ginger hair. This time I stayed on but when he took up the reins at West Brom he phoned and invited me onto the staff there.

Chapter 7

BRAZIL v SWEDEN

26 March 2008

On a day trip with Year 7 to Colchester Zoo I got to know Gemma, a young science teacher who I'd seen about but had never spoken to. Someone had told her about me working for Bolton – it's so much better when other people prepare the groundwork – and it transpired that she was actually a keen football fan herself. In fact, sitting next to her on the front seat of the coach while the kids behind got up to all kinds of mischief, I discovered that she had actually played for Oxford University ladies team as a striker. Realising that this wasn't an appropriate moment to expound my views about women's football, we quickly got into informed conversations about the merits and DeMerits of Watford players et al. and as a natural consequence I asked her if she fancied going to a match, if a decent one cropped up soon.

A week later Colin asked me to go to a friendly international at the Emirates and have a look at the Sweden side playing against Brazil. There were no Brazilians on the staff and the only Swede I currently knew had incredibly long and dirty hair, incredibly bad breath, was regularly high on marijuana and once tried to kiss me at a Christmas party. So I asked Gemma, and along she came.

It was a midweek fixture but there were still more than sixty thousand people at the game, at least three of them Swedish. The noise was fantastic and I was amazed that so many South Americans could be living in the country, let alone finding their way to N5, armed with paraphernalia ranging from pan pipes to shields that looked like they could ward off an atomic attack. I concluded that they passed security through being judged defensive as opposed to offensive weapons.

We collected our tickets and were turnstiled and escalatored up to the relative calm of the Royal Oak Lounge. John Gregg, John Griffin and a few other familiar faces of the scouting fraternity were already propping up the sandwiches and I nodded but naturally refrained from joining their throng and instead treated Gemma to a more private cup of tea on another table. John Gregg smirked at me, but understood. I chose not to expose Gemma to the boredom of scout conversation and left those keen-eyed old stagers to make what they would of my guest.

The game itself was a pretty low-level affair. It took me ten minutes to realise that it was Sweden and not Brazil playing in the yellow shirts. I felt I was not quite impressing Gemma with my expertise. Brazil scored and the place erupted, though where we were sitting there was less pandemonium. The Mexican wave began shortly after, a sure sign that the entertainment on the pitch was not all it might be. Sweden were poor and the Brazilians looked like they were on holiday. But then, don't they usually?

At half-time Gemma wanted the loo, situated at the far end of the concourse. There were more Brazilians inside than outside, playing, singing, dancing, and we struggled past at least a million to finally reach the promised land. Clearly you should never get taken short at a Brazilian football match. By the time she emerged the second half was underway and I decided that rather than plough another furrow through the Amazon body-forest we'd exit by the nearest door and sit in a couple of vacant seats, of which there were plenty, owned presumably by the Boys and Girls from Brazil who were still samba-ing around every bit of free space. It would never have happened at Highbury!

Brazil dominated but didn't score again. A 1-0 win seemed wholly acceptable and any hint of Abba was submerged beneath Carnival as we all made our relaxed way home to the beat of the Bossa Nova. Gemma said she had enjoyed the night, even if the football had been less than thrilling from the great and feted Brazil. She would be happy to come again.

The next evening I phoned Greg with a question about a Spurs reserve player. Before I got an answer he said, 'What happened to you last night then?'

I felt myself going stupidly red for absolutely no reason. 'What do you mean? You weren't at the match, were you?'

'No, but John Gregg was on the phone. Said that you were there with some young lady, wouldn't talk to anyone and then you did a bunk at half-time. Did you have more interesting things to do in the second half then?'

I begin, but then decide not, to explain. Let them surmise!

Chapter 8

KICK-OFF TIMES

The season kicks off in two stages and as the lower leagues begin I'm in Scotland, having failed to convince my wife that I should send my apologies for missing my son's wedding so that I can see how Charlton perform against Wycombe.

She'll have none of it, and we are crashing out in the Borders after the hectic activity of nuptial celebrations. That's the drawback about being a scout part-time – you just can't persuade people that it's a duty to attend matches. They still think we do it for enjoyment!

The big boys start their season next week, except for the Charity Shield tomorrow. Why can I not get excited about Man U playing Chelsea? I have a feeling it will go to penalties, but frankly does anybody care? Well, I guess the fans of both teams might, but I doubt many others will be glued to their trannies.

I spend the afternoon listening to England seemingly throw away the Ashes. I don't want to hear updates on the football scores, I prefer the whole lot together. From thirty-five miles away there are guns booming across the airwaves from Otterburn Army Range, reminding me that we are fighting a war and I morbidly reflect that there's no Bobby Robson to greet the season, nor Harry Patch, who I read watched his first football match in 1905, and I wonder how many more hundreds or thousands of fans, soldiers or otherwise, will see the start but not the end of this season. There's no end to my cheeriness.

At five o'clock the iconic announcement is followed by the iconic music: *Sports Report*. Da dum da dum da dum da dum da diddly dum da da... The brass-band sound that has heralded the football scores for more than half a century (save for a period when the idiots at the BBC tried to replace it) means we are back in business, and James Alexander Gordon begins his stuff. My spirits rise when he reads out 'Bristol Rovers...' You can always tell from one of the three sing-song tones whether it's a home win, draw or an away win, even before he gets to the score, and it's just a matter of how many Orient have put past them. A 2-1 win puts us near the play-offs, but the talk is about Norwich losing 7-1 at home and Sven seemingly working magic at Notts County, who begin with a 5-0 win. These are strange times in the Nottingham district. I've missed Charlton whipping Wycombe by 3-2 but console myself with the thought that I wouldn't have had any wedding cake if I'd been there.

Two days later the *Telegraph* has a whole section devoted to the Premiership, not surprising as most of the football coverage, even in the broadsheets, normally features page after page of stuff concerned only with the top flight. They seem to have forgotten that thousands still follow the minions of the lower leagues. I don't know why I read it; it's as reliable and as depressing as listening to the village gossip. I wonder what these guys get paid for churning out forecasts that could be emulated by the average fan from Mansfield. In today's paper there is a run-down of every Premiership team, along with the essential information of what music the teams run out to and what the bookies' odds are on the manager being sacked. What was that about 'dumbing down'?

There is also a prediction of the final league places, and I make a note of them just to see how useless they will turn out to be. In top spot, according to Alan Hansen, will be Liverpool (sure!!), followed by Arsenal, Chelsea in third, Man U fourth and Man City grabbing the fifth spot. Spurs are rated as sixth, Bolton coming in safely at twelfth, while the drop spots go to Pompey, Wigan and Burnley. Well, I guess we'd take that for another season of Premiership football, but my natural pessimism thinks it's going to be a struggle again for Bolton this year. Last year's survival could be put down to a few fantastic saves by Jääskeläinen but the team was never safe until virtually the end of the season. As with the previous year. As with this year?

I get the feeling that Gary is also a secret pessimist, certainly never one to count his chickens. Survival is the key word, but what of ambition? What is the club's ambition? Just to battle away for enough points to keep out of the bottom three? To play direct, hard, unattractive physical football, scoring mainly from set pieces, getting wins against the poorer sides but never going out to threaten the likes of Chelsea and Arsenal? Or is there a desire to break the mould, to entertain a bit, to bring a bit of glamour to the team, the club, the town? (Well, perhaps that's asking a bit too much, having seen Bolton recently on a wet and cold Saturday night.)

Is European football the target? Here's another anomaly. Clubs seemingly battle to pick up a top place so that they can get into one of the European competitions the following season, but then often go and field a weakened side against a Greek or a Georgian outfit, saving their best players for the next league game at the weekend. Is it really worth it? I'm told by Mel, the chief scout at Tottenham, that Harry Redknapp couldn't give a toss about Europe, mainly because he doesn't like to travel abroad – though Harry seemingly spends at least six hours every day driving from his home in Poole to White Hart Lane and back. Every day! Maybe Harry reflects the average fan's view, though. Would supporters prefer to see their team playing Shakhtar Donestsk on a Tuesday night in February, or giving Alex Ferguson apoplexy by frustrating the Reds in a league game at Old Trafford? No contest.

Chapter 9

EARLY BLUES

17 February 2008

There are some Saturdays when it's best not to be involved in football at all; some Saturdays when it all feels wrong. But it's not usual to have those feelings on the first day of the season. OK, the first day of the Premier season.

I'm at Chelsea to do a team report on Hull, who play Bolton next week. I meet up with Kieran, who, like me, has just come back from holiday, and we agree that it's a bit of a relief to get back into Saturday afternoon football mode after a good few weeks away from the terraces. We discuss his employers, Aston Villa, as well as mine.

'You've got in a few players, then,' says Kieran.

'Yes, but no-one who's going to knock in goals.'

Kieran chuckles: 'Well, we've given you Zat Knight.' We share the same opinion about this gentleman and have done for a number of seasons.

'I think we're going to struggle again this year,' I confide optimistically. 'The only consolation as far as I can see is that there are a good few teams who might struggle with us.'

It's an early, 12.45pm, kick-off to please the TV paymasters. Chelsea dominate the first twenty minutes but look careless and rusty. Drogba misses an early chance. Hull pack the midfield and leave one up front. It's one way traffic until Hull score from a set piece. I point out to Kieran that at the moment Chelsea are actually bottom of the Premiership and Hull top. Then Drogba hits a sweet free kick over the wall to equalise, but the second half doesn't produce the planned deluge and Hull have chances, which they don't take, to regain the lead. Predictably – that word again – the unexpected doesn't happen and in the ninety-second minute Drogba mishits a cross and scores a fluke winner.

I get home just in time to hear the rest of the results coming through, and by 5.10pm I'm already sick of football. Bolton have gone down at home to Sunderland by a solitary goal and the report on the radio suggests that they were clueless, never threatening to equalise an early strike by Darren Bent. I can't help feeling a surge of my normal 'I told you so' attitude rising rapidly. Even a Darren Bent – not the world's greatest finisher – might have been an asset at the Reebok. Why does no-one of real repute come to Bolton? Once again I wonder who is going to net for the team this year if there's not an addition made to the squad in the next ten days or so.

Other results are fairly depressing. Man City have bought their first win. Everton duly lose 6-1 at home to Arsenal, a bit of light entertainment for the neutral, and the likely relegation candidates have mostly lost their opening games, which is probably good from Bolton's perspective. But down in Div. 3 Orient have begun their home campaign with a defeat to Oldham so that's another bummer. After a week of football and before a Premiership ball is kicked the perfidy of chairmen is demonstrated by the sacking of the Norwich manager after the freak 7-1 loss in the opening game. One caller on the radio suggests a much better idea would be to sack the chairman. He has a point.

Unlike Bolton.

Chapter 10

WERDER BREMEN v NURNBERG

17 February 2008

Colin phoned while I was in the middle of a poetry lesson to ask if I could go to Germany at the weekend. Any boy in school whose mobile goes off has it automatically confiscated, but I have an understanding with all my classes that if mine rings, the lesson stops for important communication to take place. If it's not Bolton, it will be GCHQ. Sometimes I get them to call out 'Hello Colin', just so that the Bolton people believe I have a job. Sometimes when it's GCHQ at the other end they still call out 'Hello Colin'. It's a bit embarrassing.

They wanted me to look at a Werder Bremen striker who had one kidney and wore a belt under his football shirt during games. Didn't sound promising but I was happy to oblige. I visited Bremen once before when Alex, my son, studied there for a year and I liked the feeling of the old town.

There were no flights to Bremen so I was Ryanaired into Hannover on the earliest flight anywhere in Europe, where I picked up my hotel key and hire-car, fitted with a sat nav, which I'd never tried before. The very helpful Avis man gave me instructions on how to use it which left me completely clueless. A bit like my poetry lessons.

It's about ninety miles to Bremen. Sat Nav Lady began our relationship by telling me to do a U-turn on the Autobahn, then seemed to take the huff when I ignored her and didn't talk to me for another twenty miles. The Autobahn was beautifully uncrowded. In parts there was no speed limit, so I opened the Vauxhall throttle and gave it its head. I'd never driven at 200kph before and I was disappointed to work out later that it's only about 130mph. Sat Nav Lady came to life with 'Mein Gott, slow down you idiot!' and I eased off to prove that I'm a gentleman.

I carried a fax sent to me denoting that I had two tickets – who did they think I was taking with me? – and a car park pass. I got to Bremen well before kick-off time, but locating my car park was not so easy. I showed my fax at three different places, practised my 'Ich habe ein...' and waved the paper – I'd forgotten to look up the German for 'car park pass' – and each time I was met with shakes of the head, pointing fingers and a babble of language that I couldn't understand. (They must all be speaking with strong accents; I wish I'd brought Alex with me).

Giving up, I decided to park in a side road, only to discover they were all crammed with Volkswagens and BMWs. Finally I ran out of patience and opted to stick it on the corner of a quiet road and hope for the best. As I was getting out to judge the distance from the car behind, a gleaming two-seater BMW pulled alongside and the driver called across: 'Are you going to ze match?' How does he know I'm English? I'm driving a car with German plates and wearing lederhosen. Is there something about my parking which is patently Anglo-Saxon?

I meekly responded that I was and he asked, incredibly, 'Do you have a spare ticket?' Stunned into more meekness I confessed that I did and instantly obliged him with it. He warned me not to park there, I'd be towed away – and when I told him I had a car park pass, waving the magic paper once again, he instructed, 'Follow me.'

We drove to the main entrance of the ground, I parked illegally between two police motorcyclists, who appeared unmoved by me smiling at them, and I waited for him to blag himself a car-park pass. We parked together in the place that had refused me entry half an hour before. There were still a couple of hours before the match started so I explained to him that I intended to walk into town before going into the stadium. 'I vill come vid you,' he informed me. On the way I telephoned Susan to tell her that I was in Bremen, walking into town with a man who had just picked me up and volunteered to accompany me. There was a strange silence at the end of the phone. We found a place to have a spot of lunch and he convinced me to try a local Bremen delicacy, which I found just about edible. His English was not great, but better than my German, which my son once kindly told me sounded like something from the Gestapo. 'My girlfriend vould not like dis', he explained, pointing to whatever the meat was on my plate, 'because my girlfriend is a vegetable.' I managed to avoid an international incident by coughing on my whatever-it-was, though I was slightly relieved to learn he had a girlfriend.

The game was not bad. Werder were top of the table, which was a pleasant surprise to their fans, and reinforced my admiration of the Bundesliga as it was not dominated like the Premiership by three or four teams and could throw up surprises. Nurnberg were near the bottom and never in the match. Herr Klasnic did better with one kidney than most of his colleagues with two, but I'd still be concerned if I saw him stretchered off having just had a kick in the back.

Werder Bremen v Nurnberg

Wolfgang – we were on first-name terms by now – informed me that he normally had a ticket thanks to a friend but had missed out this week, that he drove each time from Hamburg, some eighty miles away, and that he was meeting his brother after the game. He told me that he was an area manager for a company that sold motorised vehicles for disabled people, watched English football weekly on TV but had never been to Britain. I didn't yet offer him free accommodation, but it did occur to me that perhaps I should keep in touch to see if he could do me a good deal on a buggy in a few years' time.

His brother arrived at our cars after the game and as we waited for the traffic to disperse I asked them both if they knew how to set my sat nav to guide me back to my Hannover hotel. Wolfgang smiled in surprise and told me that he had stayed at this hotel with his girlfriend some years before. He assured me it was good. We shook hands all round and departed, never once having mentioned the war or 1966.

He was quite right about the hotel. It was good, and I was enjoying a pleasant meal later in the evening in a dining hall populated with a few other people and soft background music. I was just into my third glass of Bavarian wine when a loud female voice told me and the accompanied gathering to 'Turn left in one hundred metres.' I had managed to find what turns sat nav Lady on; I had managed to get her out of the car without a fuss; I'd not yet managed to shut her up when I wanted her to keep mum. That's women for you.

My flight the next day was not until the evening. I resisted the temptation to sample absolutely everything that was available at breakfast, but stocked up nicely in order to last out until the afternoon. Bolton's budget allows for a lunch and good evening meal when out and about, but my natural meanness and working-class tendency to never spend money unnecessarily prevents me from going to the limits. I figured that perhaps my economies might help pay for another kidney. I checked out, drove away in a leisurely fashion ready to spend a relaxed day looking for traces of the Pied Piper around Hannover City, when I discovered that the car park barrier wouldn't rise to allow me to exit. Parking up again with a flutter of irritation I explained the predicament to the receptionist, who then gave me an access code. I smiled falsely and headed for the revolving door when a voice called out, 'Hello Les!' In a nanosecond my mind raced back to the film of *The Great Escape* where a group is captured when a German officer wishes them 'Good Luck' as they board a bus, and one of them says 'Thanks'. Should I turn round to find a gun pointed at me in revenge for 1966 after all? Or was there another Les in this hotel – how common is the name Les in Germany? – and how many German Les's would respond to an English 'hello'?

I swivelled to find a smiling Wolfgang heading towards me. Uncertain whether to panic, flee or bluff it out, I chose the English option and shook hands with him. Behind him, to my relief, emerged a good-looking young lady who had to be his girlfriend. It transpired that they had driven 110 miles from Hamburg to have breakfast here on the off-chance that they might rendezvous with me. And sure enough, thanks to a barrier that wouldn't open and a dim receptionist who didn't tell me about codes, they succeeded.

I was now entertained to a right royal unnecessary second breakfast. Wolfgang and Ingrid then proceeded to show me the sights of Hannover – places I would never have discovered on my own – buy me lunch by the edge of the town's lake, present me with a box of German chocolate biscuits as a thank-you for the Werder ticket of yesterday, and escort me back safely to the airport car drop-off point. I was overwhelmed by their kindness and the Germans went up enormously in my estimation. I invited them back to London for their first ever visit. But I never heard from them again. Klasnic, however, signed for Bolton eighteen months later. Gary's not one to rush things.

When I related the incident to my family they thought it both odd but characteristic of things that happen on my travels. My only observation was that if I had been James Bond it would have been a young and glamorous Austrian blonde who accosted me, rather than a thirty-nine-year-old thin-haired salesman who sold invalid cars in Northern Germany.

Chapter 11

BACK IN THE BIG TIME

Gary's first achievement at West Brom was to guide them to safety with a last-day win over Charlton: touch and go. In the second season they lost out in the play-offs; the third season they were promoted to the Premiership on the final day of the season; then they came straight down; then they went straight back up. Life was rarely mundane at this club. Adrian Chiles, noted West Brom fanatic, commented that Gary had brought him greater happiness than anyone else in his life. A bit of hyperbole I think but nonetheless a compliment from someone notoriously lugubrious.

A few weeks into their second spell in the top flight Gary fell foul of the chairman and for no public reason – certainly not based on results – got the heave-ho once more. I stayed on and worked under Bryan Robson, who managed to beat the odds and retain Premiership status on a memorable last day of the season thanks to a Charlton goal that defeated Crystal Palace and sent them down. Nick, my son, and I were listening on the radio to the nail-biting finish, then were dancing around in celebration, then I was on the phone to Bobby Hope, the chief scout, and to anyone else I thought might be pleased. It had been a long season to end in such a climax, but well worth the agonies. At least until a week later, when Bobby phoned me to say that the chairman had decided to dispense with the scouts that Gary used and look more to Europe. Nice one, Mr Peace; nice thank you. His dislike of Gary must run deep. I decided I wasn't going meekly and wrote to him expressing my opinion that he was a prat. He replied, wishing me well in my future career!

By this time Gary was at Forest and taking on some big-time Charlies who thought they were still Premiership players on Premiership wages. Once again I joined him, but from the outset his tenure there was clearly a battle for him. Elements of the team seemed to feel that they were in a very nice little comfort zone and didn't want anyone upsetting the apple-cart. One of them apparently told Gary, 'We'll get rid of you long before you get rid of us...'

Forest didn't do as well as hoped and the next season pressure mounted. Gary was off on gardening leave before the decree nisi was signed. Yet again, I outlasted him and when Colin Calderwood, the new manager, came in from Northampton, along with his chief scout Keith Burt, I was again invited to continue.

Forest is a club steeped in tradition and the legacy of Brian Clough persists. It seems as hard for some of their fans to adapt to reality as it would be for a recent divorcee to realise they are not loved anymore. There must be other clubs in a similar vein: Leeds United, Sheffield Wednesday – some rising back up, some showing no signs of doing so. Certainly the playing staff at Forest very much resembled little more than a decent third-tier squad, but I was happy to do reports on and help bring in Grant Holt, Rob Earnshaw, Nathan Tyson and a couple of others to boost the team.

Gary was out of management for a good eighteen months and there were suspicions that perhaps a certain chairman had been putting the boot in to scupper some of his chances. But then he got an opening at Leicester. With impeccable timing he phoned me just as I was at the front of the queue going into the Sistine Chapel after lining up for three hours. This was a real test of loyalty, but I managed to usher twenty people to go in front of me while I picked up the gist of his offer to come and work for him again.

Keith at Forest was superb, explaining that though he'd like to keep me, Leicester were a division higher and, appreciating that it's nice to be head-hunted, he would understand if I went. I had a weekend to chew it over. On Monday, I decided. I phoned Ray Train at Leicester to tell him I was on board; on Tuesday I rang Keith to tell him of my decision; on Wednesday I read in the papers that 'Megson moves to Bolton'; on Thursday I rang Ray Train again and jumped ship, or train; on Friday I was asking Keith for my job back. A week is a long time in football!

This time I texted Gary to wish him well, assuming that he'd inherited a good scouting system at the Reebok. He rang back to say that he'd inherited knock-all and was virtually starting from scratch. Did I want to join him? When, a short while later, I was offered a monthly contract with twice the salary that old pro footballers used to get, it was an offer I couldn't refuse. I got a coat, a tie, medical insurance when abroad, a CRB check and about twenty-three different forms to claim my monthly expenses. Even though it was just down the road, it had been a long journey from Preston.

Chapter 12

END OF AUGUST

The season is barely three weeks old and I'm already adopting the role of grumpy old git.

Not only are Bolton showing signs of being first-class relegation fodder, while Orient are obviously going nowhere fast this season, but football itself has got out of bed after its summer snooze with all the symptoms of vomit and diarrhoea.

Last season's 'Respect' campaign seems to have been buried and forgotten as a bad joke. But the void is being filled rapidly. Manchester City imitate a cross-section between a Russian deep-sea trawler, dredging up everything in its path, and a spoilt ten-year-old with unrestricted access to anything it wants. Joleon Lescott is wheedled away from Everton in the most distasteful manner, though he says it's not the money that's attracting him. Perish the thought, Joleon! Everyone knows you've slept in your sky-blue underpants since the age of three and you're simply fulfilling your lifelong dream. The only bit of comfort I take from this is a belief that he's not that good as a defender anyway.

I read about, and watch on TV, Crystal Palace score at Bristol City, only for the referee and linesman to decide it's no goal. This is no 'just over the line' incident. Freddie Sears bangs the ball into the net, where it hits the back stanchion and rebounds out. The Palace players celebrate; the City players look crestfallen; the well-placed referee wipes sweat from his eyes with his Optrex-sponsored wristband, fails to read the body language around him, even if he hasn't seen it, and runs happily about without a care in the world. And who's to blame? Maybe Mr Shoebridge and his assistant haven't covered themselves in glory, but they haven't cheated. In my book it's the silent, dishonest City players who clearly believe that anything goes in the modern win-at-all-costs game. When Neil Warnock and Simon Jordan emerge as the good guys, something is seriously wrong.

I foolishly decide to take my first look at Millwall, pitted against West Ham in the Carling Cup. The game becomes incidental and the headlines are made by the dozens of imbeciles with a combined IQ of minus several million, whose bricks and bottles I narrowly avoid as I enjoy a stroll along Green Street with the happy combatants. It's a depressing reminder of the yob-mob mentality that is part of the current English culture – not just football – and a throw-back (pun unintended) to the bad old days of the '70s. I later meet with a police sergeant friend who tells me he has arrested two of the intelligentsia: one from Doncaster and the other from Newcastle. Draw your own conclusions, he says. No doubt they'll avoid being fined two grand and banged up for six months and instead will receive banning orders. That should really scare them.

The next night I'm watching Eduardo score a 6.4 for his dive in the Celtic penalty area, then having the gall to convert the spot-kick. For a player who attracted so much sympathy for his horrendous injury, the word 'cheat' now, sadly, seems to fit him. What an opportunity – a moment in history, let alone morality – if he'd told the ref he'd fallen, or had simply rolled the penalty to the keeper. But my sons tell me I'm living in fantasy land if I think that could happen. I maintain that Arsenal are so superior they don't need to employ dying swans.

As if the player's actions are not sufficiently reprehensible Monsieur Wenger chimes in with his own two-francs' worth, expressing in terms of high dudgeon his disgust at the 'unfairness' that UEFA might take action against Eduardo. Unfairness: how does the word lose its meaning when translated into French? For an exponent – if there is one in this country – of the beautiful game it's a depressing but typical one-eyed view that the Arsenal manager adopts.

Bolton's opening day 1-0 home defeat to Sunderland is followed by a 1-0 defeat at Hull, and just before Liverpool dump three past them in the third league game they manage an unimpressive 1-0 win at Tranmere in the Carling Cup, in which my friend Elmander heads wide from four yards.

After the Hull game, Gary appears on *Match of the Day* expressing bemusement as to why Bolton should not convert any of the dozen chances they made. I could offer a suggestion: they haven't signed a decent bloody striker! Too much falls on the shoulders of Kevin Davies, a marvellous competitor, and Jääskeläinen at the other end to pull off miracle saves. After the Liverpool game I watch with disbelief the video of Bolton's defending. Name three players from Liverpool you would not offer free shots to, and you might mention Johnson, Torres and Gerrard. It seems, though, that Lancashire hospitality extends to all three being invited to have a pop, with the white shirts keeping their distance as though these guys were carrying smallpox.

Three games; nil points; pressure already mounting. If the next three don't produce results how much rope will there be at the Reebok?

Chapter 13

SCOUTS

Bill, my mate, thinks we're an odd bunch. Week after week, for nine or ten months of the year, he says, the same old faces turn up with their notepads to watch Barnsley Reserves, or Chelsea play Liverpool, or Bromley Town take on Eastleigh, sitting in the August sunshine and getting roasted at Adams Park, or shivering with cold and pneumonia at Crewe on an icy Monday night in January. You can usually spot them from afar, some with little books, others with clipboards, a few even with a briefcase. Mostly dressed in jackets and ties – a must at certain grounds that offer hospitality – or clad in club anoraks. And with twenty minutes of a match to go, many make an unsubtle surge for the exit so as not to get caught up in the after-match traffic, even when the task is getting away from the rural wilds of Borehamwood.

The ones I get to know and meet with regularly are a varied bunch. Greg, who has connections all over the place and currently works for Wigan, is a mine of information. Want to know about a lad who's been playing for Aldershot reserves? Give Greg a ring. If he doesn't know anything about him then the player probably doesn't exist. John Savage is an ex-detective from Lewisham who has been working for Tranmere for donkeys' years and who insists on taking back roads and CID short cuts down to Woking's ground, even when the match you're watching is at Aldershot. Kieran, an eloquent Irishman, a mate of Martin O'Neill, has a job with the Charity Commission, and having dropped out of the scouting scene for a couple of years through sheer disillusion with the game is now back with Aston Villa; John Gregg, who was summarily sacked for no reason when young Clough moved into Derby, always cheerful and smiling, and who for some obscure reason is a Freeman of the city of Berwick, is now in the employ of Walsall. John Griffin was chief scout at Griffin Park for years – coincidences abound – now works for Wycombe; Alex, a young knowledgeable guy, is on the roll at Watford, taciturn Bill at Hereford, Pete Norris at Rochdale, while a youngster called Jack, and who was a kind of protégé, coming with me to several games, has now taken my place at Forest.

There are one or two best to avoid, like Ron Peters, who manages to start fights and arguments wherever he goes and who once sued Northampton because they owed him £13.45 in expenses. Another wide berth is given to Peter Small, a customer who will twist whatever you tell him to cause trouble with as many people as he can. No-one can really figure out why. But the majority of scouts I encounter are straightforward and on the ball.

Until a few years ago we were often graced with the attendance of a small, frail, elderly gentleman who oozed poise and charm and humility. Joe Mallett, as I discovered it was, had signed forms for Charlton in 1933 and subsequently played and managed in Europe as well as South America, having coached in his time names such as Pele, Cruyff and Beckenbauer. What a wealth of knowledge and information this man must have carried and late into his eighties he was still coming up to London from the Kent coast to run his eye over prospective players. I broached with him one day the idea of getting some of his sixty-plus years of experiences down on paper, but he was of the opinion that he had done nothing to warrant interest. Ironic, when shops sell autobiographies of nineteen-year-olds! Before I could persuade him to think again, the final whistle went.

A few scouts bring along their wives, presumably so that if the game is excruciating they can at least have a bit of nookie to pass the time. Dave Cook, ex-chief scout at Newcastle who's now at Blackburn, is admirably supported by his other half, who seems as clued up on tactics as Dave. Don Smith, who has worked for Carlisle, actually sent his wife to a couple of games instead of going himself, and I recall Pete Norris treating his own missus to an anniversary celebration by catching a bus to watch Crystal Palace reserves play one night. At the other end of the scale some less liberated males run a precarious balancing act between duty to football and duty to family. I have tried several times to convince my wife that I'm having an affair and I'm not just off to watch the fourth game in a week. It cuts little ice to point out that I could be down the pub every night, or gambling away the family fortune, but the charge comes back that football takes over normal life, that it's an obsession. I argue further that there are far more pointless activities: trainspotting, collecting toy soldiers, morris dancing. I'm not in that league. I'm not!!

Football watching is so dependent on opinions, of course, which is all right if you're a journalist or a spectator, but it gets more serious if you're a scout and more and more serious if you're a manager.

The average football scout, I'm convinced, knows more about players than the average manager. Which might explain some of the bizarre buys that clubs make, when a manager gets it into his head that he wants someone, regardless of wiser counsel. Stories abound. Tommy Taylor, erstwhile of Orient and Darlington and Cambridge, apparently used to try to buy anyone who had played well against his team. Not with huge success, it has to be said. Also, Tommy publicly stated he couldn't understand why bigger clubs hadn't come in for the Orient full-back Lockwood – scorer of many notable goals. Well Tom, ask any decent scout and they'll tell you: he can't defend, which is a bit of a drawback for a full-back. When Forest do actually buy him it's on the express say-so of Colin Calderwood, the manager, despite long conversations I have with Keith, the chief scout:

'What's your take on Lockwood, Les?'

'Really nice guy.'

'Yes but...'

'Told you before, Keith, he's an inspiration going forward, but...'

'But?'

'Put a decent winger against him and he's all over the place.'

(Pause)

'Colin likes him.'

'How many times has he seen him?'

'He's going to buy him.'

(Pause)

'What do you think then?'

'Same as you.'

'And he's still going to buy him.'

(Pause)

'Well Keith, I reckon it's a bad move for Forest, bad for Orient and bad for Lockwood.'

Lockwood goes to Forest, plays eleven games in the

season and a year later is transferred to Colchester, which adds to the 'Don't say I didn't warn you!' belief that permeates much of my life.

Mel Johnson, the Spurs chief scout, and I are discussing managers' buys while wasting our time at a Watford game. The name Pavlyuchenko crops up and I mention that I saw him play in the Euros of 2008 and wasn't convinced that he could do the business week-in week-out in the Premier League. Mel tells me that he shared that opinion and that no scout at Tottenham actually recommended him. He was bought for £16 million after Juande Ramos, the Spurs manager, saw him play one game on the TV. Sixteen million! Not wishing the guy any ill-will, I'm reassured when I see him miss sitters and get carried off by the Air Ambulance whenever a toenail breaks. Sixteen million!

But it's all about opinions. And prejudices. I find it hard to reverse first impressions, especially bad ones, though it's forced upon me sometimes. I write off Peter Crouch as a big girl's blouse when he first comes on the scene at Pompey. He's 6ft 7ins and loses out on headers to players the size of Ronnie Corbett. It takes a while to believe in him, but he does now put himself about a bit more, even though his legs still look like they'll break if the wind picks up. I met a scout who once gave the thumbs down to Peter Shilton; 'Couldn't catch a shopping trolley' had been his verdict. And David Beckham was once on schoolboy forms at Orient before someone decided he wasn't bright enough for the fourth division. Good one.

Chapter 14

GAPS

I'm in the dentist's, having a front tooth replaced, when Colin rings and asks me if I'll go to the England v Croatia game. I reply with a series of 'ugh-ughs' while the dentist looks increasingly annoyed and the level of agony inside my mouth rises proportionally. He seems to stop the treatment rather suddenly.

I'd like to make some barbed comment to Colin about spotting Croatian possibles, but there are gaps in his memory about certain things. The last time I attended this fixture – the infamous 3-2 defeat and demise of McClaren – I raved on about the little midfielder Modric who ran the show, but try as I might I couldn't generate interest at Bolton, Colin being of the opinion that he was too small to perform regularly in the Premiership. Some months later Spurs sign him for double the fee he would have cost in October '07, and he becomes a key player in their team. Modric isn't playing in today's game. He's been injured in a recent match. Fifteen – thirty!

After the south versus east London battle at West Ham, it's encouraging to be able to walk along Wembley Way with both sets of fans side by side. There are masses of Croatians or so it seems, or perhaps they just make more noise and appear more obvious in the way that visiting supporters often do. I'm with my friend Andrew and it reminds us of our first visit together to Wembley some thirty-five years back when England played Scotland. For reasons I can't remember we found ourselves standing near the front among hundreds of Scots fans – and without, I recall, the slightest concern for our safety. As we walk to the stadium we talk about the two lasting memories that stay with us of that day. The first is of a Scotsman who, worse for wear, slumped over the front fence shortly before kick-off and didn't stir until the final ball had been kicked. It was his lucky day: Scotland lost 5-1. The second memory is being passed bottles of consoling whisky every time the visitors conceded a goal. We finished up just pretending to take swigs, but our friendly enemies who surrounded us gave it their all. I often wonder how many of them found their way back to the tube station, let alone north of the border. We reflect that 5-1 would be a nice score again today. Some hopes! We'll settle for 1-0.

A fax from Mr Falvey at Wembley has informed me that there is a car park space available but apologises for not providing hospitality on this occasion. You're forgiven, Mr Falvey. We take the train and buy our own refreshments at Wembley, paying eight times the price for a carton of Sprite that I paid for my World Cup tickets in 1966. A programme is now sixteen times the price.

This time we're not standing among opposing fans but are seated just in front of the press gallery, where dozens of computer screens wait patiently for their owners to come along to praise or condemn, create heroes or villains, talk sense and rubbish for the waiting masses tomorrow morning. I wander up to the top where I'm told I can collect a team-sheet and am duly ushered into the Press Lounge where I see Pat, a Birmingham scout, already in a queue. I join him, expecting to pick up the designated sheet, when I'm suddenly asked if I'd like beef or pork and which vegetables would I care for? Feeling a refusal to be ungracious, I opt for the beef and spend the next twenty-five minutes enjoying the lack of hospitality for which Mr Falvey has apologised. I don't mention this to Andrew when I return to my seat. The team-sheets were late in coming! Andrew is finishing his Sprite.

England score a penalty after seven minutes. That'll do us nicely, you can blow up now ref. But then Gerrard pops in No. 2 while Lennon and Heskey miss sitters. I recall that I'm meant to be doing a job on the Croatian team, but they are immensely disappointing, a shadow of their former selves, and the game ends up as an exhibition. 5-1. The years roll off us.

On the journey back we are seated on a tube surrounded by Croats. A whisky bottle emerges and we are invited to join in the wake. We baulk at telling them that alcohol's banned on the Underground, aware that World War One began because some people from the Balkans got annoyed. The liquid is vile, making us yearn to be back with the Scots. We get off the train two stops early to avoid being poisoned, but our arrival home is well after midnight as a result. I creep in quietly and take out a mint biscuit from my pocket that I've spirited away from the Press Lounge. As I bite off a chunk, my front tooth falls out.

Chapter 15

...AND MANAGERS

What makes a good manager?

A simple question like that appears to cause people serious brain tremors looking for an answer. When I once asked Tommy Docherty, his reply was, 'A good team and a good chairman.' I still don't know if he was being sarcastic or serious. Someone else suggested a good manager is one who knows his best team, which if true might raise questions about the last few England managers and, some might suggest, Mr Benitez up at Anfield. I'm not sure what my own answer is. Somewhere the word motivation looms, along with the ability to make good team selections and substitutions. I have a feeling that managers should spend at least the first half of a game up in the stands, where the pattern of play is so much clearer to see than when you are stuck on the touchline, but the only two I've ever seen do that are Alan Curbishley and Steve Coppell. What did old man Clough have that made him take Derby and Forest to the heights? Has the Special One got something special, apart from pots of money? How would Alex Ferguson fare working at Rochdale for a season? Would he make a difference? Or would Wenger get Exeter playing the Arsenal way if he were their manager?

Is Gary Megson a good manager?

At Stockport he worked on a shoestring budget. When he managed Stoke they went to the top of their league before a group of Icelanders took over the running of the club and Gary moved to West Brom.

In five seasons there he saved them from relegation, took them to the play-offs, got them promoted to the Premiership, then relegated and then promoted again. If managing in football is a results-driven industry then Gary's CV stands up pretty well. But I suspect that, like a lot of other people in charge of clubs in these days of instantly demanded success and pusillanimous chairmen who succumb quickly to press and fan pressure, he's one bad run away from being on the scrapheap.

'Losing the dressing room' is a fashionable expression that normally follows a vote of confidence from the Board and precedes the exit of a manager, which I take to mean that players don't have respect for, or belief in, a manager any longer, if they ever did in the first place. So is it about force of personality, or successful managerial experience? It's interesting to note that very few top players become top managers and the likes of Ferguson, Wenger and Benitez never blazed a trail of glory when they were actually kicking the ball. Is it, therefore, the awareness of intelligence, trusting that the man knows what he's talking about and doing? And what part does man-management play? When to encourage, to praise, to bollock, to threaten, maybe do all or none of those. No blueprint as far as I can see, but I have to believe that eleven players who have enough regard and respect, maybe even love for a manager that they'd walk through walls for him, will go further than a team who see him as fundamentally less important than they regard themselves. Managers can, of course, influence this perception. Is it a coincidence that after Phil Brown humiliated his team by keeping them on the pitch for a half-time public drubbing, Hull dropped like a stone and avoided relegation by a whisker? I wonder if he'd do that again.

Why do coaches and managers try to complicate things? Football is such a simple game with the potential to touch on the beautiful as the Brazilians claim, almost always compelling at any level. One of Bill Shankly's sayings was that the game was so simple, yet made complicated by people who ought to know better. I've played football with a group of youths in a back street in Peru; with kids in an African village who didn't have a proper ball and played with a rolled-up newspaper; in the plaza outside the Pantheon in Rome with Canadian teenagers who didn't play football, plus the passers-by, from young women to very old men who eagerly kicked the ball back every time it strayed outside our circle. All attracted to the fundamental magic of booting a ball from A to B.

All it really consists of is getting the ball between three sticks, or stopping it going there. But to see the way an industry has been built up around this task, not to mention an air of mystery, of esoteric knowledge, of special vision and understanding that are beyond the comprehension of the ordinary mortal, puts the game on a level that it often doesn't deserve. Of course there are tactics and tricks and experience that can be communicated to great effect. But there is also a load of hogwash that surrounds a basically simple idea.

I'm convinced that sometimes managers kill natural talent through an insistence that players conform to a system: no, son, you're not going to run with the ball and beat three defenders, you're going to play it across the park and make sure we retain possession. It becomes a mindset and something I still don't understand. Why does Michael Carrick, with his obvious ability, not score more often? When United were chasing the game at Arsenal last season he spent the last twenty minutes virtually stuck in the centre-circle. How can Steve Lomas play 505 games for West Ham and score only one goal (a shot through the keeper's legs in a 7-1 trouncing of Hull)? Even if you're a defender and it hits your backside and goes in off the referee, the law of averages insists that you must get on the scoresheet at some point. Unless you adopt the belief that 'I'm a player who doesn't score goals.'

Or is it that the problem lies with communicating instructions through to players who are not terribly bright or receptive or fluent in English? Bolton employ three analysts whose job it is to receive match reports from scouts, break them down into component parts and put them back together again with relevant details which are then passed onto the coaching staff and the manager, who then communicates them to the players in preparation for a game, who then regularly cross the touchline at the start of the match and forget to do the basics that they've been told to do. When I once sat next to Tony Pulis and asked him if he ever got frustrated that his players failed to follow simple instructions his terse reply was, 'Every bloody week.'

Whilst working for Forest, I meet up one Saturday with Colin Calderwood before a cup match against Premiership Charlton. Along with a few other Forest scouts we chat about his long-term vision for the club – a five-year plan which I think at the time a bit optimistic – and then go to the changing room to look around and to see Colin's diagrammatic blueprint of how to win the tie. I study it privately for a good two minutes, regretting that I've not finished my degree in hieroglyphics, and wonder if I can borrow it later to submit to the Tate Modern. How, I ponder, will Nathan Tyson and his boys make sense of those pretty lines and coloured squiggles and bits of green that might actually be phlegm where Colin has sneezed over it? But make sense they obviously do. They win the match 2-0.

Chapter 16

OCTOBER 3

This game is mad.

Mad, fantastic, depressing, ruthless... what emotion does it not touch? What other activity can bring so much euphoria, albeit short-lived, to thousands of people at one time? What can turn educated and intelligent people into slabbering morons shouting obscenities alongside people they would normally never want to come within a mile of? What is the power of this game? It's not, of course, more important than life and death, despite Shankly's famous aphorism; we are reminded of that from time to time. And it may not have the lasting support that some people find from a faith, though there are striking resemblances to following a religion. I recall as a kid walking around the outside of Orient's ground in the summer months and peering in at the empty stadium with feelings of awe. Hallowed ground. I know Brighton supporters who refuse to ever shop at the supermarket which now stands on their old Goldstone Ground: Jerusalem occupied by infidels. Good for them!

But I'm glad it's not my job.

I'm watching Middlesbrough play Reading at the beginning of the month to run the rule over Gary O'Neil as a possible replacement for the injured Sean Davis. My verdict is that he could possibly replace a museum attendant, but given the amount of running he doesn't do – or doesn't in this game – I wouldn't slot him into the fray at Old Trafford next week. That's it for O'Neil: career finished! I meet up with an old college friend who I've not seen since his wedding thirty-nine years ago, and we naturally talk about this perk of scouting. He's impressed and maybe a little envious until I happen to see Mel Johnson, the Spurs chief scout. Except he isn't any more.

With undisguised bitterness Mel, who has been knocking around the football world for donkeys' years, discloses that he's been given the sack by Tottenham, a few short weeks after being assured by Harry that his job was secure.

'I'm taking them to a tribunal. November 5th.' (I refrain from the obvious quip.)

'Why did you get the push, Mel – what did they say?'

'No reason. Harry brought in Ian Broomfield.'

'Ian Broomfield...'

'Say no more. I was warned by everyone to keep my head down, get on with my job. You know what people say.'

'But why him?'

'Rumour has it Harry's been trying to get him in for a long time. Do you think it's friendship? With Broomfield?'

'Why else? Old pals act?'

Mel gives me a look that says, work it out, but doesn't articulate. 'Funny things are going on down there. You looked at Harry recently? You think he looks well?' I consider for a moment and wonder if Harry ever looks well. 'Big secret you know,' Mel continues. 'He spent a week in hospital end of last season. All kept hush hush.'

'And then in comes Broomfield.'

'In comes Broomfield. First he gets rid of the scouts and then he says to me, "We're going to have to let you go, Mel. Pack your stuff and go say your goodbyes. You can keep the car for a few weeks" and I'm out by lunchtime. Four years of travelling the world, four years of total commitment. I've never been sacked before and now I'm fifty-nine. Where do I go now?'

I'm shocked and saddened and angry for Mel. Bolton are playing Tottenham today and lead at half-time. It seems that I want Tottenham to lose with one-tenth of the intensity that Mel does. I wish him well and offer him the name of a good solicitor who is married to my daughter-in-law, if he ever needs one. He's a decent guy and deserves better.

Middlesbrough see off Reading at a stroll, Orient score the only goal at Wycombe and Bolton draw 2-2 with Spurs. On *Match of the Day* I'm pleased to see that once again a team report that I've done on Spurs the previous week has made a difference. My warnings about Crouch's aerial ability and Kranjcar's right shooting foot are heeded to the letter, until Kranjcar scores with a right-foot shot and Crouch heads in from a corner. But something else emerges from the game. Bolton score from open play and with a bit of panache. They look good for a while – adventurous, attractive. Is it becoming Beautiful Bolton Wanderers?

I calm down after a little reflection and decide it must be an aberration. I'm sure Gary will sort it out. Bolton have strolled through September undefeated but the next game is at Old Trafford, where I can only hope they kick the opposition off the park and bulldoze their way to a respectable defeat. Beauty is only shin deep.

Chapter 17

LEYTON ORIENT v GILLINGHAM

26 September 2006

It was still early season and Keith at Forest had asked me to do a team report on Gillingham, playing down at Orient in a midweek fixture. It was the Os' first season back in the old Third Division, aka Football League Division Two, now for some crackpot reason called League One. They hadn't had too great a start, but had managed a home win against Millwall earlier in the season.

It had been a few years since Millwall and Gillingham were entertained on a level footing down at Brisbane Road, and their travelling supporters might have noticed a difference in the ground. At each corner a block of flats, aptly named after an Orient legend, housed owners who, if they wished, could fall off their toilet seats and instantly watch what was going on down on the pitch. Those with a bit more decorum might sit on their balconies and be entertained for no less than the price of a mortgage. To show that South London humour was not dead and buried, when the Lions' followers saw the residents sipping their wine and politely applauding the Orient attacks they broke into a familiar rendition of 'You're supposed to be at home...'

Hospitality for scouts was not what it once was at the Orient, when soup and sandwiches were a welcome respite from what you had to watch happening on the pitch. Nowadays, under the Barry Hearn austerity scheme, scouts were charged a pound for a half-time cup of tea. Well, actually just for the cup. The tea was on the table but a fearsome lady collected your dosh to furnish you with something to drink from. From a mixture of principle and plain tightness, I would smuggle in my own cup and the tea tasted better for it. Teaching two of the sons of the chief executive at Orient, as I was currently doing, I kept dropping massive hints about the wished-for return of the soup run, but to no avail.

Another drawback was that scouts were now seated quite high up, above the real directors' seats, and adjacent to the section housing the away supporters. Not a massive problem for most scouts; not a massive problem when it's Carlisle United or Hartlepool United who have brought their smallish contingent; quite a problem when you happen to be an Orient diehard and you're within gobbing distance of morons from Gillingham who have made the journey up the Thames in their hollowed-out wooden boats and are now slagging off your team with foul language and awfully unoriginal badly-sung chants. Well, you wouldn't expect anything creative. The hugely unfrightening stewards who stood thinly between the sections provided little comfort that if anything kicked off they wouldn't be first for the exit. I surmised that the seating manager at the ground was working on the assumption that there's not much kudos in these fans spilling over and attacking a group of gentlemen in jackets and ties who were scribbling notes and able to defend themselves with nothing more than writing pads or the very occasional clipboard.

It's difficult though to remain anonymous and impartial when it's your team, but help was at hand in the form of Orient defenders who presented the opposition with an opening goal in similar fashion to someone being given a Bafta award. In case anyone in the flats happened to miss the presentation as they popped back inside to top up the Martini with a bit of ice, the same players repeated the performance a short while after and Orient went in at half-time 2-0 down with heads bowed and euphoria resembling drunkenness swishing across the airwaves from the nearby Kentish men. I was sitting with my son Nick and we shared the sense of relief that no-one could identify us as supporters of the team who were heading for a heavy defeat. Our heads too were bowed, mine with a pretence of making notes on the pad I was holding.

The second half picked up where the first left off. Gillingham wrapped up any lingering uncertainty with an early third goal; Gary Alexander, the Orient striker, scythed into an opponent at waist-high level and along with everyone in Waltham Forest looked amazed when he was not shown a straight red card; and with half an hour to go John Rudge edged past me for an early exit back to Stoke. He'd seen enough and laughed as I said, 'You're going to miss the comeback, John.'

The Gillingham crowd became more obnoxious as they became more smug. With a quarter of the match remaining Orient made a forlorn substitution and brought on Jabo Ibehre, a great runner with great pace and great enthusiasm and a great record for resembling a headless chicken when he has to finish off a move or make a decent pass. Well, he might as well get a bit of exercise.

Within a couple of minutes Jabo had sprung to life and at the speed of light had gone past a defender only to be brought down in the area. Matt Lockwood, the long-serving Orient full-back, converted the penalty, but it was a token, not enough for us to reveal our true colours to the mob across the way, who momentarily had fallen quiet. But the psychology of a goal started to kick in. Within another five minutes, Lockwood had abandoned his left-back position to pop up at the far post and knock in a second. This time I became aware that there was an Orient fan-base somewhere in the ground and I couldn't help but become a part of it. Nick was also jumping and we were dangerously close to attracting attention.

Then it happened. One of the reasons that football never ceases to captivate: the knowledge that you never know what you might see at a game; maybe something you've never seen before: a linesman wearing a hat; a punch-up between two goalkeepers; a goal being given when the ball has actually gone wide. Tonight it's a comeback from 3-0 down. But not just a comeback, an Orient comeback and one that takes place within the last half-hour. But not just an Orient comeback from 3-0 down that takes place within the last half-hour: a comeback that's brought about by a player scoring a hat-trick. A full-back. A full-back scoring a hat-trick in the last half-hour!

And then Orient hit the bar!

Nick and I are on our feet, pointing, jeering, laughing, chanting with accompanied V-signs at the now silent and sick-looking loudmouths who just want to escape with a point. All sense of scout propriety has gone out the window. I'm a raw fan again, and yes, you wanna come across the dividing line for some and make our night perfect? Well we're ready for you here, you muppets...

The report I sent next day to Forest was created purely from memory. All relevant written information lay scattered among the detritus of celebration somewhere in the East Stand of Leyton Stadium.

Chapter 18

BREAKTHROUGH

Chelsea play Bolton twice in a week, once in the Carling Cup and then three days later in the league. I'm doing a team report after a 5.30pm kick-off on the Saturday, and Colin has asked if I can get the report to the analysts by Sunday lunchtime. He reminds me that the clocks go back, so I do have an extra hour. Very thoughtful! Doing a team report is a good three or more hours' work, consisting of individual player reports, formations and changes, substitutions, strengths and weaknesses of a team, specific patterns of play, overall observations and, the most time-consuming of the lot, diagrams of all set pieces – attacking corners, defending corners, attacking free kicks, defending free kicks, throw-ins, penalties... all copied down in the heat of the moment during a match as the ball is swung across from the corner flag and twenty bodies writhe around in the area to get possession, then transposed onto pitch diagrams for the analysts to do whatever they do with it.

It goes without saying that the accuracy of these diagrams can sometimes be flawed. Watching replays on *Match of the Day* can occasionally assist but only if you can make your television record and play back properly and only if the programme producers allow the match any prominence. I have suggested to Colin that each scout be provided with a Sky Sports package that allows us to review the whole game and slow it down at crucial moments. His laughter indicated that he thought I was joking.

Clubs don't go overboard with facilities for their scouts. I did once receive a fax machine courtesy of West Brom and occasionally some clubs have sent templates for match reports which have generally avoided the proofreading stage:

Question 9: Is the player right or left footed?

Question 10: Which foot does he prefer?

Question 16: How many players come back into the penalty area to defend corners?

Question 17: How many are left outside the area? (I must send that one to the exam board for next year's A-level maths exam!)

Bolton do, however, have access to a computer system known as Scout 7. At one of the Reebok meetings we are introduced to this state-of-the-art piece of technology, given a private password and sent on our way with the assurance that it will make team and player reports a doddle. Kids' play. Provided you have kids around to work the buttons. And provided you have a computer.

After several hand-written and faxed reports are sent through I decide to embark upon the technology trail. I buy a laptop and consult a list of instructions from Lee, the computer whizz-kid at Bolton, which explains the way to operate Scout 7, though I'm sure there is something additional which he has added that I failed to put down. I rack my brains in vain to think what it was. The first impressions are exciting. If I want to, I can see who is playing for a team in the Azerbaijani second division or for Perth Glory in Australia and I can create my own little cabinet where my player recommendations can be read and recorded, even if the players themselves never see the light of day at the Reebok.

Chelsea demolish Blackburn 5-0 and the game ends at 7.30pm, allowing me to reach home at 9pm. Having downed some supper, I'm ready for *Match of the Day*, followed by the Football League show which some clown at the BBC insists has to go on every week well into Sunday morning. By 1am TV watching is over and I decide it's time to join the 21st century and make a start on the match report. Scout 7 now really comes into its own, offering the teams, the line-ups, the scorers and substitutes and pretty diagrams of pitches and penalty areas onto which I can put players and balls and movements to demonstrate set pieces. It's wonderful, or at least it would be if the match was on the system. But it's not yet. I cut my losses at 1.17am and decide an early Sunday start will be the answer. I still can't remember what Lee said.

By Sunday morning we are up and running. I get a text from Lee saying that he won't be working on the report until mid afternoon so there's a bit of respite that allows me a coffee break. I forget to ask him what it was that I forgot. But the pretty pictures come onto the screen and I'm soon embroiled in the task with a vengeance, impressed by the fact that without any help from me I can see the teams, the substitutions, the times of the goals and the scorers. Nevertheless, the amount of information that needs to be put down takes me well past lunchtime, one hour, two hours, three hours. How do Chelsea attack? How do they defend? What are their five main strengths? What are their five main weaknesses? (Weaknesses? Five? After a 5-0 thrashing that could have been 9-0?) My concentration is boosted by listening to a radio commentary of Bolton playing a lunchtime game against Everton. As I begin the first of the sixteen diagrams I need to draw, Gary Cahill puts the lads 2-0 up. I switch off happily in order to concentrate on my artistic talents. I'm enjoying this.

After diagram 12, the fourth attacking free kick formation, I tune in again to see how Bolton are doing. It's now 2-2 and the deflation is acute. A team coming back from 2-0 down are much more likely to go on to win the match than lose it. Bolton still haven't won a league game at home. I smash the radio and return to the computer. There are only two diagrams to go and I'm looking forward to texting Lee soon to announce my success when, without warning or reason, the laptop goes off. I sit for a good three minutes looking at the black screen, totally stupefied. It is at that moment that Lee's forgotten advice returns: Make sure you save your work as you go along.

Whether my skill at forgetting things and failure to do the basics qualifies me to perform in the Bolton back four I have yet to decide. I telephone Lee to explain away the forthcoming absence but he's not a genius for nothing. Like a caring operator at the end of an emergency line, he gently talks me through recovery, both mine and the machine. Can I see a little white box? Yes I can. Can I put the cursor on the ball in the centre of the diagram... and I'm back with good old S7 – old friends now so I feel the abbreviation is justified, having made the technological breakthrough that has been threatening for years. My audible sigh of relief down the phone, however, is superseded by a yell of triumph coming from Lee: Bolton have just scored a late third! The sun breaks into the kitchen where I'm working; I reassemble the bits of the radio in time for the final whistle; a commentator informs us that it's two years to the day since Gary took over at Bolton; I'm tempted, but refrain from sending a congratulations card along with the final two diagrams which are finished, saved and sent. For a few Sunday afternoon minutes, God's in his heaven and all's right with the football world.

Chapter 19

LEST WE FORGET

Aldershot seems as good a place as any to attend a match on the day before Remembrance Sunday. The town itself feels like an extension of the army base that nestles alongside it. There are soldiers, in and out of uniform, around the streets, army vehicles and parade grounds visible from the train as it pulls into the station. And today there appears to be a special regard for the couple of squaddies outside the ground selling poppies, which everyone seems to be wearing; a special feel about the minute's silence impeccably observed by the two and a half thousand crowd; and particularly warm applause for the guys in uniform who stand on the pitch before the game and who, in a few weeks' time, may well be fighting for their lives in Afghanistan.

(I'm reminded of the old connection between football and warfare, especially significant for an Orient supporter. History tells that whilst the Clapton Orient team of 1914 may not have been conquering all and sundry, they did provide the first and most numerous of volunteers – 41 – who went off to fight as part of the 17th Middlesex, known as The Footballers' Battalion. An especial hero was a free-scoring centre forward by the name of Richard McFadden who, in peacetime, had already saved a man in a burning building, rescued a drowning boy from a river and then eschewed publicity. A Company Sergeant Major in the army, he won the Military Medal, was a feted leader and, along with two of his Orient teammates, paid the ultimate price. It's

72

barely a year since I joined 180 Orient supporters on a pilgrimage to their graves and memorials in France, and I still dip regularly into the book which records their exploits*)

Along with a dozen other clubs, Aldershot is one of the teams allocated to me by the Bolton bosses, who have scouts covering every club in the country, from Premiership to Conference, plus those in Scotland and Wales. The network is impressive: sixteen scouts, including a couple who concentrate on Europe; more extensive than many Premiership clubs, though none in the category of the Man City super-scouts who pocket £60K a year for the arduous task of travelling the world to watch football matches.

There aren't any Man City scouts at Aldershot, as far as I can see. I'm not expecting my trip to be productive, but it's good to keep tabs on the teams I'm meant to know, and every now and then a bright spark will pop up from the lower leagues or even the Conference and I keep Colin informed if anyone catches the eye. As usual, half my mind is on the Bolton game, today at Villa Park, and I hear on the radio that on the stroke of half-time no-one other than my friend Elmander has netted for the team, his first league goal for eleven months. Unfortunately, Villa have already scored two, but a goal just before the break can be a good psychological fillip. I'm hopeful as I go back for the second half to see Aldershot hold on to a 2-0 lead over Bury and book their place in the FA Cup second round. There are no hidden gems on the field as far as I can see, though some of the Aldershot defending is effective, if agricultural.

When, at the end of the game, I see snatches on TV of Bolton's defending, agricultural would be a complimentary expression unless it specifically referred to the stuff cows leave on fields. My ever-misplaced confidence is again proven correct. Bolton's second-half comeback has manifested itself in the shape of letting in three more goals, and were it not for Jääskeläinen the 5-1 defeat could have been a cricket score. I watch in horror as Knight resembles a piece on a chess board as he's left static in the penalty area for two of the goals, while his fellow ex-Villa and normally reliable defender Cahill, in his attempt to break into the England squad, seemingly decides to go for Man of the Match by contributing splendidly to Villa's fourth. What remaining hair Megson has must be in real danger as he watches the circus.

Bolton have now conceded thirteen goals in the last three matches. The undefeated run of a few weeks back fades into irrelevance as they now sink to just above the bottom three. I force myself to watch the debacle on *Match of the Day*, but at the end a bulletin over on World News informs us that the death toll in Afghanistan has risen in the time it's taken Lineker and Co. to run through the day's games. I think back to the lads at Aldershot, to a young ex-steward at Orient killed so recently in the Kandahar Province, and I can't quite work out where a game comes into the scheme of things or what I should really be feeling. I know, though, it's not happiness!

They Took The Lead by Stephen Jenkins.

Chapter 20

BOLTON v PORTSMOUTH

20 December 2008

I'd submitted a team report on Portsmouth, who had just lost 3-0 at home to Newcastle.

A fortnight later I was at the Reebok, having been invited up for a weekend's meeting followed by the match against Portsmouth. It was a bad weekend for a trip north, as two days before I was due there the car developed bird flu and needed a period of recuperation. I booked a late train to Horwich Parkway.

Travelling by public transport can be both environmentally smug-making and emotionally wrecking. The ticket cost me more than if I'd travelled to Bolton in a Rolls – a real incentive to use the train – but I got a seat in Coach B, the quiet carriage where mobiles and other equipment are meant to be in silent mode. I took out my latest Robert Harris novel and settled back. After ten minutes a phone rang and I was immediately on edge. The young woman three seats along had a brief but audible conversation about Kenny, who wouldn't be able to come up for the weekend as he needed to see a specialist about his allergy to bacon. I decided not to leave my seat to confront her, giving her the benefit of compassionate leave, or the equivalent. But my nerves were jangled and I couldn't relax in case anyone else should casually break the rules of the compartment.

At Crewe, a bald-headed, tattooed and muscular young man sat in the seat opposite me, looking as angry at nothing as anyone I'd ever seen. I avoided his gaze but couldn't avoid hearing the music coming from his iPod. My dilemma deepened as I contemplated four options. I could move seats, though that might seem obviously provocative and cause him to flip; I could let my Bolton pass fall accidentally onto the table and hope to engage him in pleasant football chit-chat; I could take him out with a pre-emptive SAS strike, shoving my fingers in his eye sockets before ripping the offending wire from his ears; or I could pour Christian forgiveness on him, reckoning that he'd just come back from Afghanistan where he may have seen his mates blown up and therefore had every right to feel pissed off with our wet and flabby society. Before I decided on which course of action to take, I was completely floored by a family of three children plus sweeping, middle-class, I-talk-in-a-loud-voice-so-everyone-can-hear-how-I-treat-my-darlings mother who was far worse and more irritating than her Giles, Jeremy or even the squawking Hermione. Compared to them, soldier boy seemed positively attractive, and I instantly decided to let him off. Instead I glared across the aisle at the year-old baby girl, who didn't seem to understand my message and went on squawking. By the time I changed trains at Manchester, I was a bag of nerves.

Bolton went two up within the first ten minutes. Fans around me were laughing and some of the other scouts were cracking jokes. I wasn't.

Two-nil is a dangerous score. Especially 2-0 after ten minutes. 2-0 gives you a false sense of security, and all it needs is a goal at the other end and then the whole confidence balance changes and you are on the back foot. A team pulling one back just before half-time goes in cock-a-hoop while the team still leading is deflated, as though they've already blown it. What's needed is a third goal to create a comfort zone, but Bolton don't do third goals.

Too many teams nowadays don't do third goals, and then the fourth and fifth and so on. Even teams that actually lead by three or four at half-time come out in the second half, having disembowelled the opposition already, and fail to score again, depriving their fans of a real feast. Do modern footballers sit back and get away with as little effort as possible? Do teams losing by four goals to nil suddenly feel that their pride is under attack and defend more desperately? Or has the age of compassion infiltrated the professional game, so that players think it's insulting to rub the opposition's noses in the dust, and that they will be berated by the experts sitting in front of the Sky cameras? It's rare nowadays to get anywhere near a cricket score in the way that my boyhood witnessed with some regularity: Spurs drawing 2-2 in a cup match at Crewe, winning the replay by 13-2. (The story is that Crewe arrived at Euston on Platform 13 and departed on Platform 2 but I've never seen this verified.) Not much sympathy there for the stalwart lads of Crewe who had fought out a valiant draw just a few days before. Or the Orient beating Chester 9-2 in a League Cup match.

Orient were bottom of the First Division at the time in their one and only whistle-stop visit to the top flight and I suppose finding it hard to beat most teams in that league (with the exception of Man U, Everton and Liverpool, who featured among their mere half-dozen victims!) decided to beat up the team from Division 4 as a bit of an entertaining and heartless distraction as to just how crap they were in the league. At 9-0, I recall shouting with enthusiasm for them to get No. 10, but instead Chester scored a consolation. The old boy standing next to me was disgusted, saying how conceding goals lowered morale. When Chester scored again he threw down his bobble hat and walked out in disgust.

Portsmouth started to recover from the early blitzkrieg and were looking dangerous.

Against Newcastle, Portsmouth appeared disorganised and hapless, the writing clearly on the wall for Tony Adams unless there could be a speedy improvement. Their only threat on goal came from the nine-foot neck of Crouch, coming in regularly at the back post to see if he could direct crosses into the net. Unfortunately for him, Newcastle stuck two tall defenders around him to negate the impact, and he didn't have a good day. But nowadays he has learned to jump, which took him a while to master from his early performances, and he's the kind of player you don't want to leave alone inside the penalty area. In my report to Bolton, this was underlined in red and written in capital letters.

Portsmouth score just before half-time.

Crouch comes in at the far post. Unchallenged. Heads the ball into the net.

The second half was not enjoyable and I didn't feel loved. Bolton held out at 2-1. I caught my breath and then the train back after the game, exuding a sense of relief and annoyance like some cheap aftershave. At Manchester I decided the quiet carriage was not worth the hassle and so found a spare seat in a bay of four. As the train pulled away, the other three seats were suddenly filled. I looked across and once more Hermione met my gaze.

Chapter 21

TRICK AND TREAT

Scouts often don't get the chance to see their own teams regularly, which is perhaps inevitable but still a pity. It can be embarrassing when someone asks you how X is doing since his transfer, and you really haven't a clue because you've seen as much of him on *Match of the Day* as the rest of the world. Also it means that you don't get a first-hand insight into the players, the strengths and weaknesses of the team, the way they play over ninety minutes.

So when Bolton take on Chelsea three days after I submit a match report on the Blues, I take the chance to go and watch them at Stamford Bridge. It's a week when the two teams play each other twice, first in the Carling Cup and then up at the Reebok in the league. I am initially reassured when I see the team sheet that Drogba is on the bench and Anelka and Terry are not in the squad, though I then notice that Kevin Davies and Jääskeläinen don't feature for Bolton. Given the offer I suppose I'd take the swap.

Three days ago Blackburn were insipid in their 5-0 defeat and I can't imagine Bolton caving in so tamely. I even go so far as to put a pound on a 1-1 draw at ninety minutes at odds of 11-2.

Though it would mean extra time and – who knows – going through on penalties, plus a late night home for the second day running, the boost to Bolton would be amazing, and the winnings would pay for my petrol.

It doesn't go to extra time.

Four goals prevent it, all going in at the wrong end: Bolton's. The lads do have a couple of chances and Matt Taylor misses a good opportunity to equalise but at the end of ninety minutes it's a dispiriting performance and Chelsea even have the gall to bring Drogba off the bench to join in the fun for half an hour. I get my first real look at Klasnic since I went to see him play in Germany and he looks OK, but my friend Elmander comes on at half-time and provides a less favourable impression. He doesn't look strong enough to compete against top-class defenders, doesn't jump for headers and looks awkward when he's running. Apart from that he's fine! Zat Knight wins balls in the air as he might be expected to do at 6ft 5ins but why, I wonder, does he win so few when he's up in the opponent's box for corners and set pieces? I think his goal tally so far this season is equal with his own goals. In this match his most memorable contribution is a sixty-yard back pass that's hit so powerfully that Ali Al Habsi in goal can't reach the thing (and daren't pick it up) before it goes off for a corner.

It's a depressing evening, ameliorated only by the fact that Chelsea clearly employ Miss World hopefuls for their reception staff, which brightens the visit of ageing scouts attempting to grow old disgracefully. And probably a lot of other heterosexuals with equal interest in football and prawn sandwiches. It's a real treat. My pre-match, half-time and after-match sandwiches and drinks are served by a young Colombian lady who leaves Jennifer Lopez standing. I don't normally have thirteen cups of tea but manage to keep needing a refill on this night. Conversation is thwarted a little by the fact that the nearest I've got to Colombia is Peru and she doesn't seem that impressed by my knowing the capital of her country. Even my fail-safe line – 'Has anybody ever written a poem about you?' – falls flat when she says her boyfriend has, and Vas, my barber, who is accompanying me for the evening, saves me further blushes by suggesting it is time to leave. He does acknowledge, however, that the staff who greet us, press lift buttons for us, bid us a welcome and a farewell are a lot nicer looking than the average customer he gets in his shop. But it still doesn't really compensate for Bolton's performance, and the only consolation is that in four days' time there will be opportunity for revenge when the teams meet again – this time at full strength. Roll on Saturday.

I think Halloween is rubbish: a recent American money-making import designed around the nonsense of ghosts and ghouls and begging kids knocking at my door at regular intervals. This year it falls on a Saturday, so at every football ground in the country there will be sellers of masks alongside the sellers of scarves, attempting to wheedle money out of badgered fathers who might cough up for the sake of a quiet life.

I'm at Millwall watching a Colchester midfielder by the name of Wordsworth wander across the field and use his sweet left foot to score a goal and create a host of golden chances which his colleagues don't take. He doesn't quite merit the accolade of poetry in motion but he's worth a mention on Scout 7. My mind, however, is drifting northwards and I keep wondering how Bolton are faring in their return match with the Premiership leaders. At half-time I attempt a quick exit down to the lounge to see the scores, only to be blocked by a youth wearing a Halloween mask and demanding payment to pass. I just manage to refrain from pushing him down the stairs but he doesn't get a sou from me as I edge past him ungraciously. The TV screen announces that it's 0-0 at the Reebok, but at the moment I begin a minor celebration there is a flash that Chelsea have been awarded a 45th-minute penalty.

Last Saturday Lampard scored a penalty against Blackburn. He has an outstanding recent record of converting penalties, but although he hits them hard they invariably go low to the keeper's right. If the keeper goes early it's definitely saveable. The match report I sent in specifically mentioned this fact so I wait with bated breath to watch Jussi interrupt Frank's successful record.

Jääskeläinen goes early.

Dives low.

To his left!

Lampard scores. In the other corner.

On the way back up to my seat I accidentally kick the kid with the mask, but I'm still hopeful of a Bolton comeback. Millwall win this game 2-1 and Wordsworth hits the bar. Once again I make a quick dash for the TV to see how Bolton have responded after their 4-0 midweek drubbing and the late first-half penalty. I'm optimistic that they might still spring a trick or two.

They lose the game. 4-0.

Driving home I stop and buy the scariest Halloween mask I can find, determined to frighten any knocking children in the way that Drogba and Co. have clearly frightened the Bolton defence. I'd feel better if I could spread the annoyance.

I'm on the phone on Monday to Colin in real November mood. I need to know where the breakdown occurs between drawing diagrams of penalties and the ball being picked out of the back of the net. He phones me back an hour later, having spoken to the analysts.

It transpires that in addition to my masterpiece they showed Jussi twenty penalties taken by Lampard, nearly all of them going to the 'keeper's right side. But Jussi decides to employ psychology and play a double bluff; he stands slightly to his right, inviting Frank to shoot into the wide open space to the left where Jussi subsequently dives and makes a spectacular grab at thin air. Penalty No. 21 goes into the same area as the previous twenty.

'Goalkeepers', Colin asks rhetorically before ringing off, 'why do they even try to play tricks?'

Time of the year maybe...

Chapter 22

STORIES

Strange things can happen while scouting.

I was in the Jimmy Dickinson Lounge at Portsmouth talking at half-time to Pat, a curly-haired middle-aged guy who works for Birmingham. A few feet away a suited and bespectacled man was drinking with a woman of about forty. As the man drifted off to answer the call of nature, the woman sidled up next to Pat. 'Do you fancy coming to my place after the match?' she asked him.

Pat was understandably lost for a moment and could only utter a strangled 'Pardon?'

She repeated the invitation, whereupon Pat replied, 'But you're with that man who's... who's just gone off.'

The woman didn't bat an eyelid. 'Yeah, but I'm trying to dump him. Do you fancy it?'

Pat managed to stammer out an excuse, something to do with a train he had to catch and the woman shrugged, looked around the lounge eyeing up the alternatives and departed with 'Suit yourself.' I didn't know whether to congratulate Pat or commiserate with him, and he didn't seem to know whether to be amused, complimented or shocked. We did both keep an eye on the woman as she sauntered back along the bar, intrigued as to her next possible move. But at the end of half-time she was still there on her own, now looking distinctly upset; the boyfriend seemed to have done a runner. I was torn between continuing my match report or going over to console her, but before a decision could be made, she flung a glass noisily onto the floor, flounced past Pat and in a loud voice shouted 'Bastard' at him before making a stunning exit. As she left, every eye was turned towards my Birmingham colleague and I edged as far away from him as I could to allow him the full opprobrium heading his way.

Birmingham lost their next fixture heavily.

Keith at Forest asked me to go to Basingstoke to look at a player who had come to his attention. It's a bit of a drag on a Wednesday night, but people outside the tube line have no conception of how much fun the M25 can be at rush-hour time. The number of occasions I've been asked by my northerly brethren (where clearly maps haven't been brought yet by the missionaries), 'How far is Wycombe (or Havant or Bournemouth!) from you?' There is still a misconception that ten miles along the country lanes around Stockport or Nottingham is the same as ten miles through the middle or round the outside of London. However, Basingstoke was reached with a good half-hour to spare. It was my first visit there and I spoke to the gentleman sitting behind the reception desk, giving my name and club in time-honoured fashion. Without searching, he replied, 'We don't have a ticket for you.'

'Oh, I know the club put one on. They said they'd sent a fax.'

'Yes, we got the fax.'

I smiled blandly and waited for the punchline, thinking that I must be missing out on the brand of humour that Basingstoke is renowned for. It didn't come. 'So, the ticket...?'

'We're not giving out free tickets to you lot. Clubs like yours can buy their own. £7 at the gate.' I waited just a second for the *Candid Camera* smile to appear that I knew was not coming. Welcome to Basingstoke! And when the game started, just to top off the evening, the players were wearing shirts without numbers. Whoever the player was that attracted attention, I assume he's still doing it down in the wilds of Surrey.

It's amazing what a jacket and tie can do for you. Car parking at Charlton used to be provided but now is not. Not that it matters as there is a massive Makro just down the road, five minutes' walk from the ground. Going to watch the newly-relegated outfit in their new League One surroundings, I turned up at 2.30 only to be met by Makro Man at the entrance to the car park. 'Have you got your Makro card, sir?' he asked in a thick Indian accent. I thought quickly, wondering if I should engage him in entertaining tales from my visit to the Punjab. I really didn't want to be searching around for a space with half an hour to go.

All I came up with was: 'Actually, I haven't brought it.'

'We can't let you in, sir – the football people are all parking here when they shouldn't.'

'Well look,' I said, with all the authority of a white shirt that I could muster, 'do I look like I'm dressed to go to a football match?' I could see the hesitation in his eyes, the risk and repercussions of upsetting a valued customer and I just hoped he didn't recognise the Bolton crest on my tie. Seconds passed. Authority won out. 'OK sir, but please bring your card with you next time.'

I assured him I would and thanked him for using his common sense. I hoped he went home feeling pleased at the compliment. I slept easily, knowing I hadn't told him a lie.

Chapter 23

MR BROWN

Somehow or another Mr Brown is given my name as someone who does part-time tutoring. He rings me up to explain that he has a daughter and a son, twins, who are both heading towards their GCSEs next summer. Both are bright but the boy is lazy and needs pushing. Could I give them some help in English for a couple of terms?

I ascertain that Mr Brown is an old school pal of Tunji, a friend and ex-colleague of mine who occasionally goes to watch Arsenal reserves. He and Mr Brown apparently grew up in Lagos, went to university together and then went their different ways, with Tunji teaching science while Mr Brown made a packet doing something that Tunji never makes clear. I don't like to pry but I'm intrigued when the two students arrive at my house in a chauffeur-driven Merc. I feel better about charging £25 an hour rather than my normal £20.

After three weeks of inferential comprehension interspersed with forays into the world of iambic pentameters, Dapo guides me away from grammar and onto the world of football. We digress for ten minutes, mentioning that he might like to read *Fever Pitch* so as not to appear to be wholly off course, and he learns that I work for Bolton as a scout. The rest of the lesson deteriorates inexorably.

A few days later I am visited by Mr Brown himself. Inviting him in, I prepare my defence for the wasted lesson with Dapo and am about to offer him a refund when he smiles broadly and announces that his son has informed him of my Reebok attachment. I breathe a sigh of relief but am confused as to why he should pay a visit just because he's learned that I work for Bolton. It then becomes clearer, albeit depressing.

'I have a nephew. Very good footballer. Excellent skills.' Oh dear! If only I had a pound for every person who has told me about their outstanding five-year-old goalkeeping grandson, or their thirty-one-year-old brother-in-law who is setting Wales alight playing for Haverford West Reserves... I listen politely, nodding appropriately. 'His manager says he is the best player he's ever seen for his age. Outstanding.'

'How old is he?' I enquire with as much feigned interest as I can muster.

'Fifteen. Sixteen next July.'

'And his position?'

'Can play anywhere. Midfield. Striker. Even plays as a centre back.'

'Utility player, that's good,' trying to keep the level convincing.

'Very intelligent boy. He's got top grades in his school in all his subjects.'

I try to prepare the ground for Plan B. 'That's very useful. Too many youngsters are prepared to sacrifice their education just on the hope that they'll make it in football.'

'But this boy will!'

So much for Plan B.

'He's got everything he needs to make it. All he needs is for someone to spot him and recommend him.'

I am aware of the crunch coming. Not wishing to upset Mr Brown, I ease gently into the intended refusal. 'Well, usually lads of his age are picked up by youth scouts, maybe if they've been seen playing for their school or district sides...'

'The scouts in his area are rubbish though,' he interrupts. 'I would rather my grandmother gave her opinion than those guys. He really needs to be seen by someone with a professional eye, someone who knows about football and can spot potential.'

I search quickly for the next riposte but Mr Brown continues. 'I would really appreciate it if you could look at him. I would class it as a great favour, and when he makes it as a top professional I know he will not forget you.'

A flash instantly comes and goes of him running down the wing at the Emirates while I watch from an executive box and drink champagne. While not bowled over by the Brown promise, I am at a loss to construct a convincing refusal, reasoning that it's not too much of a burden to go and watch the lad play once or twice. Mr Brown chimes in again. 'He's playing in a tournament before Christmas, over a weekend. He'll be playing in three or four matches, so you could really have a good look at his ability.'

'What weekend is it?' I enquire, hoping that I can show him I'm obligated to do a match report at Tottenham that Saturday, but when he tells me I discover there are no pre-ordained commitments. 'Well,' I concede, 'I guess I could make it. I'm not down to do any particular matches that weekend and I can clear it with my chief scout.'

'Excellent,' he replies. 'You will not be disappointed. I will telephone him and tell him tonight.'

'Oh, by the way, where does he go to school? Whereabouts is the tournament?'

Mr Brown beams widely. 'Beautiful new school, just recently built. State of the art facilities. An hour from Lagos.'

Chapter 24

TELLING COLIN

The conversation I have with Colin takes on a slightly surreal air.

'Colin, I've had a shout about a lad who's meant to be really good.'

'Go on. What's his name?'

I suddenly realise that I don't know this basic piece of information. 'Oh, can't remember exactly. I'll text it through to you.'

'Who does he play for then?' Another basic question with another basic non-answer.

'Well, he's not signed up for any club yet, but he is playing in a competition coming up soon.' I can feel Colin is smelling a distant rat. 'I said I'd go along and watch him in three weeks. I'm not doing a match report that weekend.'

'Where?' Cut to the chase, Colin.

'Er, well actually it's near... Lagos.'

There is a pause. 'Lagos.'

I pause too. 'Just outside.'

'Lagos, as in Lagos, Nigeria?'

Colin's geographical expertise goes up in my estimation. He must have had a good teacher. Or maybe he's played there.

'You're watching a lad whose name you don't know play in some obscure competition in Nigeria. Have I got that right?'

Apart from 'Yes' I don't know what to say.

'Are you intending to submit an expense form this month? I'm just asking so I can warn the chairman that we'll need to sell a player or two.' Scouse humour, not very subtle.

I reassure him. 'It's all paid for, Colin. I'm going as a guest of the lad's relations.'

I can hear him shaking his head, but there's also a whiff of relief that I haven't landed him in it completely. He does need time to think though, but reminiscent of his playing days his foot is on the ball for only a second before he threads the telling pass through to the inside-right.

'Go on. But don't use your initiative when you're there. And don't take up any offers from the hotel. OK?'

I haven't the foggiest idea what he's talking about but decide it's politic to quit while the green light is showing.

Chapter 25

IN AND OUT OF AFRICA

I've never been to Africa, so there is a tweak of excitement about the prospect. A week before the proposed visit I am being fast-tracked at the Nigerian embassy for a visa, thanks to a lady who is a distant relative of the Browns.

'We're flying KLM,' Brown informs me. 'Better than Turkish Airlines,' he adds. 'We leave Friday morning, then there are games on the Saturday and Sunday and we fly back overnight on Sunday.'

It sounds like a hectic schedule but I'm not paying so I don't feel objections are in order. I'm relieved to know that Brown will be coming too. All the travel and guide books that I've looked through say the same thing about Lagos: get out of it as soon as you can.

We fly from London City to Amsterdam on Friday morning, leaving at 9am. All the flights are on time except for one: KLM. Ours. It eventually leaves at 10.20 and we land at Schiphol just as the Lagos flight is departing. Good old KLM! The woman at the desk smiles and happily tells us that we can be accommodated in a local hotel and fly out tomorrow. As we are still in Europe I take charge and tell her that it's essential we fly today. Gradually the smile disappears and eventually, with a shrug of the shoulders and a couple of phone calls, we are booked on a flight to Ghana where we will transfer and fly Virgin Nigeria to Lagos. I'm taking in two African countries for the price of one.

It's dark and late when we finally reach Lagos. We're met at the airport by a chauffeur in a shining white

BMW. Brown is staying with his friend who owns the car, but as this guy also has a live-in cook and security guard as well as the chauffeur there is no spare bedroom, so I'm booked in at a nearby hotel. The drive from the airport is a unique experience. I've read that there are fourteen million people in Lagos and they're all on the streets to meet us. There are no traffic rules and every second vehicle seems to be falling apart. Miraculously we arrive at the hotel intact, not much like any hotel I've ever stayed in, though it does remind me of a converted convent that houses travellers in a small Australian town called Beechwood. My room is the size of a small hall and the bed in it is wide enough for six. The windows have no glass, only mesh; there is a second room – a lounge of sorts – with a second television, a bathroom in which water only drips from the taps and no toilet paper. As I'm improvising with serviettes from the plane, the electricity fails and everything is plunged into darkness. I cut my losses and head for bed.

Before being collected in the morning, I decide to try a breakfast of yam and cereal. The yam is not my cup of tea and there is not a cup of tea anywhere in the hotel. The cornflakes come with powdered evaporated milk but still take twenty-five minutes to arrive. The chauffeur arrives at 9am, not a minute too soon, and we are quickly heading towards Ibadan, an hour's journey away. The games, I'm told, kick off at 11am so we have plenty of time. In theory, at least, but that doesn't allow for a hold-up on the freeway in which we find ourselves embroiled. For nine hours. I vow never to moan again about the M25 and find this whole experience amazing. There are hundreds, thousands of vehicles jammed together at a variety of angles, some trying U-turns, others crossing the central reservation to speed down the freeway in the opposite direction. Scores of youths and children emerge outside to sell us drinks, fruit, mobile phone cases, autobiographies of Bill Clinton and anything else that might be of use in passing the time. I decide to get out and have a stroll to unstiffen my legs but Brown vehemently prohibits it.

'Please don't use your initiative while you're here,' he informs me, and somewhere a bell in my head gives a tinkle. There is not a policeman in sight but we learn from the grapevine that a tanker has crashed ten miles down the road and cannot be moved until the insurance representatives come and take photos. Thankfully we have air-conditioning, unlike most other vehicles around us, but incredibly, despite the heat and frustration of hours, there is not a sign of bad temper or road-rage. I'm impressed by the toleration levels and assume this is part of everyday life.

We reach Ibadan just after six, but are stopped and pulled over by a police roadblock on the outskirts. Brown winds down the window and as a young, black sweating face peers in at me and the other occupants, asks, 'Hello officer, what can we do for you?' A conversation then ensues which seems to involve shouting, laughing, looking at me, nodding and shaking of heads before a wad of money is handed over to the policeman, who then comes round to my side of the car and opens the door. Every film I've ever seen concerning hijacks and summary executions flashes through my mind as he reaches in towards me, but instead of a bullet through the temple he shakes my hand and informs me, 'You need another striker to help Kevin Davies. You should have signed Michael Owen.' Out of a sense of amazed relief I almost laugh out loud as I shake his hand and agree vehemently. As we drive off I ask Brown how this apparent extortion can be so good-natured and learn that it's a kind of unofficial tax. Not only are the police paid a pittance, they also have to buy their own petrol for the police cars.

The town itself is poor and ramshackle and the obvious poverty depresses me, driving through in the BMW. A mile out of town, however, we come to the venue for the football competition – a newly built, gleaming-white school that reminds me of the pictures in old films of Foreign Legion forts rising elegantly from the wastes of the desert. The competing teams are just emerging from the changing rooms and after standing around for twenty minutes while Mr Brown and Joseph, the chauffeur have conversations with several other people I'm finally ushered into the Principal's office to be greeted by a large laughing lady who, I learn, paid for the whole school to be built and now acts as its head teacher. She exudes warmth and generosity, has a bible on her desk, thanks me for coming to look at the boys playing football and then asks me if I know anyone who can build her a sports stadium.

Five minutes later, the lad I've crossed the equator to see enters the office, greets Mr Brown, who then introduces me, and finally kisses the head teacher, who turns out to be his mum. Things are falling into place. Bolo is a tall, lithe, good-looking youth with a pleasant shy face that lacks any hint of swagger or arrogance. He is told to sit opposite us, to sit up straight and to answer all the questions that I am now going to put to him. Unaware that I was expected to conduct an interview, I duly oblige by asking him as many things as I can think of and sounding professional into the bargain. To convince them that I know what I'm on about I throw in questions about zonal marking and diamond formations, hoping that Brown and the lady will be both baffled and impressed. After ten minutes I know everything there is to know about Bolo, even down to his boot size. Not having brought a notepad, though, it is all stored in my head. The observers are impressed.

We decide to stay in a local hotel so as not to miss the next day's games. This one is more upmarket and in the morning Brown informs me that it's part of Nigerian tradition in some hotels to offer the services of a lady, but that he declined on my behalf to save me embarrassment. I don't know whether to feel relieved or disappointed but I am determined to pump Colin when I next speak to find out exactly how he knows these things.

The games are underway by the time we reach the school but Bolo's match hasn't kicked off. There are several teams in the competition, each playing twenty-minute 11-a-side games on good-quality grass. I can see from the kit worn that the kids here must come from the upper echelons of Nigerian society and I wonder what kind of interest is taken in those in the downtown areas.

Bolo captains his side and starts off in the centre of midfield. He touches the ball in the first five seconds but then isn't involved in the next five minutes. I am already formulating a speech to deliver to his mother and the rest of Nigeria explaining that, yes, the lad looks to have potential, but he needs to mature and work on his technical ability before he could be considered, when he chests down a ball on the halfway line, glides effortlessly past two opponents with really impressive acceleration and then unleashes a thirty-yard left-foot drive that even Jussi might have let fly into the net. My speech preparation is aborted in mid-sentence. It's a Susan Boyle moment and I begin to take my mission more seriously.

By the end of the day I'm totally sold on the lad. He has tremendous control and vision, soft feet to kill a ball easily, can use his head in both defence and attack and wallops the ball well with either foot. In fact there is not an area of his game that seems weak. I feel like a prospector who has just found a nugget and when mum, Brown and I meet together after the competition ends I am genuine in my enthusiasm. When Bolo arrives I am prepared to promise him that Bolton will be seriously interested in monitoring him and, I'm sure, in inviting him to the UK for a trial as soon as it can be arranged. Bolo smiles and looks a bit overwhelmed. He then begins a conversation in Yoruba with his mother, occasionally incorporating English words and phrases but not enough for me to catch the drift.

Mr Brown joins in the discussion but I can't gauge from any of them in tone or expression what's being discussed. After ten minutes they all stop and the lady beams at me with a face to match her lovely floral dress. She never stops smiling as she tells me, 'Bolo has decided that he wants to be a doctor. And he's a very good boy and he will become a very good doctor. We need good doctors here I'm sure you know. We need good doctors more than we need good footballers. So he will become a doctor.'

Bolo himself adds, 'I want to thank you for coming here Mr Les and I hope you don't mind my decision.'

Not for the first time since arriving in Africa, I don't know what to say, but the three other people in the room look so content and relaxed that I see any attempt to persuade him to change his mind would feel not only useless but immoral, and I gaze silently at this lad for a few minutes with a mixture of admiration and humility. All I wonder is how I'm going to explain this to Colin without sounding like a failure. Maybe Bolton will need a new club doctor in a few years' time.

Chapter 26

BERWICK RANGERS v
STENHOUSEMUIR

8 April 2006

I'd been in Scotland for a week or so enjoying a break at my holiday home in the Borders. It's a different way of life from the metropolis but I was developing withdrawal symptoms, not having seen a match for over a week. The nearest fashionable clubs are in Edinburgh – Hearts or Hibs, a good hour away – or Newcastle ninety minutes south. But there is Berwick Rangers, only half an hour's drive, playing on Saturday, and even if it is Scottish Division Three it's a match.

I'd been to see Berwick play on two occasions, many years ago, for reasons that I couldn't now remember or imagine. They get a crowd that averages around 350, most of them shepherds, and play in a ground that is three-quarters open and extends behind the goals like an American prairie. It would be useless and interesting to know just how many bodies could be packed into the ground were it ever to be filled. Of course, you would have to segregate people by height as there is no upward slope behind either goal. Imagine a lad of five-foot-nothing at the back of 2,000 people, all on a level. Be a great afternoon out. (Perhaps this is the birthplace of the overused phrase about a level playing field.)

They did, of course, once pack in several thousand for a memorable match against Rangers in a Scottish Cup tie, and, as the zenith of their achievements, beat the mighty Glaswegians by a single goal. The other thing about Berwick, as every football trivia mogul in the world knows, is that they are the only English club to play in the Scottish league. Quite how this fits into Anglo-Scottish relations, I'm not sure. Do the good folk of Dumbarton or Arbroath doubly celebrate wins over the Wee Gers as not only a football feat but a re-run of Bannockburn? Or does the town of Berwick put on a kilt every other Saturday and pretend that the great 1483 takeaway never really happened and that they are all subjugated clansmen together?

I telephoned Forest and asked Carol Washington, who has been organising tickets since the days of Clough, to fax through a request for a ticket. Realising that Shielfield is not quite White Hart Lane, I decided that the jacket and tie routine might be a little stuffy and provide scant protection against the chilly April winds blowing in off the North Sea. 'Casual' was the word I maintained for my appearance; 'scruffy' was my wife's choice.

The car park was on a wet field, providing space for the listed elite. If this was the place for guests, I was intrigued to know what was left for the ordinary punter. It was a good job I was wearing my second-oldest shoes as by the time I reached terra-firma there was a cake of mud attached to the soles. I stamped off what I could before approaching the main door – actually the only door – that was guarded by a man in authentic commissionaire uniform. He could have come straight from Highbury. I announced myself – Les Padfield, Nottingham Forest – and had to repeat it for him to understand. I'm not sure if he was hard of hearing or merely Scottish, but as the penny dropped I was stunned into waking up when he said, 'Wait there, I'll go and get the chairman.'

In less than a minute a well-dressed youngish man was shaking me by the hand and introducing himself as Robert Wilson, the chairman and current owner of the club. I was led inside and up the carpeted stairs, fearing to look behind for any sodden trail I might be leaving, and then into an area where there were other smartly dressed male occupants wearing blazers that denoted the crests of either Berwick Rangers or Stenhousemuir. I was introduced to a few by my name and club, asked what I'd like to drink, and began polite conversation with a couple of elderly gentlemen who spoke in considerately slow accented terms so that I could understand. Robert returned with my drink and I felt I ought to apologise for my dress-code. But while I was still wondering whether this was terrific, generous hospitality that a small club lavished out on all visiting scouts, or whether scouts were as rare to Berwick as visitors from the planet Zog and therefore to be feted as an interesting, alien species, Robert enlightened me. It turned out that, despite his clearly Scottish nationality, he was, in fact, a rabid Forest fan.

We spent the next twenty minutes discussing the present, past and future fortunes of Forest. Robert mentioned in passing his affiliation with Berwick and that he had ploughed a few score thousand into the club to keep it going. I discovered he was a meat-dealer by trade and concluded that the industry must be doing well in the north of England. It transpired that when things at Berwick got too tedious to watch, he zoomed off south to support his favourites. He then quizzed me about my presence at the match.

'I suppose you've come to watch the Stenhousemuir lad Templeman. He's no bad for a sixteen-year-old.' I'd never heard of the lad Templeman but I didn't want to appear totally ignorant of the Scottish scene, which I was, nor confess that I'd just turned up because there was nowhere else to go. So I responded with a few banal pleasantries, 'Yes, I hear he's quite a prospect... been attracting some attention...likely to move on sometime...' and picked up on a few details about this lad in the process. Could I have by chance stumbled upon a find, I wondered?

The game itself was kick and rush, similar in standard to when I saw a Post Office XI take on the Essex Police 6th team at Hackney Marshes. No, that's unkind, but it was about the level of the Conference South. Berwick outmuscled their opponents and the sixteen-year-old looked every bit a sixteen-year-old. He may have had a bright future; he may have been having a poor day; he may turn out to be the next Denis Law – I struggle to name a current Scottish hero of similar ilk – but on this showing it would have been embarrassing to pass his name on as someone to watch. I didn't tell any of the assembled gathering this: scouts are meant to be notoriously circumspect and I didn't want to break rank. Instead I enjoyed the company, the hospitality, the friendliness of both sets of directors, the honesty of all who seemed to be associated with the clubs. The players there may not be world-beaters but neither were they prima donnas, diving to win free kicks and sympathy, driving off back across the border in flashy and expensive cars, having heads that run the risk of getting stuck between the goalposts. It was a pleasant, albeit unproductive afternoon and as I thanked Robert and wished him farewell, I was given an open invitation to any future game at Shielfield, and we swapped mobile numbers so as to stay in touch.

Three days later, on my way south, Frank Barlow, who had taken charge temporarily at Forest after Megson's departure, telephoned me about the forthcoming weekend. He asked in passing about the Berwick game and I recounted my impressions of the standard of the football, mentioning that there was a Stenhousemuir lad who had been recommended, but that I hadn't fancied him. I heard him exclaim at the other end, then laugh, then swear. It seems that the local Nottingham paper had had this lad's name plastered over its sports pages as a prospective player and star of the future for Forest. Frank had been at a loss to understand where the story had originated and the chairman had quizzed him about rumours such as this, not without some displeasure. His plea of total ignorance had not been met with much grace. Rumours, said the chairman, had to have a base in something.

Frank thanked me for putting him in it. And I learned at first hand the power of Chinese whispers when it comes to the press.

Chapter 27

THE HORSE'S MOUTH

A college friend and I meet up at Waterloo for the first time in forty years through the Old Codgers Reunited website. He's lived and taught in Oldham for his entire career but many moons ago transferred allegiances from the Latics to Bolton, where he's now a season-ticket holder. Inevitably, we spend most of our two-hour coffee session talking football whilst his wife beats a retreat and does some shops.

It's interesting for me to hear the views of a fan who watches the team home game after home game, and like the vast majority of seasoned, committed supporters I know, he has little but criticism for his favourites.

Pete may have more cause than most, but I know Chelsea fans who are regularly bemoaning their side's performances, Arsenal followers who think Wenger has got it all wrong, United supporters who claim that Ferguson doesn't understand tactics. And of course, there's Benitez and Liverpool!

I wonder how many thousands of the population spend their Saturday afternoons and evenings in a regular state of self-imposed depression. Why it is that hordes attend games with the almost certain knowledge that they won't enjoy what they see, and for most of the time are not disappointed?

Pete says that, over the years, watching Bolton has been like spending your holiday at the dentist. For as long as he can remember they have played direct, uncomplicated, muscular football, that is to the beautiful game what Maria Callas is to oxyacetylene

104

welding. Ugly football has been the term used by some people, perhaps a little unkindly but possibly as near a fitting description as can be found. The difference at the moment, Pete says, is that whereas they used to play ugly football and win, now they're playing ugly football and not winning. Those two combined make a dangerous duo.

Why is it, I wonder, that some clubs become associated with a particular brand of football which seems to stay with them for years and years, sometimes decades. From the early '60s West Ham have been renowned for playing attractive, cultured football, which may have reached its zenith in the days of Moore, Hurst and Peters but still seems to be an expectation with the fans despite the actual reality of much of the stuff they churn out. Tottenham has always been a place to go to for goals; Newcastle have been inexplicably synonymous with failure for more than fifty years, despite massive near-maniacal support from a large fan base. Just walk about the city and see the number of inhabitants who sport replica shirts every day of the week and then take them off to freeze at matches. Each time I go to Crystal Palace it's with a sense of gloom: it's highly unlikely I shall see an entertaining game, whatever the score. Orient won't score goals, unless they're playing Newcastle; Millwall, situated next to a recycling plant, traditionally offer up rubbish for two thirds of the match and then come up with a winner. Fulham are always rubbish in the first half, while Carlisle live on their outpost mentality, their performances being as unpredictable as Lakeland weather.

Does the location influence the play? Bolton strikes me as a pretty dour and uninspiring place, an area of traditional no-nonsense toughness. Is that why its football looks the same, even going back to the days of the uncompromising Nat Lofthouse, famed for knocking goalkeepers unconscious before bundling the ball into the goal? I must try to find out if there has been a period since the war when the club established a reputation for bright, attractive football.

It clearly is possible to turn an image around. The 'Boring Boring Arsenal' of George Graham days has now given way to a decade of Wenger, and many scouts would agree that of all the teams in the Premiership, on their day Arsenal play the most attractive and entertaining football of anyone. So why not at Bolton? Could Gary introduce a bit of flair and panache into the Reebok setting? Would the finances stretch to incorporating some ball-playing wizard? Is it part of Gary's managerial mentality to even try it, or would he point to the disastrous short-lived attempt by Sammy Lee, who seemed to want to break the Allardyce mould and promptly landed Bolton at the foot of the table? I must ask Gary what he thinks, if he's still in a job the next time we talk!

Chapter 28

LIVINGSTON, I PRESUME

Robert Wilson telephones me at the end of the summer break. He has now sold Berwick Rangers to a consortium of fans and after a few months of exploring the freedom-from-responsibility wilderness is considering taking the plunge back into the mire, rescuing a club from the brink of extinction, along with three other joint owners. He can't yet divulge which club it is, but it doesn't take a genius to put two and two together.

Livingston are a relatively new club, though they trace their roots back to the old Edinburgh team of Meadowbank Thistle. Having worked their way up to the Scottish Premier League in rapid time, they now find themselves back in the third division, enduring a massive penalty for the maladministration of the previous owner – an Italian who many considered to be completely bonkers and who cut off the electricity to the stadium to teach the fans a lesson in gratitude. Holiday bookings to Italy fell by two-thirds in the Livingston area.

I'm a mile north of the border for a short break some weeks later and decide to give Robert a call. Livingston have a midweek match against Annan Athletic (a name to stir very few footballing – or any other – memories) and Robert invites me to the game. He lives in Berwick but works seventy miles north in Edinburgh and says that if I can meet him by Waverley Station he'll drop me off after the game on his way back home. I decide to drive six miles from my abode, park in Kelso and catch the Edinburgh bus, a two-hour journey that doubles the car time but halves the petrol price and adds to my green credentials. Moreover, with tram installations flowing fully in an attempt to turn the Scottish capital into something akin to Hamburg or Budapest, I'm keen to avoid the added chaos that driving and parking would encounter in the messed-up city centre.

On the way to the ground Robert tells me again about a lad who plays left-sided midfield for the club and has been attracting attention. Andrew Halliday is just eighteen and already scouts from Fulham, Hearts and other places have turned up to run the rule over him. I meet him and other players before the game and am impressed by his quiet level-headedness and pleasant, polite manner. If his football matches his character he may well have a bright future.

It's a nice set-up at the club: a new all-seater stadium, good facilities and a really friendly atmosphere emanating from the owners right up to the fans, who cheerfully fill about one-twentieth of the ground. As far as Scottish clubs go, it feels like they are misplaced in the lowest league, but I'm told they have constant battles on their hands. Not only, it seems, were they relegated by an unprecedented two divisions, but knives are out to get them for refusing to play their first fixture on time, when they were still fighting the original punishment. There is a consensus among many people that the SFA is riddled with small-minded and vindictive individuals, most of whom come from other Scottish – and less successful – clubs. Some now want to dock a further fifteen points from the club.

Annan are despatched 2-0 and Livingston go top of the division, at least for the night. Andrew Halliday, returning from injury, comes on for the last twenty-five minutes and impresses with some good runs and the use of both feet, but it's important to remember that he's not pitted against world-class defenders. After the game I talk for a while to his manager and the Annan boss, who comes in and happily accepts a whisky, (what else!). He's not devastated by the defeat but does say that he wished he'd played his great-aunt at centre-half instead of the lump who gave away both goals. I worry about the player's return journey to the south-west and hope he doesn't sit near his acerbic manager.

We leave the ground at 10.50pm and Robert is surprised to learn that I didn't actually take the train from Berwick but the bus from Kelso. I feel rather awkward at the fact that it means a bit of a detour for him but he says it's only about ten miles extra. It's still raining as we bypass Edinburgh and head south, leaving the A68 to funnel down to the small border town where I left the car. We talk about the game and the young lad Halliday and I tell Robert that I shall certainly put his details on the Bolton system, but Scottish Division 3 level is unlikely to bring the posse charging up over the border, although if Fulham have shown interest, why not Bolton?

The street lights of Kelso, all five of them, appear in the distance at just the moment the car headlights pick out the sign that says 'Bridge Closed'. We grind to a halt and look in vain for a diversion sign, but there is none. Robert has no map in his car, his sat nav is on the blink and he's not familiar with this area. He's also working in the morning and is now about eight miles and fifteen minutes away from his best route home. I make an instant decision.

'Robert, drop me off here and I'll walk over the bridge and into Kelso.'

'You can't do that, it's almost midnight.'

'It's no problem. Kelso can't be more than four or five miles away, you can see the lights. I can do it in an hour or so.'

'But it's pitch black.'

'I've got a light on my mobile. I'm not going to have you drive round and round in the countryside looking for non-existent roads. And you're working tomorrow, I'm not. I'll be fine.'

Reluctantly he concedes, turns the car around and heads off back to the distant main road. I watch his red tail lights fade into the deep blackness like some departing spaceship, put on my mobile torch, which I realise is not quite as powerful as I thought, and head down the inky road towards the bridge, thankful that it isn't raining. I calculate that if I hit Kelso by 1.15 I'll be in bed by 1.30.

I can't get across the bridge. In the dark I manage to work out that there's a huge scaffold across it with plastic sheeting on three sides. In the gloom I feel like I'm walking into some massive tent. I decide to try to edge my way around the side, but peering down into what I can't see but can hear is fast-flowing water, I decide it's not a good night to fall into the river. I edge my way back.

Devoid of any good ideas I consider calling Colin to illustrate my dedication to Bolton Wanderers Football Club which has, indirectly, landed me in this fine Laurel and Harvey mess. He probably won't answer his phone at midnight, but it would feel gratifying just to be able to make him aware of the sacrifice. Instead I walk back up the blackened road, though why I'm not quite sure, and start to laugh. Hysteria or hypothermia, I haven't a clue where to go or really what to do, and it's too cold to camp out for the night. Through an out-of-

110

body experience, I look down upon this lost and lonely Londoner marching blindly into a new day with only the Scottish night-time wildlife to keep him company. And I think: what a tosser!

I ring 999 and ask for the police. What sounds like a twelve-year-old girl speaks to me in a broad accent, but at least it's a human voice.

'Hello,' I begin, deciding against putting on an 80-year-old voice for effect, 'this is not really an emergency. I'm not dying but I'm stuck on a road and I don't know where I am.' Even as I hear those words come out I feel completely stupid.

'Where exactly are you?' comes the reply. It makes me want to laugh again.

'Look, I really don't know, but if you could put me through to Kelso police station I might be able to explain. The last place I remember driving through is somewhere called Nenthorn.'

'Can't you drive back there then?'

The question is reasonable: I haven't explained that I've been dumped. I do explain but now she probably thinks I'm a jilted old lover.

'I'll just look it up,' she continues. A minute later she's back. 'I can't find Menthorne anywhere on the map.'

There follows a second attempt to communicate the place name. The good news is that she finds it. The bad news is that she can't get through to Kelso. The computers are down and I presume good old telephone lines have gone with them. Studying her map she says I could get to Kelso by crossing a bridge and walking about five miles. Oh dear, this is becoming tedious, but I try to explain it's a bridge too far. She tells me that she'll ring me back in a couple of minutes, and I continue my march back into oblivion, there being nothing else to do. Then on my left I see a flickering light. Civilisation! I gravitate towards it like a moth, enter through a gate and am suddenly engulfed by a choir of barking dogs who come charging out from kennels, mercifully chained. I squeeze past them but before I can knock on the door it's opened suddenly by Wee Willie Winkie.

Dressed in a cotton nightshirt, sporting a hat of sorts, carrying a torch in one hand and a poker in the other, a minuscule little man is glaring at me through rimless 1940s glasses. At which point my phone rings.

Don't you hate it when the police ring you just as you're talking at midnight to a Scottish pensioner in a nightgown? A three-way conversation then ensues which ends when Willie understands my predicament and with the magnificent generosity for which Scots are renowned offers to drive me into Kelso. 999-girl hears the offer and sounds as relieved as me: another nutter sorted.

Driving an open-top jeep, Willie is still clad in nightwear but wears a leather jerkin and a hat as some concession to the cold. I ask him to drop me off at the top of the town so he can get back unarrested. The final 300 yards to the centre I make on foot, back to the comfort of my car, which has been clamped. It appears the authorities have introduced new laws whilst I've been up north for the afternoon. I phone Colin to tell him but all I get is Liverpudlian Voicemail. It's only six miles back to my house and it's not raining. I get in at 3am and scald my arm making a pot of tea. Who was it that told me I should get out more?

A month later Halliday comes south for trials at Charlton and eventually signs for Middlesbrough.

Chapter 29

FGR

I ring Colin to tell him that I'm unavailable for any midweek games as I'm spending five wet, cold November days with my sister-in-law in the West Country. She and her husband Geoff run a farm and the prospect of some wild walking in fields full of sheep and cows is an offer my wife can't refuse. It is, after all, our wedding anniversary.

Colin rings back ten minutes later to ask if I'll be anywhere near Forest Green Rovers. I have no idea where Forest Green Rovers play. Colin asks me to hold on and then tells me it's in Nailsworth. I have no idea where Nailsworth is. Colin asks me to hold on again and then tells me it's in Gloucestershire. Running out of further ignorance, I make a quick mental calculation and then tell him I'm staying about thirty miles from Gloucester. 'I just wondered if you're around that way if you could look at the lad Constable from Oxford. They're playing there next Tuesday night.'

'Next Tuesday's my wedding anniversary, Colin.'

'Oh well, we'll put another ticket on if it's any help.'

My wife declines the chance but Geoff decides to go with me. It's a foul, wet, windswept late afternoon and he insists on going in the Land Rover in case of flooding. He's been to New Lawn – an amazingly inappropriate name in such a place on such a night – once before, but still manages to almost miss the hairpin bend with a sheer drop which we approach at 50mph. My life once again flashes before me and hardly feels worth preserving but we career round the bend, over a nice shrubbery, and head towards the limestone village beneath.

It's two hours to kick-off and we decide to explore the nightlife of Nailsworth but decide not to join the three teenagers outside the post office. A hotbed of vice, a recent drive-by shouting is all the talk of the village.

We motor up a steep track to New Lawn passing huddled fans making their way to base camp. This is not the End of the World, but you can see it from here. A car park steward embarks on a raging argument with us, informing the universe that he doesn't care if we represent Real Madrid let alone Bolton Wanderers, we're still going to pay £3 for the privilege of parking between the soggy cow-pats. His language becomes even more choice when I ask him for a receipt. By the time we get inside the ground I've calmed down a little and a plate of chips with curry sauce lowers the blood pressure to below danger levels.

New Lawn is a curious mix of one new stand, one from an old ground behind the goal, a stand that appears to have been lifted randomly from someone else's ground on a raiding party and a long open terrace for visiting supporters, just the job on a night like tonight. I wonder how many of the faithful Oxford followers remember, not too many years ago, travelling to places like Old Trafford and Highbury for their visits. I reckon it must be like marrying Janet Street-Porter after you've been divorced by Keira Knightley.

The game kicks off and Oxford play into the teeth of a gale. They are top of the Conference and FGR have won only one home game all season, so Oxford should be clear favourites, but in conditions resembling Hurricane Harry anything can happen.

The Rovers keeper is constantly berated by his team-mates for taking goal-kicks that go sailing straight out at the other end of the pitch. My man Constable is well policed by the Rovers' defence but then provides a moment of real quality by turning his marker inside out and smashing in a non-wind-assisted picture of a goal that flies past the hapless keeper. It's his fourteenth goal of the season and I'd be surprised if he's scored many better.

With the home side struggling to avoid going further behind the auguries look good for the men in yellow until suddenly all the lights go out. Absolute blackness envelops the ground and across the valleys beyond. It's like sensory deprivation and a little bewildering: we know the players are on the pitch but we can't see them. And then after a couple of minutes we don't even know if they're there or not. Pitch black!

I'm tempted to quickly strip naked and run to the centre-circle and back before the lights come on again, but resist the urge. Below us somewhere the PA announcer is shouting up in his loudest voice that 'it's not our fault, it's the whole area,' as though the idea had even entered anyone's mind that Rovers are trying to get the game they're losing abandoned. He keeps repeating the same message as if talking to a totally demented crowd. (Well, given where we are…) And then someone has the nice but dim idea of passing us a cup of coffee to spill in the gloom.

I am full of admiration for the fans and stewards during the blackout, especially those from Oxford who have travelled a hundred miles only to be treated to a re-run of 1940s London. Gradually a few mobile phones provide specks of light, but it's the humour that shines through the darkness. I personally am convinced that the game is a goner: I can't see how they are going to get the lights working again. To be honest, I can't see anything.

But work again they do, coming back on and instantly tripping all the sockets in the press seats just behind us. The air is blue, but it's mixed with laughter as overweight bodies scramble frantically to climb between each other's legs to plug their laptops back in. One local reporter topples forward and nearly dislocates my shoulder in his attempt to save himself from a horrible death. The whistle blows for half-time.

After that, the second half is an anti-climax. Oxford hold on to their single goal lead, with Constable patrolling the opposing penalty area without looking intimidating. The final whistle brings gloom to the faces of the home fans but understandable wet joy to the away supporters, who will need every bit of encouragement before embarking on their return journey that should see them back in the city of dreaming spires around midnight. I try to imagine such a trek if you'd just seen your team lose.

Geoff squeezes out of the car park before the solitary visiting coach on its southbound trip blocks the narrow road, and we head for home and near disaster again. Geoff discusses sheep-dipping with another farmer on his hands-free, and we all but miss the same hairpin bend that almost killed us on the way down. The rattling of the Land Rover begins a serious argument with the chips, curry and coffee trying to sleep inoffensively inside my stomach and we have to stop three times for me to be sick. On the third occasion a gust of wind removes the only hat I own and whisks it into the inky blackness of the West Country prairies. I don't even think about trying to retrieve it.

As I crawl into bed just after midnight, poorly, befuddled and down one hat on the evening, my wife asks, 'Is something wrong, dear?'

'Just indigestion,' I reply.

'Not again,' she grumbles and goes back to sleep before I can wish her Happy Anniversary.

Chapter 30

GROUND RULES

I haven't yet fathomed quite why some clubs are more accommodating and welcoming to scouts than others. Does the decision come from the chairman, from on high? Does the manager have a say, or is there a club secretary sitting in a little office exercising his or her dictatorial powers with relish?

Around the London area clubs differ widely, even at Premiership level. Do a match report at Tottenham and there are two VIP tickets with a meal and drinks, and refreshments before, during and after the game: hospitality unsurpassed. If you're not on a match report, though, you find yourself on the other side in the Legends Bar where it's tea and coffee only, and annoyingly a designated seat where, come every Spurs attack, twenty rows in front of you stand up – heaven knows why – meaning you either have to join them or sit and watch the action on the big screen in the corner. Which makes it feel rather pointless being there.

Arsenal's welcome has improved since Highbury days, and the tea and sandwiches and ex-Coldstream guard commissionaire who checked that everyone's tie was in place are now replaced by three varieties of sausages and a choice of savoury and sweet offerings which do nothing for cholesterol control but are very tempting. At Fulham there are also nice things on offer but the room in which they are served is like a cupboard at the top of the stand – standing room only – and of all the grounds I visit Fulham is the only one which never provides a second ticket. West Ham's hospitality seems to ebb and flow like the North Atlantic that stretches to their erstwhile Icelandic owners. In recent seasons, scouts have been entertained to pleasant refreshments in a trophy room, then to a small room with tea and biscuits, then to a melee where reporters and scouts vie for an outside cup of lukewarm tea while a clone of Hitler watches that you don't put your plastic cup in the wrong bin, and this season back inside around a couple of designated tables but only for designated refreshments. I recently helped myself to some soup that was adjacent to the tea urn, but no sooner had I broken my roll and taken my third sip of liquid than an angry lady approached me with the news that the soup was for paying punters only, not for scouts. My smile and apology made little impression on her, though she hesitated and then withdrew when I offered to pour the contents of my bowl back into the urn.

Scouts have no god-given right to expect hospitality: a decent view and a team-sheet are all that can be expected. But it does a club no harm to have a reputation for being welcoming. I did receive a request from Bolton once to report any club where hospitality was poor. They were going to reciprocate but I think changed their mind and decided to keep the moral high-ground. It's easy to lose sight of the privileged aspect of the job. Such is the attraction of the game that many people who can't afford the ridiculous prices for tickets, even if they could get them, would give their eye-teeth for the kind of seat at the kind of games that become commonplace for scouts to attend.

I've taken people to games where they've been almost overwhelmed just to be in the stadium. Vas, my barber, was on the phone to his friends for most of the first half at Wembley, just telling them where he was; a niece had a lovely birthday treat when she came with me to watch her beloved Chelsea beat Liverpool; and a dear friend, in her last months before succumbing to cancer, was thrilled to watch her Gunners from the directors' box and then have her photo taken alongside a visiting Sven.

Lower down the scale of thankfulness there are also times when I come away from a dire match just thankful I haven't had to shell out for the entrance fee. And it's not just lower league stuff either. One of the most tedious games to watch over the past couple of years was a goalless encounter between Chelsea and Liverpool that passed as a Carling Cup tie. A bit of stimulant in the Cup itself might have been welcome. And a thrilling 0-0 clash featuring West Ham and West Brom was mind-numbing in its lack of excitement. I'm regularly reminded of the fan who seriously considered taking his club to court in order to try to redeem some money under the Trade Descriptions Act.

Travelling and parking arrangements can also take their toll. The London Borough of Waltham Forest undoubtedly manages to raise money for its Christmas staff bonuses every time Leyton Orient play a home game. Even if it's midweek in the middle of winter, out come the parking officers in their droves, followed by tow truckss, flooding the surrounding street looking for any vehicles that might have parked one millimetre over a line for a fraction of a nanosecond. I was once towed away, quite illegally, by their enthusiastic upstarts and spent four months recovering my £180 release fee. Beware all ye who travel east.

It's not surprising that many scouts, like some fans, leave games early. The joy of escaping from certain grounds, such as Upton Park, can be truly uplifting.

At Millwall scouts used to be parked up in the away supporters area where the visiting team's and fans' coaches were locked in behind iron gates for at least 40 minutes after the game, and then given a police motorcycle escort right down the Old Kent Road until they reached the motorway. Hanging about on the wrong side of the gates with some snarling Millwall fans who are teaching their eight-year-olds the art of abuse does not come high on the enjoyment list.

At Wycombe it's the local buses that are given priority to leave the ground first, but being buses they don't exactly hurry. I have spent a good hour on occasions sitting in my car in the unploughed field that is the car park, looking down and into the picturesque little ground and the woods beyond it. I suppose there must be worse vistas from football car parks.

On my first visit to Oxford's new stadium I decide to take the train, having read on the website that I will need a further bus-ride to the Kassam. What the website doesn't tell me is that when I get to Oxford no-one will be able to tell me where to catch the bus. Three different people who I think resemble possible locals with a mild football interest haven't an inkling; the Information lady deals only with trains and has never heard of the Kassam; having been guided to a bus-stop outside I finally find a notice that informs me of a bus going to my desired destination every half-hour, but Monday to Friday only.

A bus pulls up and I enquire of the driver where I might catch a football bus but he informs me that he isn't from around these parts and hasn't a clue. Wandering into town I peer around for someone who doesn't look like an undergraduate reading Greek philosophy and just might have heard of football.

It's not easy! By now it is 2.25pm, thirty-five minutes to kick-off. I finally reach the ground at 2.50pm, ten pounds lighter with a promise from the taxi driver that he will be waiting for me after the game to lighten my wallet by another tenner.

Chapter 31

OH DANNY BOY...

Prejudices run deep. Halfway through December and Bolton are the only Premiership side not to have kept a clean sheet all season. It can't be that Jääskeläinen has suddenly taken on the mantle of an accident-prone waiter; after his sterling efforts of last season he surely hasn't deteriorated that far. But having shipped twenty-one goals in the last seven games, the team is now languishing one from the foot of the table and I stoke up my bias against certain players to the point of unquestionable certainty. Step forward Messrs Knight, Elmander and Muamba.

I'm watching *Match of the Day*, desirous to see just how Bolton can take the lead three times against the sheikhs of Manchester, and then manage to offer equalisers and almost a winning goal each time.

It's pleasing to see Klasnic score twice. He's now got a few goals under his belt – which, I presume, he's still wearing – and looks a good acquisition. Cahill scores a beauty and for a while Bolton don't look too ugly. From just watching the highlights, though, my three bêtes-noires sink deeper in my estimation.

Elmander comes on as a sub and pulls a face in the penalty area. Knight defends an innocuous high ball by tapping it into the centre of the field which nine-year-olds learn is the Danger Area and are told never to put balls there. City gratefully pick it up and score their first goal. Later, Muamba sprints clear of the defence, zooms in on goal for a brilliant one-on-one, and then slices the ball wide as though it's been struck by an unchalked snooker cue rather than a professional footballer's boot.

I've never actually met any of these three players and my antipathy towards them is on purely sporting lines. It's always difficult though to disassociate the professional from the personal. With players like Bobby Charlton and Bobby Robson there was no problem: excellent players and excellent people. It's more difficult with the likes of Didier Drogba and Craig Bellamy, undoubted masters of their art but the kind of people I don't want at my funeral.

It might well be that the Bolton three all have four-figure IQs, are all committed Christians and give away half their salaries to charity. I don't know. On the field of play, though, their reactions look not only too slow for yelled instructions from the touchline but too slow for smoke signals. I can't but believe that someone has given Gary some really dodgy advice.

Or it may be that the manager himself has given an enthusiastic green light to these players and seen something in them that I (and a few thousand other scouts) haven't. Views can not only vary but can change too. I recall my first sightings of Danny Shittu. Gary is in his first season at West Brom and looking to bolster his defence with a view to making a push for promotion. I spot this lad playing for Charlton reserves and watch him a couple of times. Built like a brick-outhouse, strong and frightening, though not the nimblest when turning on a sixpence, I pass him on for consideration. A month later Gary rings.

'I went to see your lad Shittu last night.'

'And?'

'You must be having a laugh. He had a mare. Looks a real liability.'

'Well, he's not the most mobile, I will say that. But I reckon he can do a job at Div. 2 level. No higher than that.'

Gary laughs to show there are no long-lasting hard feelings. 'The only thing I will say is that my dad has seen him play. He thinks he's a good prospect too.' I feel privileged to share the same dock as the famous Don Megson, even if we are both found guilty.

West Brom don't sign Shittu. Instead he goes to QPR, then Watford and into the Nigerian national side. I see him a few times more in passing and he looks forever the same: strong, solid, a threat in the box from set pieces, but very limited in his manoeuvrability.

Four years down the line Gary brings him to Bolton where he's offered a three-year contract. I refrain from expressing any opinion, hoping that in the months since I last saw him play he might have developed gymnastic skills or taken part in *Strictly Come Dancing*. But the first time I see him in action little has changed. It's almost embarrassing to see some of the skilful, subtle and tricky Premiership forwards giving Danny the run-around. For all his willingness, strength, enthusiasm and niceness – and he is apparently a really lovely guy – he's out of his depth at this level.

So I look forward to the last game of the season when Danny boy scores the winning goal with a flying overhead kick to keep Bolton in the top flight.

Chapter 32

TOTTENHAM HOTSPUR v CHELSEA

21 March 2009

I used to teach Jo's mum in another life. Then our families became friends, she fell in love with a Belgian engineer, I became best man at her wedding, after which she was whisked off immediately to live in a land south of Brussels, soon producing three healthy bilingual boys. How one became an Arsenal supporter, one a Chelsea fan and one a lover of waffles is two-thirds of a mystery, especially given the fact that neither parent was sad enough to be attracted by football (though I do remember my ex-pupil and one of her classmates watching me play in a cup final in the days when she was an immature and impressionable schoolgirl, so perhaps something passed down in the genes from that aberration).

Jo's 16th birthday coincided with Chelsea playing Spurs and me being required to do a report on them before they played Bolton a fortnight later. Jo had only ever seen one other Chelsea game and it occured to me that it might be a nice birthday present if I took him to White Hart Lane. As usual, there was no guarantee of a second ticket until a couple of days before the game, but his mum booked two Eurostar tickets regardless. If the match didn't come about, she'd take him shopping in Oxford Street. Jo would be thrilled. His mother shops for Belgium.

It worked out and I met him at St Pancras, got a train across to the ground, and we were royally entertained to pre-match lunch and drinks in the VIP

Tottenham Hotspur v Chelsea

Suite with hospitality that leaves most other clubs looking Scottish. We ate our meal with Dave Cook and his wife, who together seemed to be running Newcastle's scouting system, and shared jokes and funny stories with them. I was surprised that anyone working for Newcastle at that moment could raise even a smile.

I warned Jo not to be too disappointed if, having come all this way, he saw Chelsea lose. They were, after all, not the invincible side they had been a year or so ago. He told me that Tottenham were his second favourite team anyway. It's a win-win situation. Unless it's a draw.

Reluctantly forgoing the wine and mint-chocolates, we took our seats and I began to draw pretty diagrams. Before kick-off Jo saw Abramovich sitting a few rows in front, accompanied by a face that I'm sure I'd seen on the cover of a magazine at my dentist's. Jo said he wanted his autograph but I demurred. The richest man this side of Mongolia was in deep conversation with *Vogue*-face and I told Jo ---

He was up and away with a confidence that comes from being sixteen and living in a country that runs Europe without running itself. I heard him say, 'Roman, sign my programme please.' And Roman did. And then had his photograph taken on Jo's mobile by Mrs Billionaire. On the way back up to his seat Jo spotted Capello. The performance was repeated and I sat amazed at and jealous of his bravado and success. I'd seen Fabio at a number of games and had been tempted to try out my Italian on him with 'Mi scusi signor, e posso avere...' but courage had failed me each time. Even getting Sven to sign my team-sheet I had had to pretend it was for my wife.

Chelsea were indeed off the boil and lost the game 1-0. I worked out a masterplan during the match as to how Bolton could inflict the same result on them, jotting down movements and tactics at corners and free kicks with faultless accuracy, aided by Jo who reinforced my observations with his own quick, absorbing eyes. Or at least I think he did. I had slight worries that his loyalty to Chelsea might go so far as to ply me with false information about Drogba's movements as Lampard's corner came across, while I desperately searched for a replacement biro for the one that had just expired on me. I trusted his European sense of fair play! At the final whistle he didn't appear too suicidal and we returned to the VIP lounge for post-match coffee. He looked through a window to see the Chelsea team coach parked directly below. Then he was off again, with me in tail at a respectable distance like some shady camp-follower.

At the foot of the stairs he saw more fodder. With frightening assurance, he called out, 'Defoe! Defoe!' and then, 'Bentley! Bentley!' and each time the names responded as though they were hypnotised stooges on a Derren Brown magic show. Outside there was a gathering of fans and a kind of security person keeping them at arm's length away from the emerging John Terry and teammates. But not Jo. Terry was signing up as though he thought it a new improved contract, then Jo was at the entrance to the coach selecting the autographs he wanted whilst allowing lesser lights to board. It's as though he was enforcing some new piece of legislative Brussels policy: Directive one double one five subsection three: 'Designated players are required to sign the programme of one J. Descamps, Charleroi representative, before being allowed onto allocated team transport. Failure to oblige will mean automatic refusal into EEC countries when next required...' By the time he quit there were eleven autographs in his possession.

I looked on in awe at this success, the fruit-machine part of my brain trying to estimate what kind of price his multi-signed programme would fetch on eBay. What lessons could I learn from this demonstration of successful pushiness, to overcome my own innate reserve? Don't take no for an answer? Speak with a French accent? Adopt the Nike advice and Just Do It? As the Spurs manager came out from a downstairs door I swept into action to emulate my teenage friend. I was about to greet him with, 'Hello Harry, remember me? We used to play together for East London Boys forty-five years ago when I was the inside right and you played on the left wing...' before I asked him to sign my shirt with 'Good to see you again Les and thanks for all those great passes', but taking in my first two words only, he nodded perfunctorily and swept past me as though I was an unfamiliar face, leaving me holding out my hand like I was just about to start a session of robotics.

Jo and I travelled back to his grandmother's in role-reversal mode. He had an air of quiet but unsurprising success; I feigned reading my unsigned programme, wearing a lack of confidence like an overcoat. Why didn't Harry greet me?

Jo refused my offer to escort him back to St Pancras in the morning in case somebody mugged him on the tube and took his precious programme. But I talked to his mum in another role-reversal scheme. My ex-pupil was now a counsellor and I reckoned she could advise me as to how I could encourage people to respond to me more positively. I e-mailed her about this after I'd tried to cheer up with a week in the Isles of Scilly.

She didn't reply.

Chelsea beat Bolton 4-3 after being 4-0 up. Does anyone read my report?

Does anyone know who I am?

Does anyone have any valium?

Chapter 33

SOMETHING OLD, SOMETHING NEW

Southampton is not the greatest place to visit on a freezing December night when it's just beginning to snow. To begin with, even on bright sunny days, the M25 and M3 motorways never feature in the Thomas Cook brochure of Amazing Sites to Visit as Soon as You Can, and in the dark and in the wet and in the rush hour they lose all their appeal. It's a tedious three-hour journey before the signs appear that you only see by the seaside: To the Docks; Isle of Wight Ferry; To the Seafront... Coastal places never cease to have a fascination for me. Unfortunately, signs to St Mary's are a little harder to come by and I have to follow instinct to make sure I'm heading to the right area, before I see the growing number of men and boys all walking in the same direction. My police training in putting two and two together always comes in handy and I decide to park up, shelve instinct, and follow the crowd.

It's the semi-final of what was originally called the Associate Members Cup, now termed The Football League Trophy but for a couple of seasons going by the roll-off-the-tongue title The Johnstone's Paint Trophy. I wonder if there's been a less eloquent sponsorship name yet. The Saints are playing Norwich, who have picked up well after their opening-day drubbing, and the winners are going to Wembley, que sera, sera. I have to keep reminding myself that these two are now third division sides. Along with the likes of Leeds and Charlton it's a league this year that boasts some big clubs with big support. For teams like Orient, who for a couple of decades have farmed in rougher territory, it's a bit like Friends Reunited with these clubs visiting and entertaining on supposedly level footings like they used to in the '60s and '70s. How wide the divide has been.

Somewhere or other there's a car park allocated by Southampton but I recall spending forty minutes once trying to find it, and then forty minutes after the game being boxed in by policemen closing the road to allow spectators to amble from the ground. Tonight I decide to park and walk, even though the snow is now really sleet which wets so much more easily and I've forgotten to bring a hat. My blue Bolton jacket with the Reebok logo prominently displayed keeps me warm and well protected on top of fourteen layers of clothes, but also instantly attracts two very enthusiastic, very knowledgeable and very irritating punters heading for the match who fall into step, one on either side of me, immediately I get out of the car. I realise, from their attire, that one is a Saints fan and the other a Norwich supporter, and it's amusing hearing the two of them banter in their respective accents, the south-coast burr that lends itself only to soft and placatory noises and the East Anglian Pam Ayres lilt, agricultural inasmuch as this is how you'd expect a scarecrow to talk.

Between them they express opinions about Bolton, England, climate change and Silvio Berlusconi, pump questions at me, which one asks and the other asks a second before I have a chance to reply, and show a better knowledge than I have of players performing for Bolton. I go along for the ride but I'm pleased when the mile or so trek comes to an end without me having shown too much ignorance. As we say our farewells, with the two still arguing about whether Adam Lallana is better than Wes Hoolahan, one of them tells me, 'Oh, by the way, you left your lights on.'

They disappear without another word whilst I stand rooted to the spot. This final piece of information has not been delivered with any sarcasm or venom or hint of regret; it's just a straightforward fact that for some reason outside my understanding was not mentioned twenty minutes earlier. It makes me wonder if it's me that is diagonally parked in some parallel universe.

The balance of action is weighed in my head. I hate getting to a match late. Many scouts may leave a game early but hardly any arrive after the start; it's just not done. On the other hand I hate having a car that won't start when I'm 105 miles from home on a winter's night. It's now 7.20pm, twenty-five minutes from kick-off. I decide that if I leave the car, there is a chance it will still start, but if I trek back there is no chance I'll be seated at kick-off. I shall also miss out on the orange juice and prawn sandwiches that I anticipate are awaiting me upstairs. The deciding factor! I go into reception and pick up my ticket.

Seeing Southampton in their traditional red and white stripes, Norwich in their traditional yellow shirts and the officials in their proper colours of black shirts and shorts appeals to my irrational sense of conservatism. One of the many pet hates I've developed is teams wearing away colours when they have no need whatsoever to change. Of course, it's nothing to do with commercialism and the sale of replica shirts. Of course not!

The first half of the game is free-flowing and impressive, Southampton taking an early lead whilst the Norwich fans channel their disappointment into chants of 'Play up Pompey'. There are a number of decent players on the pitch and a pleasing amount of good honest endeavour. However, there are only two that I decide are worth a mention on Scout 7: Adam Lallana and Wes Hoolahan. I regret not paying closer attention to the opinions of my two escorts. At half-time I see that Bolton and West Ham are scoreless after thirty minutes in an important bottom-of-the-table clash. I did a report on West Ham a week ago and saw them as a really weak outfit. If things go pear-shaped tonight there will be rumblings at the Reebok.

After the break the Canaries come back to lead 2-1 with Hoolahan running the show until he's inexplicably subbed on eighty-five minutes. (Hoolahan's name reminds me of a time when I was asked by John Mortimore, working for Southampton, to go to Southend to check out a player he'd had a report on by the name of Hooligan. It wasn't April 1st and John wasn't renowned for practical jokes so I duly obliged. Gavin Holligan, as he turned out to be, made a stir for a short time but then vanished into the woodwork.)

The Canaries fans are in good voice and working out their route from Norwich to Wembley until virtually the final kick of the match, when Southampton snatch an equaliser. It's straight to penalties without extra time – another first, but pleasing in the circumstances if I want to get home before the weekend. Norwich score and miss and score and score, Southampton score and score and miss and score. It's level pegging but after Southampton net their fifth, there is an amusing interval. A solitary spectator, seemingly overcome with the fifty per cent prospect of going to Wembley and unable to contain his exuberance any longer, rushes onto the pitch, evades three stewards, one of whom falls ungraciously onto the wet turf, begins a circular run up towards the players standing in the centre circle, and upon reaching it jumps straight into the arms of the Southampton striker N'Diaye.

He's not the first nutter I've seen on a pitch, but he is the first one who is aged six. N'Diaye seems honoured at being chosen; if he'd been the same colour as the child it might have been assumed he was a father welcoming the overjoyed offspring. But it's a random choice and he appears to be unsure whether to hug the child, apply for a CRB check, simulate anger with him and hand him to the stewards or put him on his shoulder and give him a flying angel off the pitch to rapturous applause. Similarly, when eventually the stewards catch up they seem confused as to how to handle the little miscreant. Eventually one carries his top half and the other his legs, though what sanctions befall him when he reaches the far side I can't see. I'm intrigued though at the options.

This could, of course, all be part of a Machiavellian master plan hatched in the Southampton boardroom, for the delay in proceedings seems to adversely affect the next Norwich penalty-taker. His shot is saved; the Saints are heading for Wembley; I'm rapidly heading to the car.

My fears are well-founded. The ignition turns the engine over once but too sluggishly to fire, and then gives up the ghost completely. I sit disconsolately staring through the windscreen, wondering just how many hours, on a night like this, it will take Green Flag to come and get me moving. I haven't even brought any jump leads. Or sandwiches. Should I find a hotel for the night?

As I take out my mobile to look up the number, there is a sudden bang on the window. A grinning face sporting a red and white hat, next to a less happy visage above a yellow and green scarf, is saying something to me. It's the return of the two musketeers, just what I need, and I'm in no mood to either congratulate or commiserate, given their hand in this predicament. However, I try to wind down the window but of course it's electric, so open the door instead, hoping they're not going to turn nasty when I can't offer them a lift.

'Steer her out, mate,' says Red Hat, 'and we'll bump start you. We knew you'd need a push.'

I am unable to express my overwhelming surprise and gratitude before I'm duly moving down the road, with not two but five burlies now creating velocity at my rear. The clutch is released, the engine fires, I rev up and all I can do is to hoot twice to express my thanks to the figures standing dangerously in the middle of the road who now disappear into the gloom of my rear-view mirror. The journey back is done in record time. Radio 5 tells me that Bolton have won 3-1 with the help of another Robert Green howler, South London takes on a picturesque hue in the returning sleet and I hit the sack with childish delight. For a few moments I recall advice from the French writer Apollinaire who says that in pursuit of happiness we should sometimes stop and enjoy a happy moment. Then I decide that's just a load of cobblers for a winter night. Father Christmas has come a few days early.

Chapter 34

QPR v TRANMERE ROVERS

25 January 2003

West Brom had a sniff about a midfield player at Tranmere and I was asked to go to QPR to do a report on him. Jas, my Derby-supporting friend, accepted the offer of a game; anything, he said, was better than watching the Derby score filter through on the television drip by drip. Especially these days.

We bought Travel Cards rather than try to negotiate the traffic from the east to the west of London. The Central Line, which we took at the Bank, would deliver us at White City, ten minutes from the ground. We were deep in conversation about the ruin of the Rams when the tube train started to shake and make strange and worrying noises such as I've never heard in all my decades of underground travel. As the front carriages emerged into Chancery Lane station we realised there was something amiss. There were ominous bangs and judders; we could see people outside running down the platform, away from the train which had now ground to a sudden halt, half in and half out of the tunnel. The apparent panic of those outside caused fright for those inside and people headed for the doors, which had not opened. In a few seconds, there was a voice that came across the intercom, the driver's or the guard's we didn't know, but it sounded shaken, telling people to get to the front of the train immediately. As if that message was not enough to begin a panic, the owner of the voice forgot to turn the intercom off, and the next presumably intended private communication everyone picked up was his shout of: 'Mayday, Mayday, Mayday.'

Within seconds there was pandemonium with people swarming in different directions towards the doors and the end of the train. From the carriage behind there now emerged a white cloud, which I and most other people wrongly assumed was smoke. It was enough to cause screams and more chaos. In a moment of unfelt calm I recalled reading that more people die from panic in situations like this than from the actual incident and I found myself standing on a seat as bodies swarmed by, wanting to call out 'Don't panic!' but realising I'd just sound like Corporal Jones from *Dad's Army* and would almost certainly cause more panic. Bizarrely, I began to wonder if it would be fire or suffocation that brought about our end and whether the kick-off time at QPR would be delayed. A couple of men were now trying to kick out the windows of the door. On the other side there was a guard struggling to open it. I felt sure that if a leg went through the window an artery would rupture. I'd lost Jas in this melee but, in a way that I can't recall, the door was finally wedged open, people started to squeeze through and I found myself pulling back one half while the guard held back the other.

Now that the door had been forced, my fears of being entombed in a fiery carriage had abated and I was still holding the door open for a dribble of people coming from the back of the train when brown-suited and helmeted men arrived with breathing apparatus and told me to get lost. I duly obeyed and made my way up the stairs, though stupidly I never looked back along the platform to get even an idea of what had happened. Some remote control button had been

138

activated in my brain and I followed its orders. At the top of the station there was a scene of chaos with Police, Fire and Ambulance services in abundance, people sitting on the pavement looking shocked and tearful, some being comforted by paramedics, others standing around aimlessly. I bumped into a youth leader I knew and learned from him that he had a group of kids in a carriage where windows imploded. I wondered what had happened to Jas but then saw him across the road. He was looking rather white, which considering he's Indian was quite worrying. Before he could continue making excuses for Derby County, we gave each other a hug of relief and then appeared not to know what to say. I suggested to him that as we both appeared uninjured, had no great desire to hang around and give our story to the media, still had a valid Travel Card each, and had two tickets waiting for us at Loftus Road, we got a bus and tried to pick up another train further along the line. There was, after all, a match on down the road! Neither of us seemed to question the aptness of that decision and in the next street we grabbed a bus that I knew went to Oxford Street. We sank into our seats but after five minutes I realised my sense of disorientation had not been accounted for: the bus was going the wrong way.

Back in the street I suggested we got a taxi instead to a station up the line. The problem was that we had only £8 between us and I wasn't sure how far that would take us. When I explained our predicament and asked the taxi driver how far we could go, the milk of human kindness raised its welcome head. 'Blimey mate, I thought I'd had a bad day, but you've bloody beaten it.' He took us all the way to the ground. En route it occurred to me that we ought to phone our wives to reassure them, just in case they had heard the news. Neither had and carried on with their respective lives disappointingly unconcerned. At the ground news of the incident was filtering through and they were considering delaying kick-off. I put it down to telepathy. Jas and I suddenly realised that we looked a sight. When Jas blew his nose he found it filled with black stuff resembling soot.

The game was lousy, which seemed fitting. We'd had enough excitement for one day and both felt, without expressing it, a relief that we were actually sitting there in one piece. The Tranmere player didn't do badly; in fact he didn't do anything: he wasn't even on the bench. Even without him, though, the northern outfit won the day but within a couple of hours the events on the pitch were relegated to the 'Forget Quickly' bin in the brain. Devoid of money, we were forced to use our Travel Cards to get home. It's probably good to have had to use the tube straight away, but we made sure we stood near the connecting doors. The Central Line was closed for months following the discovery that the wheels had fallen off the train. Rather a fundamental problem for that kind of transport, I would have thought. Dozens of people had been injured and traumatised but thankfully nobody killed.

Jas was off work for a week, unable to sleep through constant flashbacks. He contacted London Transport and they firstly sent him a bunch of flowers and later a cheque for £400. I waited patiently for my own trauma to kick in, but each night I dreamed only about meeting Keira Knightley on a beach near Tranmere, walking along the promenade and, using bought doughnuts as visual aids, taking her carefully through the offside laws.

Some people have all the luck.

Chapter 35

CHRISTMAS CARDS

Following the madness of Christmas Day it's a relief to go to The Valley twenty-four hours later to watch Charlton play Swindon. The hype of Christmas seems to get worse by the year, and cometh the day there is so much stress about whether the vegetables will be cooked at the same time as the stuffing, so much over-excitement from toddlers inundated with ridiculous amounts of presents, so much exhaustion when you've seen the family come, drink, moan, feed, lounge and go, that the thought of watching a ball being booted around feels like a ticket to freedom. As a small concession to counter bah-humbug I wear a festive tie and don my Christmas socks that play 'Jingle Bells'.

Boxing Day games have been traditional for as long as I can remember, but I'm always amazed when considering that up to the mid '50s Christmas Day often housed a full fixture programme, with teams getting a train, along with the opposition, to play the return match the following day. Even the thought of trains on Christmas Day makes it feel like another century. (Which, I realise stupidly, it was!) And these were not always local derbies. I look back through some old programmes and see that West Brom travelled to Newcastle, Orient ventured up to Norwich. (Norwich! Getting there at any time from anywhere in the world is a mission, let alone on Christmas Day!)

Imagine the reaction of modern players to this situation. Two games in two days! There would need to be wholesale counselling available. And at Easter, of course, right up till the late '80s and before any concept of rotating squads, teams played on Good Friday, returned the call on Easter Monday but actually slotted in a game on the Saturday first. Three games in four days, and amazingly no reported incidents of players' legs falling off.

Of course, fitness levels are higher now and the pace of the game quicker, though not necessarily more physical when you look back at bits of old footage to some of the less refined tackling that used to pass as the norm. Though logic might dictate that if players are indeed fitter these days they should surely be able to endure more intense activity than their less-fit fathers and grandads. So perhaps it's in the mind, or maybe the contract or the agent's pay-packet. Certainly there is often sought-for sympathy nowadays for players having to turn out on a Saturday having played a whole game – a whole 90 minutes! – the previous Wednesday night. How do they do it?

Colin has suggested that I have a special look at a couple of Charlton players, Sodje and Burton, but when I tell him that I already know what these players are like and that neither in my opinion is anywhere near Premiership level, he asks me to run my eye over them and put in a report nevertheless. He's the boss. I don't argue. I just hope the sandwiches on the scouts' table aren't turkey.

The game pans out with a few unexpected turns:

5 minutes: Sodje goes up for a high challenge, cracks his head open and gets taken off by the trainer. Not a great start.

15 minutes: Sodje returns with his head stitched and bandaged. How the crowd love a sight like this.

20 minutes: Charlton take the lead.

25 minutes: Sodje lunges at an opponent and gets a straight red. There is not much protest though the referee and the unfortunate recipient of the tackle get the treatment from the more extremely short-sighted of Charlton supporters.

30 minutes: Sodje arrives to sit on the seat just in front of me. I get a close up of his track-suit and the bandage round his head, in case Colin's interested.

35 minutes: The referee turns down a good shout for a Charlton penalty. Burton protests vehemently and stupidly and gets booked. The ref's chances of coming top of a Christmas popularity poll in south-east London takes a plunge.

40 minutes: Burton tries to handle a high ball coming into the goalmouth. The referee gets upset again and gives him his second yellow.

Despite his stupidity, the crowd applaud the striker off the field but seem desirous to bestow some different greetings towards the official who, not adding to his approval rating, books another Charlton player before going off to half-time mulled wine and poisoned mince pies.

The second half begins like the Alamo and the crowd seem to enjoy the unfairness of nine v eleven. Swindon camp in the Charlton half but don't seem to fathom how to take advantage of the two extra players. A siege mentality takes hold both on and off the field. I turn my attention to some other players who look more interesting than the two dismissed men. Eventually the pressure pays off and to no-one's real surprise Swindon equalise. The Charlton crowd fall silent for a few minutes, but then, realising they are still on level terms, come to life again. When Swindon score a second it feels like curtains for the home side, allowing more blame and vitriol to be levelled at the referee. Which it is! With fifteen minutes to go Swindon play keep-ball and attempt to see out time. Charlton appear resigned, their attacks lack conviction and their attackers enthusiasm.

But it's Boxing Day, pantomime time. And I have a feeling something's behind the curtain. With four minutes of added time played, Charlton's poorest player on the pitch flies upfield on his magic carpet, challenges in the penalty area, and as the cry goes up from the keeper and visiting fans – 'He's behind you!' – an ambling Swindon defender allows the ball to be stolen and then lobbed over the goalie and into the net for a ridiculously unlikely equaliser. The Valley erupts as though it's a cup-winning goal; a delirious fan in front of me turns and tries to hug me. 'You couldn't write the script!' he slobbers. I think I just did.

Chapter 36

OUT WITH THE OLD...

It's the eve of New Year's Eve and I'm on a train heading for Hyde Park Corner when I get a call from my son. 'Megson's gone.' In the next two hours I get eleven texts and three calls all giving me the same information and asking if I know what my position is. I don't, though I'm touched by a message from Keith Burt at Forest which says, 'There's still a job here for you if you want it.' He's a good stick.

I'm depressed, annoyed and disappointed at the news, though not altogether surprised. The final straw, it seems, has come as a result of last night's 2-2 draw at home to Hull City. I followed the game on the internet and having submitted a match report on Hull recently was pleased when Bolton took a 2-0 lead with half an hour to go. Was this to be the first clean sheet of the season? Then Hull score through Hunt, the player I'd cited as the major threat up front; Megson makes a hugely unpopular substitution, taking off the goalscorer Klasnic and replacing him with McCann, not a crowd favourite; Hunt pops up again to squeeze the ball over the line, only inches from the rescuing leg of Robinson the full-back; Hull get a point, Bolton drop two and both remain in the relegation zone; the crowd boo vociferously at the end of the match.

Inches. A matter of inches is the difference between one point and three, between Bolton staying in 18th place or rising to 14th, between Gary being in or out of a job this morning. Had Bolton won the game, taking the current run to two wins, three draws, one defeat,

I'm sure the news would have been different. But it's on such small margins that careers in football hinge. That and possibly weak chairmen.

What motivates Phil Gartside, the Bolton chairman, to drop the axe at this point in time? He can hardly cite results which, despite last night's giveaway, have picked up again in December. The answer surely is fan pressure. In the modern game, that has become an often ridiculous and unreasonable force with which to contend. Reflecting society in general, followers of clubs are not, it seems, prepared to wait and work for success: it has to be achieved now. Therefore any club that endures a bad period of results over a month might automatically expect to have its boo-boys demanding a change at the top, and either in an effort to curry favour, or through fear of looking strong, the chairman will often take the easy option, pin the blame and consequences on the manager and get rid of him.

Despite the statistics that show that fewer clubs progress better under a new manager than they did under the old one; despite the fact that compensation may cost a fortune; and despite the fact that at least two of the country's currently most successful sides have been the ones to stick with their man for over a decade, during which there will have been periodic and strident voices for the manager's removal. Where now is the owner of the banner unfurled at Old Trafford in 1990 that read: '3 Years of Excuses and It's Still Crap. Ta Ra Fergie'?

It's clear that the opposition from a section of the Bolton supporters has been orchestrated. There is a photo of a big sheet that appears in the papers the next day and on the internet carrying the message: 'Megson Out!!!' When I speak to Gary, twenty-four hours later, I observe that such a sign was not suddenly constructed when Hull scored their second goal. He tells me that there were in fact three identical sheets all displayed together, and that he'd first seen them at the West Ham game which Bolton had, inconveniently, won 3-1. Some fans, obviously, were just waiting for the first opportunity to unfurl their demands. Which raises the question of what actually motivates them coming to a game. I also express my feeling that football nowadays suffers from chairmen who give in easily to opposition when fans and the media launch a campaign. I know of some who so dislike abuse shouted at them that they take themselves down from their seats to the boardroom for a relaxing drink whilst their team is sweating away on the pitch. That's guts for you!

Gary is disappointed but philosophical. What else can you be in this game? There is an element of surprise that the boot has come at this moment when results have started to pick up and when he felt convinced that they were turning a corner. He intimates, though, that there might also be undercurrents in the decision. He'd made clear his vehement opposition to any idea of Gary Cahill being transferred: footballing suicide. Without being paranoid, if the speculation becomes reality then it might confirm his suspicions. Watch this space, he says.

Chapter 37

MIXED FEELINGS

The FA Cup third round day sees my first game of the new decade, and I drive to White Hart Lane to watch Spurs ease past Peterborough 4-0. Spurs are not great and some of their players look casual to the point of arrogance when they are on the ball. But Peterborough are more disappointing. Coming as underdogs by a country mile, I would expect them to give it a go, but they play with one smallish striker upfront, never try to get to grips in the midfield and invite Spurs onto them for most of the game. Only their keeper Joe Lewis seems to relish the battle and keeps his side in the game until well into the second half. I decide that he's worth putting on the system but as he's already an England Under-21 player I'm sure he's known to someone at Bolton.

Watching an FA Cup game still provides me with a touch of romance, despite all the Jonahs who talk wisely about it having lost a lot of its magic, and managers – usually foreign ones! – who field under-strength teams because they think league positions are far more important than Wembley steps. Lose the sense of history that football carries and you lose yet another bit of the mystique the game has. But if you grew up in Spain or Italy or France then I suppose memories – yours, your dad's or grandad's – might not include ones about Radford's goal against Newcastle, Colchester humbling Leeds or non-league Yeovil putting one over the mighty Arsenal.

Mr Lee Mason, the referee, clearly has little sense of FA Cup romance about him. He's had a fairly easy afternoon, booking three players for tackles that would hardly have warranted a finger-wagging a few years back. His moment of true altruism, however, comes and is lost for all time in the ninety-second minute. With Tottenham cruising to a 3-0 win, a Peterborough midfielder, Coutts, has a sudden glorious rush of blood to the head and takes a run of some thirty yards past two defenders and into the Spurs penalty area before being rudely bundled off the ball for a stone-wall penalty. Well, a probable penalty. Or at the least, a really good shout!

It's at the end where a few thousand noisy and enthusiastic fans have encouraged their hopeless team all afternoon. There are only two minutes to play. Mr Mason has a clear view of the incident and would not be called names by anybody in the ground if he blew his whistle to the delight of the travelling Posh. Does he enter into the spirit of the occasion, send the visiting fans back up the M11 with just a little souvenir, give the Spurs fans an amusing chance to see their keeper try to save a penalty against the plucky, albeit outplayed, lower-league side? Does he heck! With true Scrooge sensitivity he waves play on and then as the ball travels to the other end of the field adds insult to injury by awarding a spot-kick to the home side for what most two-eyed people in the ground would judge as a totally innocuous challenge. Which Robbie Keane, having had a poor game, selfishly converts. A plague on both your houses!

Meanwhile, up at the Reebok, Bolton are taking on Lincoln City, currently sailing around in sea-area 87 of the Football League. It's the first game after Megson's dismissal and I can't quite figure out what my own feelings are about it. Had things not changed then I

149

would have been agonising about the 0-0 half-time score, certain that a bad result would be a direct threat to the manager's position. But though I have nothing against Chris Evans, temporarily in charge, there's a part of me that wants to stuff the message that it wasn't all the manager's fault down the necks of those unreasonable Bolton buffoons who bayed for blood. And what better than a defeat to Lincoln City?

A sudden sense of disloyalty and betrayal swells up within, followed by heavy and useless self-analysis. I am still employed by Bolton on a month by month contract, still here at Tottenham as their representative, still on good terms with everyone I know at the club, so where exactly do my loyalties lie? Are they with Bolton? Or Megson? For this afternoon at least, I'm not quite sure, though I don't feel strongly or confused or brave enough to fall on my sword.

I wonder, anyway, what this nebulous thing called Bolton Wanderers is, or Chelsea, Luton Town, Accrington Stanley and the like? It's not the players who, with rare exceptions, have very little long-lasting loyalty to a club. The days of playing proudly for the local team that you supported as a boy in the area where you grew up are long gone. Clubs, to many, perhaps most, players are no more than places of employment and the higher the wage they offer the more loyalty they will buy on a temporary basis. Frank Lampard has regularly been seen kissing his club badge in front of adoring fans after scoring a goal. Chelsea through and through seems to be the message, though when he was apparently offered less than the £130,000 a week he demanded a season or so ago it looked like Frank might be heading for another flower-bed in which to plant his loyalty seed. Emmanuel Adebayor is so dedicated to Arsenal that he taunts their fans a year later whilst playing for Manchester City. Michael Owen walks away from Newcastle without so much as a 'thank you and goodbye' having been well paid for sitting in the stand most of the season. Talk to scouts from these clubs and you get quite an insight into players' real characters.

Neither is it the manager. How many current ones have a sense of real belonging? Crowds may adore a successful man and chant with gusto that 'there's only one Harry Redknapp', but when a bigger offer comes along will that adoration count for much? Clubs become mere stepping stones on a managerial ladder until the final chop comes, as it invariably does, a few million pounds down the line.

Neither is it the owner, or at least rarely these days. More and more clubs are bought and sold as commodities. Half the teams in the Premier League are now foreign owned, the source of ownership often clouded in mysterious, not to say dubious, provenance. Just who are these oil-sheiks, Americans, Chinese property developers, Icelandic spectral names, and how much do they understand, let alone care about, the peculiar place that football holds in the British psyche? A Manchester City scout told me that at a recent club meeting one of their foreign owners admitted that the oil barons were looking to retain their economic domination after the oil ran out in thirty years' time by building up other empires. In their perspective the club is just a small part of that investment.

Football long ago, probably with the advent of the Premier League, sold its birthright for cash. It's the commodification of the beautiful game, reducing it to part of the global entertainment industry, mere poker chips to be gambled and traded on the international market. And the dereliction of duty from those in charge of our national game has been disgraceful. Fans may welcome the short-term flow of cash into their club's coffers but sooner rather than later it will all end in tears. I have a horrible feeling that when the plug is pulled on a high-profile club, as is a real possibility, others will follow not too far down the line.

To Portsmouth and Palace and Rotherham fans and those from the very lowest clubs football is not a business, not even merely an entertainment. A placard outside Fratton Park summed it up: 'Pompey: Not a brand. A religion.'

So what is Bolton? It's not Megson, nor Gartside, nor Anelka nor Klasnic. It's not me probably for much longer. It has to be those people who invest their memories as well as their hopes in the team they support: the record-keepers, the ones who went to Wembley in 1958, the kids who support the team because their dad and uncle and maybe even their granny does, the people who knew Nat Lofthouse, the guy who's sold the lottery tickets for thirty-five years and has seen managers and owners and players and scouts come and go. That's where Bolton exists.

Bolton knock in four second-half goals without reply and a spark of excitement creeps in uninvited when I think ahead to the fourth-round draw. I watch the results teleprint in whilst sharing a drink and a plate of chips with Cliff Jones and Peter Baker, two old Spurs legends from their first-ever double team. I confess to them both how, as a boy, I used to hate them, especially when they put five past Orient, but they are both charming and unassuming in their forgiveness. The discussion turns from the modern game to that of their era and when they express to me the dilemmas they felt as players between loyalty to club and loyalty to managers, a sense of reassurance returns. Here are two highly respected, highly talented and successful old pros mirroring some of the arguments that are going round in my own mind. Forty years on! Perhaps I'm normal after all.

Chapter 38

FRANCE v NIGERIA

2 June 2009

For the second time in four days, Colin asked me to look at the Nigerian national team. He had had various calls from agents about players who might have been available the following season, and wanted a possible opinion. The first game was at Craven Cottage on a Friday night; the second was in St Etienne in the middle of France on a Tuesday. I was free so I said I'd go.

The day started at 4.55am with an hour's drive to Heathrow. From the car it's a shuttle bus to the terminal, then a plane to Lyon, then a bus to the train station, then a train to St Etienne, then a taxi to the hotel at Quartier Montreynaud to arrive at 2.05pm. At 2pm the hotel stopped serving lunch. I dumped my bag, slipped on summer shorts and went to look for a place serving a light snack.

There wasn't one.

The place was a dump, an intersection for about nine roads at different levels plus trams plus trains but no cafés. Is this France? The best I could do was a soggy takeaway pizza from one place, washed down by a café-au-lait from another. This was the glamour side of scouting. I had over six hours to kill before the kick-off at 9pm. 9pm!! What time do these people go to bed? Being Nigeria I guessed there was every chance they wouldn't turn up till 10.30 anyway. I decided to walk away from the non-café nine-ways traffic intersection to find a relaxing park to while away an hour or two.

There wasn't one.

One old woman I asked, 'Excusez-moi Madame, y a-t-il un parc ici?' directed me to an underground car park; another enquiry prompted a teenage girl on her way home from school to run off and probably report me instantly to the police. The best I found was a sandy strip adjacent to some flats with a bench and some children's swings and roundabouts. After five boring minutes sitting on the foreign-language-graffiti-ridden bench I decided to have a go on the slide. On my second slalom down I noticed a policeman in the distance, but I couldn't tell whether or not he had his revolver drawn. I beat a retreat back to the hotel, intent on having a nap and a long afternoon lounge in a luxurious bath.

There wasn't one.

Trying to relax in a Radox shower has its drawbacks and comes a poor second to a bath, especially when there is no shampoo or shower gel provided. The Hotel Ibis in Montreynaud is not the place to spend your honeymoon. I watched a French TV equivalent of *Countdown* and found I was as good at making words in French as I was in English. The thought occurred of what this programme would be like in Polish: 'consonant please Carol, consonant please Carol, consonant please Carol...'

It's not hard to waste the afternoon. At 6.30 I wandered down to reception to check the whereabouts of another hotel from which I had to collect the match ticket. I assumed it was on the way to the ground, which was only about fifteen minutes' walk from the Ibis. Not the case. I discovered it was on the other side of the town and it was now 6.30 and I hadn't had dinner. A taxi whizzed me across in thirty hair-raising minutes and I found myself at the reception of a much plusher hotel, surrounded by, of all people, Nigerian footballers. I was tempted to engage Danny Shittu in conversation but the taxi was waiting outside for another Le Mans lap back to my hotel. Dinner took ages to be served and eventually came with a million chips. I was forced to take another taxi to the stadium. The driver was the third one who didn't ask me why I was going to the match. Are they so uninterested or is there an unwritten law that says taxi drivers don't talk to the English?

Colin had asked me to report on three Nigerians, all of whom had names beginning with O. From Nigerian agents on the telephone via the broad Scouse of Colin Harvey there's a good chance that something may get lost in translation, especially as I estimated there were currently twenty-six players in the Nigerian squad whose name began with O. Obinna was recognised though, and came on as a sub for twenty minutes in both games, barely touching the ball. Odejayi apparently played for the national team but wasn't in the squad for some reason. But Colin said to look out especially for a lad sounding like Oleche who acted as a midfield motorman.

There wasn't one.

No-one had ever heard of a midfield motorman whose name resembled Oleche. I met his agent at the match and even he'd never heard of him! In the lounge I found out that Gérard Houllier and Arsène Wenger were not looking for him either. Eight hundred miles, thirty-six hours, planes, trains, taxis, buses for a non-existent Nigerian whose name began with O... Justification?

There must be one!

Somewhere.

Vowel please Carol.

Chapter 39

THE BLEAK MIDWINTER

The year is a week old and life has ground to a standstill. The heaviest snowfalls for years bring about daily cancellations of trains, buses, planes and football matches. I'm convinced that the problems are caused as much by the mental approach to difficulty as by the actual disruption of ice and slush, especially when the South-East of England is in the firing line. When something out of the ordinary happens two things seem to occur. First is the question of who is to blame. Second is how can we turn this into some crisis that allows us to wrap ourselves up in protective cotton wool in case we bruise our big toe and suffer post-traumatic stress as a result.

Various people apart from God have been blamed for the current cold snap, the consensus laying the blame at the door of the Meteorological Office, who predicted a barbecue summer followed by a mild winter. Some Bolton fans were accusing Megson before he left and Ferguson says it's the fault of referees.

Whoever carries the can, the outcome sees kids kept at home when their school is round the corner, snowball fights being banned by crackpot head teachers afraid that lawyers are hiding behind every sledge and police officers deciding that football matches should be cancelled, not because the pitch is unplayable or the terraces (where they still exist) are dangerous but because the route from the nearest tube station to the ground is a bit dodgy and someone's zimmer frame might just slip as they step up the kerb. Health and

Safety is the new gospel, preached and adhered to as rigorously as any fundamental religion. (When I told a friend that Fulham post notices behind the goals declaring 'Beware, flying footballs' he thought I was pulling his leg.)

On Monday I decide to watch a reserve fixture between Arsenal and Chelsea. These are the kind of games where good players who are just out of reach of first-team football for those clubs could be flagged up for loans to teams like Bolton, even if they are not going to be bought eventually.

Currently Portsmouth are playing Kevin-Prince Boateng in their first team after more than a year where he lounged around for Spurs reserves; Hull City have Richard Garcia, who never made it further than West Ham's reserves, while Matthew Etherington, having failed to impress for a long time in the same second XI, now commands a regular place in Stoke's team. The game is at Barnet, kick-off 7pm. At 3pm it's called off because they can't de-ice one corner of the ground, which is surprising as there's such a slope at Underhill you would imagine any water would run straight off before it managed to freeze. Whatever happened to the old braziers that melted frozen pitches in former days?

The following evening the only game within reach is Bromley Town versus Thurrock. Neither Conference South team may be hiding a budding Beckham, but it's a game and it's local and they produce nice cakes for scouts so it's worth a visit. Or it would be if the local boys in blue hadn't deemed it too much of a public hazard to allow a crowd of 250 or thereabouts to walk the hundred yards from the nearest bus stop, despite about 240 of them turning up in cars.

Of course, I don't discover this until I get to the ground and my offer to a local sergeant to sit in my car and hear thousands of cheering fans encourage Stoke to beat Fulham in a part of the country that really is snowed-under, is politely declined. I go home and watch an enthralling special BBC programme about The Big Freeze.

Bolton travel down to London on the same day in preparation for the game at the Emirates the following night. Under-soil heating and the latest in modern technology will ensure that not a flake of snow appears on the lush turf and although there is no closing roof on the stadium most spectators will avoid getting wet should the blizzards begin.

I wonder about teaming up with Chris Evans and Co. on the Wednesday morning to elaborate a little on my recent team report but I figure he will have his hands full and any last-minute information might just confuse the players. Instead I spend the morning trying to explain to my wife why I need to go to Arsenal again tonight when I was there last week and I'm due there again on Saturday. She assumes I'm doing it because I want to and doesn't believe me when I tell her I'd much rather be shopping with her in Bluewater.

The blizzards pay another visit to the capital at 1pm. By 2.30pm the transport system has gone into a sulk and decided it's no longer fun to carry people around from place to place. Lots of offices close early so that people can stand for longer on platforms and wait for trains that don't come; bus drivers insist that roads are too slippery and ungritted to drive safely; London looks skyward and seems more intimidated by falling flakes than it was by falling bombs. With no available public transport, the Arsenal game is called off at 4pm, just about the time that the few thousand hardy souls from Bolton will be arriving in the metropolis. They will be pleased.

I spend the afternoon in Bluewater.

The following morning I telephone Colin and suggest to him that I should take off for the weekend to look for players in North Africa or southern Spain – anywhere where there's a bit of sunshine. I notice that Mali are pitted against Angola on Sunday but he reminds me I'm doing another match report and then has the gall to tell me that he's off to Europe later today. Lucky old Europe! Colin doesn't speak a word of Italian or German or Spanish. He hardly speaks any English as a matter of fact, but when I point this out he insists that Scouse is a universal language and that he's never had any trouble communicating in any part of the world. Or at least, I think that's what he says. I secretly hope that the runways up north are snowed up. But I don't tell Colin this.

Three days later, as the snow wreaks the kind of havoc on footballing fixtures that might be expected after an atomic attack, I'm back at the Emirates to watch one of only two Premiership games deemed safe enough to play. Men with blowtorches have been burning ice off the steps all morning whilst the turf inside the ground looks impeccable. How far grass technology has come from the days when most blades would disappear by mid-December to be replaced for the rest of the season by hard mud.

Yet another team report is required on the Gunners, who play Bolton next Sunday. This will be the first game in charge for the new manager, the first report he's seen from me. Maybe I should add a rider, pointing out just what a hazardous and life-threatening journey

I've made to get here, along with pictures of my six trusty huskies.

The game itself is a good old-fashioned blood-and-thunder affair that feels like a throwback to former times. Everton have come to get something from the game and take an early lead. The referee, Peter Walton, decides to ignore the common interpretation of the law which seems to insist that anyone falling to the ground MUST have been fouled and several players look bemused and indignant to receive neither sympathy nor free kick having just been fairly and squarely walloped by an opponent to relieve them of the ball.

Two Arsenal players actually fall to the ground with no-one anywhere near them. Gallas manages to overcome some mystery complaint but later Denilson, much more spectacularly, crumples as though he's just been shot and is carried off on a stretcher.

Best of all though is the second-half blizzard that sweeps across the ground for a good twenty minutes, almost whitening one end of the pitch, floating right into the Directors' Box, wetting all the diagrams I'm trying to draw and bringing an announcement over the tannoy advising Everton supporters to leave the ground quickly as train services back up north are now on ice. This brings a cheer from the home fans almost as big as the one that greets their 93rd-minute equaliser. A 2-2 draw seems appropriate (though really Arsenal have got out of jail) on an afternoon when it's been eleven versus eleven but twenty-two versus the elements. Later, on *Match of the Day*, Leon Osman, the first Everton scorer, can't hide his boyish delight when describing playing in these conditions, 'with snowflakes getting into your eyes so you couldn't see the ball coming down.' Original excuse, at least. I wonder if his enjoyment at performing in the Arctic is shared by the Brazilian contingent. Could it be that Denilson's problem is frostbite?

Chapter 40

OFFERS AND CALLS

One of the perks for scouts is that they are sometimes offered tickets to watch high-profile games just for the fun of it. When Colin rings me early one morning it's with such an opportunity. Would I like to see England take on Malta tomorrow evening? I immediately think to myself that I'm coming out of a coma, having no knowledge whatsoever of England playing any international fixtures this week. Have I badly missed something? I can tell that my hesitation has caused amusement as Colin continues liltingly: 'It's being played at Blackpool, kick-off half seven. Don't you fancy a trip up to Blackpool?'

As this is not April the first I come clean. 'Colin, I wasn't aware that there was any international match tonight. Is it Under-16 or something?'

'No, full international. I'm looking at the team selection right now.'

I begin to doubt my surroundings. 'So, who's playing then?'

'Well,' he continues, with dramatic pause for effect, 'there's Alex Scott at full-back' – my mind is trying to connect with an Alex Scott – 'Karen Bardsley in goal, Sue Smith as striker. The rest are still to be finalised.'

Another very unfunny bit of northern humour. I thank Colin and tell him to try elsewhere but he stretches the joke to its limits. 'What's this then, I thought you people in the south were supposed to be liberated, equal ops and all that. What have you got against women's football?'

'Just about everything. It's poor, it's boring, it's non-physical, it's just not worth watching. I'd rather eat a plate of cold sick than sit through ninety minutes of that.' I suddenly panic, hoping that my daughter in the kitchen hasn't overheard those last remarks. 'Thanks all the same, Colin but I'll give this one a miss.'

She has heard! I'm in real trouble, trying to explain and justify my belief that women are just not cut out for competing in games like football and rugby. It's just not... well, it's just not feminine! I'm really struggling so I dig myself deeper into a hole. 'Even when you listen to that Jacqui Oatley woman who commentates sometimes on games, it's awful. Her hysterical, screechy voice' – unlike John Motson – 'it's all wrong. And then that Gabby girl hosts *Match of the Day* sometimes and tries to talk tactics with Hansen and Lawrenson. It's... It's...'

'Nan went to games with you and Grandad when you were a boy. She's told me that.' Betrayed by my own mother, whose motto was 'If you can't beat them, join them.' The look of contempt on my daughter's face ends any further attempted explanations. I suspect it's as well that she's not in uniform or else I might just have become a victim of police brutality. She simply exits the room without a word.

When she's at a safe distance I call out: 'Thank goodness there are no women scouts. Might have to call them Guides!' She doesn't even slam the upstairs door.

Later in the day I try to put the man-thing in a different way, attempting to explain to my wife the similarities between a passion for football and passion for a woman. You lavish heaps of money on both and often look forward with anticipation, only to be frequently deceived and disappointed, sometimes with a sense of betrayal, even boredom. Great Expectations give way to Hard Times. You cherish the memories of the good moments but find it impossible to recapture them. Sometimes they become tainted by the troughs that followed the peaks. But despite the let-downs, the tears, the frustrations and the jealousies, when you see others doing it so much better, you come back again and again, a dog craving its food, a moth heading to the flame...

My wife says she's never heard so much garbage...

I'm in the loo, just settling down with Bill Bryson, when Colin rings. 'Can you go to Peterborough on Saturday, have a look at Joe Lewis again?' I wait a moment for some Liverpudlian punchline that doesn't come, wondering if this is another send-up, but then I remember that I did a report on this young keeper a few weeks back. Peterborough is the most distant of my allocated clubs and most of Saturday will be taken up with the task. But if it's what the new manager wants I shall obey, and besides, I've never been to their ground so it's another one I can tick off on my duffel-coat list.

Susan declines the offer of a trip up the A1 to savour the delights of the Cambridgeshire city. The place has apparently never featured on her Ten-Places-I-Must-See-Before-I-Die list; the heavy sarcasm drives me out for a long slow jog.

I'm in the shower, recovering from the exertions when I hear her calling. 'It's Colin on the phone. Again!' I drip downstairs and grab the mobile which I've left on charge in the kitchen. A puddle develops by the oven. 'Change of plan. Can you go to Portsmouth instead?'

I'm overwhelmed at the mention of so many exotic places. 'The boss wants you to look at Boateng.'

'Boateng!'

'I know. I've told him you've seen him and know about him.'

'I could tell you what his sister-in-law has for breakfast!'

'Well, if that's what the manager wants...'

'I shall obey...' I finish the sentence for him.

Kevin-Prince Boateng. I saw him first playing for Hertha Berlin in a tournament in France. Best player on show and despite my innate prejudice against his silly name I passed him on to Gary and the Nottingham Forest staff. Not surprisingly he was quickly snapped up by Spurs, but that was when the plum turned pear-shaped. Not commanding a first-team place he sauntered about for the next two years in reserve-team football where his attitude, temperament and body-language conveyed a message that here was a player who believed he should be waltzing on higher planes.

The conventional chicken-and-egg scenario: impressing on the odd occasion when he came on as a first-team sub to please the crowd with his skills and showboating technique; it seemed all a bit beneath him to try to convince anyone regularly when turning out on a cold Tuesday night in front of a couple of hundred hardies at a reserve match.

He's the kind of player to put scouts into a dilemma. Recommend him and you could be inviting a whole lot of trouble into the changing room. Managers have resigned because of disruptive players who upset the team, the balance, the atmosphere. Give him the thumbs down and there's a chance that another club will snap him up and unlock his real potential.

Offers and Calls

My own predisposition to take a chance has led me to suggest a couple of times that he might be worth the risk, though it's never been with a clear green light of approval. This season Portsmouth have taken the chance, but then all kinds of crazy things are happening at Portsmouth this season.

'Have an open mind on him,' Colin advises.

'I always have,' I assure him. 'It's not what's in his boots that's the problem, it's what's between his ears.'

This time my wife is persuaded that Portsmouth has more to offer than Peterborough. She has some friends there, a walk by the naval dockyard is a pleasant way to kill a couple of hours, and it's a trip down to the seaside if nothing else.

I'm approaching the roundabout that leads off to the M25 when the mobile rings. Susan answers and a veil drops over her face. 'It's Colin,' she says in a voice drained of surprise or emotion. She holds the phone to my ear.

'The Portsmouth game's been called off. Waterlogged pitch.'

I'm on the roundabout but manage not to take the exit leading south.

'Right thanks, Colin,' I reply, heading back for the London exit.

'Could you go to Peterborough, look at the keeper?'

I go past the London exit.

'Liz cancelled the ticket.'

'Ring them and get another one.'

'What's their number?'

'I haven't got it. Look on the internet. I'm driving to Nottingham.'

'I'm driving to Portsmouth!'

'I'll get it through to you.'

By now I have done three complete circuits of the roundabout, Susan is feeling giddy and if there's any CCTV someone watching us will conclude that we are either potential terrorists or an old couple trying to re-invent the Keystone Cops.

We take the road up to the Dartford tunnel in meaningful silence. I try to move into travel-agent mode, thinking of the numerable, outstanding and unmissable delights that can be gained from spending three hours in Peterborough city centre on a damp January afternoon. I'm struggling.

When the number comes through I pull over illegally and ring the club to ensure there will be a ticket. A delightful lady called Margaret is full of apologies that she can only offer me a seat and a tea pass: Premiership scouts are normally entertained in the Executive Suite, but all those seats have now gone. (Another reason for Bolton not to be relegated.) Would I like one ticket or two? I don't dare ask Susan if she'd like to watch the game.

The London Road ground boasts some old-fashioned charms. The seats are wooden and hard on the backside; the pitch, recovering from the snow, is like a sponge; and it must be unique in that the queue for the mini-bar where I collect my free tea doubles up as a queue for the Gents. I notice a lack of ladies waiting to be refreshed.

Peterborough lose two defenders in the first half, both of whom are inexplicably applauded off by their fans for sheer stupidity, and Derby win the nine v eleven encounter by 3-0. The keeper, Joe Lewis, is nonetheless impressive and I would be astounded if he stays with this club next season. After the game I rendezvous with Susan, who has spent some time in the shops but most sitting in the cathedral, enjoying the silence, she says. I rather suspect she's been saying prayers for the miraculous nobbling of my phone.

On the way back, Colin rings.

I let it ring.

Chapter 41

FADS AND FASHIONS

After a few years of scouting, when the majority of games are watched from the relative oasis of decorum in directors' boxes, it's easy to forget the often amusing, often depressing, sometimes exhilarating, sometimes sickening experience of being among the paying public. The accusation of snobbery is possibly justified, but if it's a choice between your own little box with refreshments at Southend or sitting in a draughty stand at Gillingham five yards away from a moron who clearly has racist mucus running down his nose, it's not much of a contest And the fan base differs from ground to ground.

Given that there are idiots and hooligans in every club, except those who haven't got enough supporters to yet qualify for that status symbol, the prevailing ethos often varies for no apparent reason. Move six miles down the road from Millwall, where for decades the crowd has been notoriously hostile and volatile, and you find at Charlton that they may actually applaud a visiting goalkeeper, rather than automatically throwing hand-grenades because he's not one of them. Some of the gentry folk who watch Arsenal seem to retain a smattering of the old Highbury superiority complex that may be a throwback to the 1930s. They seem to expect their side to be on top and regard it as an aberration of nature if the Gunners are not winning comfortably.

Supporters of Man Utd traditionally go very quiet and withdrawn when things are not going their way;

no loud, raucous, enervating encouragement pulsating down from the terraces (or plush seats), at least whilst the players are struggling. Brighton supporters must be among the most middle-class of fans in the country, pronouncing every syllable in the abuse they levy at officials and opponents, whilst their counterparts from Everton and Liverpool are less precise in their articulation of obscenities, but it doesn't matter because nobody outside the city understands a word they say anyway. In varying accents, though, all seem invariably to latch on to the same kind of chants.

Someone, somewhere, must begin these mantras, and then they become fashionable and widespread. It would, for example, be intriguing to meet the lyricists who create the chants that eventually permeate every ground in the country and often, I've noticed as I travel around, even abroad. (I recently heard Charleroi supporters chanting 'You're not very good' to the melody of 'Knees up Mother Brown'.) Is there a bard sitting in a tavern just outside Huddersfield who one day has the inspiration of putting the words 'Sacked in the morning, You're getting sacked in the morning...' to the tune of 'Guantanamero'? And what does he do to make it universal, once the idea has been turned into something practical? Does he blog it, or share it with a few friends behind the goal at his local ground, waiting for others to join in and then for it to be adopted by visiting fans and spread like evangelicals with the gospel? Or perhaps there is a consortium of supporters who meet every Tuesday afternoon in a car park in the middle of Walsall to sift through new chants, approving some and rejecting others and then publicising them on the Web. For snatches of songs that are sung (in the loosest sense of the word), week in and week out by tens of thousands, it seems rather a shame that the original writers receive neither recognition nor royalties. I have suggested to some scouting colleagues that we could perhaps create words for 'An Ode to the Beautiful Game' and sing it in directors' boxes to the melody of Mahler's 6th Symphony, but no-one seems to think it a great idea.

More interesting though is how teams also seem to copy trends with sheep-like dedication. At least half the sides I watch currently begin a game by performing a public huddle and then go round giving each other high-fives and cuddles, as though they have just met and haven't been putting on boots and jockstraps in the same dressing room for the past hour. I heard once that a team gathered together on the pitch to discuss tactics as they thought their dressing room had been bugged. Fair enough. But from that sensible arrangement it seems now to have become an obligation for many sides, but with what effect, I wonder. I think opponents who snarled at me, or did a war-dance à la the All Blacks, might be more intimidating than eleven blokes resembling (in Geoffrey Boycott's words) a group of schoolgirls at the start of a hockey match. Perhaps I'm not into bonding all that much.

On the field of play there are other trends that didn't exist ten years ago and, I suspect, won't be around in ten years' time. Which coach, in which club, first came up with the idea of crowding all ten of his outfield players into a small area on one side of the pitch whenever a goal-kick is taken? And for what purpose? What do you do with the ball if you actually win it, apart from pass it to a colleague who is five yards away with a defender down his shorts, or hold onto it until another teammate breaks out of the tight little knot? Of course, to allow this tactic to have any credibility, both sides have to play – which they duly do. So within an area no bigger than a fifth of the pitch we now have not ten but twenty full-sized bodies trying to reach the ball first. A little reminiscent of the kind of football I used to play at primary school.

My young scout friend Jack and I debate and disagree about the common tactic of employing a holding player. Was it Makelele who first introduced the idea for Chelsea, playing it effectively but at the same time providing a kind of template for lots of other clubs? I argue a case that for much of the time this role is a waste of a player, often a talented player. Scott Parker at West Ham springs to mind. Watching him perform makes me angry. The vast majority of his passes are sideways or backwards, lots no more than ten yards in length, he does a 180-degree turn with the ball at least a few times in a game, and only when West Ham are chasing the game, which they are a lot of the time, does he venture on dangerous forward runs. Also I think it sends a message to the back-line: you can't pass the ball properly so give it to me and let me do it. Onus off the back four. One player less in an attacking role. Trend adopted.

Who was the first player to rip off his shirt in supposed celebration of scoring a goal, and how many thousands have followed suit? The significance of such actions still, I confess, eludes me, unless you are intending to chuck the garment into the crowd as a memento and play the rest of the game bare-chested. But what does top-half exposure signify in terms of the game, apart from a card from the referee? Were it to catch on in women's soccer it might be more interesting, but I struggle to see meaning in this ritual. Who will be the first player to remove his shorts and run around waving those above his head? Now that might well show just how happy a player is at scoring.

Chapter 42

PRINCE OF PORTSMOUTH

A week later I'm once again heading to Portsmouth, only this time by train. Someone at Bolton is really keen to know what Boateng is currently doing. It's a slow journey down to Fratton and I'm just through Clapham Junction when I look at the sports page of the paper I've bought. Boateng, it tells me, is injured.

I'm resigned now to the fact that scouting this player seems to be fated and the two-and-a-half hour trip down to Portsmouth will be little more than a waste of time. A mixture of sailors and Sunderland supporters make the journey a touch more interesting than it might have been as they swap stories about sailing ships and building ships. It's a nice atmosphere.

One wizened old boy, who looks about 120, notices my Bolton tie and strikes up a conversation. He's not missed a Sunderland match since 1982 – (more like 1922!) – he says, and only three since 1958. He recounts the numerous encounters with Bolton and his memory is fantastic, even if his looks are not. I marvel at such an active mind inside an obviously decaying body and I just hope he makes the walk from the station to the ground without expiring.

Squeezing through the narrow alleyway that leads to the main entrance of the ground I'm suddenly in the midst of a noisy demonstration, with TV cameramen, police and scores of chanting protesters all crammed into the narrow cul-de-sac. It's not that Pompey are bottom of the Premiership which has sparked this outburst. Far more seriously, the club is facing a winding-up order in a couple of weeks unless someone can pull their irons out of the fire.

Inside the Jimmy Dickinson suite, I discuss this with Greg and a couple of other scouts, who are bemused that football can be run in such a chaotic way. No-one, it seems, knows who actually owns Portsmouth. How can that be? We all agree that the introduction of foreign players into the English game has raised the standard of play enormously, but the advent of the foreign owners has been – with a couple of exceptions – a pretty diabolical move, though not one that wasn't predicted.

It's another aspect of football selling its soul, of money turning heads and changing the good old game into a modern dirty business. Coinciding with stories of managers on the tax fiddle and ex-chairmen siphoning off millions from their clubs, it becomes a pretty depressing conversation. For any club to go out of business, be it Portsmouth or Accrington Stanley, it's an emotional wrench. I worry that if Pompey do go under it will have the domino effect that some people predict. I feel almost inclined to go outside and join in the noisy protests.

I moan further to Greg about my wasted journey but when the team sheets appear the Prince has done a Lazarus and lines up in midfield. Well done the newspapers and the Portsmouth press agency for such accuracy. Well done the Portsmouth admin people who have given Greg and me complimentary programmes for the match against Coventry three weeks back.

KPB has a decent game and despite his under-whelming work ethic helps Portsmouth to beat a superior Sunderland 2-1 to go into the fifth-round FA Cup draw. I still don't know what to recommend about him, but I can't really see him fitting into the Bolton set-up unless it radically changes.

On the walk back to the station I team up again with the Ancient of Days, who explains in great detail just how and where his team have lost the tie. I'm intrigued with his perception. Also, he's not only stepping out at an impressive pace for an octogenarian, he's eating a McDonald's cheeseburger and having a conversation in Gaelic on his state-of-the-art mobile at the same time.

There's hope for me yet.

Chapter 43

GM CROPS

Two ex-Bolton scouts, now working for other clubs, are talking to me before a match at The Valley. They ask if my job is safe under the new manager – answers on a postcard! – and how long I've been working with the club. The conversation then drifts round to their involvement with Bolton, and a few eyebrows are raised around the table when stories are related.

'You wouldn't believe some of the goings-on after Big Sam left,' one of them tells me. I'm curious to know more but there is an initial reluctance on the part of both to go into details. I deflect the direction to try to work round it.

'Did you not want to move with him, then? I thought he took most of his staff to Newcastle.'

Number Two joins in. 'We were quite happy to stay with the club. It was a nice set-up, a nice club to work for. Things had been fine for all the time we'd been there.'

'And then what? Gradual change?'

The doors open. 'Gradual!' chimes No. 1. 'There was nothing gradual about it!'

I probe a bit deeper: 'From what point: the coaching, tactics or what?'

'Just about everything,' adds Two. 'We always had regular meetings up at the Reebok and were put up in the hotel there. After Sam left they couldn't even organise that. We were shipped out into some local hotel. You wouldn't believe the chaos.

'But that wasn't the main thing. The very first time we met under the new regime the whole atmosphere was awful. The message was that everything that Big Sam had achieved was rubbish, the way the team played was crap, Big Sam was crap and things were going to change wholesale.'

'And remember,' returns his mate, 'that Sam had achieved fantastic results during his time in charge. Much better than anyone could have hoped for, even if the style of football was as unattractive as his looks.'

'Soon as he was gone people changed, personalities changed. Big time. We couldn't believe just how different they were.

'You know, they appointed some people to important positions who knew nothing about football. At the end of the first meeting, one of them came up to me privately and asked me to help him out. He said he was out of his depth.

'But that wasn't the worst thing. At that meeting, the first one we had, the scouts who were there were told that they were a bunch of effin useless dickheads.

'Except the language was a lot stronger than that. And there were ladies present at the meeting!

'Right to our faces. We were accused of only going to games to get the refreshments, and leaving early because we weren't interested in what we were doing. I thought at first it was a wind-up, you know a kind of joke session, but it soon became clear that it was all meant. Bit of power with some of these people and they think they're gods. Didn't take us long to leave them to it. We both told them to stick their jobs.'

'Not that it got them very far,' adds his mate. 'Half a season – less – before the team was propping up the table and they got their comeuppance. Except, of course, that they're all back in business up the road now.

'I heard that Big Sam got wind of what was going on and what was being said. Must have been hurtful to hear himself being rubbished by people he'd worked with, but he would have known that the chickens would come home to roost, sooner or later.'

'Don't know how much he knew about what had gone on before he came,' adds the first, 'but your mate Gary didn't exactly inherit a bed of roses when he landed up there. I think he didn't do too bad a job considering.'

You and me both, mate!

Chapter 44

ROOM WITH A VIEW – NEARLY

There are worse places to spend an afternoon scouting than Craven Cottage, especially if the sun is shining. Go by tube or leave the car in a nearby side road and you can amble through the park that borders the Thames, absorbing all the ambience that a wide and busy river offers. Before the modern stand was built it was possible to watch the football match from the top of the South Terrace and then when it became too excruciating turn a half-circle and look at the rowers on the river. I recall actually seeing Oxford losing the Boat Race one Saturday whilst Fulham were losing the plot.

The Cottage itself, a listed building, stands as a sentinel to the past, whilst all around has been developed into a modern all-seater stadium. On occasions, when Fulham play reserve games here, scouts are accommodated inside the Cottage – a lousy place to watch a game, stuck right in the corner of the ground, but wonderful for its homely atmosphere. All it lacks is a view of the Thames, just the other side of the new stand.

Fulham must also be the most welcoming ground that I visit regularly. Pick up your ticket from the Johnny Haynes Stand and then walk around the edge of the pitch to the far side before finding the 1975 Bar where sandwiches and sausages lie in wait. But on the way virtually every young attendant greets you with a smile, an enquiry about your health and an offer to guide you by the hand to your destination. By the time you arrive at the Bar you feel like it's your birthday.

Scouting for Moyes

Before watching Fulham play Villa I indulge in the delicacies on offer in this crowded little room, squashed but comfortable in a corner of the bar, making eye-contact with a few other scouts who have managed to find sufficient elbow room for their hands to reach up to their mouths. It's all very cosy! And then I notice Martin Peters edging his way along the bar with his wife in tow and finally coming to a stop within chatting distance. I don't normally go up and begin conversations with the rich and famous, even my boyhood heroes, but when one of them lands up virtually in your lap it's an opportunity too good to be missed.

I ask him how he's doing and add that it's a pleasure to see him, explaining quickly what happy memories he has provided for 33 and three-quarter years by virtue of his goal in the World Cup final that saw off the Germans. He looks a little embarrassed: real modesty. When I ask him why he's here at this match his wife informs me that they've come down with Villa. I am surprised by her northern accent: I always assumed for no good reason that any Mrs Peters would be a thorough going Essex lass. Enquiring further of Martin how he has left his West Ham roots to take up with a Midland club, he tells me, in his first full sentence, that he's the stadium manager at Villa Park. I am surprised for the second time at this information, but I'm more surprised by the northern twang that comes from his lips as well as his wife's. In fact, not surprised: alarmed. It's not how I remember him. It's not what I expected. It's not Martin Peters.

It may be his doppelganger but it's not him. After five minutes of conversing with him, I feel ridiculous in attempting to apologise but his very kind wife says that he's always being mistaken for the England legend. Often, she adds, he just signs the programmes of kids who have been sent by their dads and sends people away happy. It doesn't make me feel too much better and I decide on the way out to walk straight past Prince Charles, who is drinking tea by the door.

Fulham, who play Bolton in a week's time, are awful. They very often are when I come to see them, but usually manage to redeem themselves with a second-half improvement and scrape a win. Today they never look like rescuing a point and sink to two first-half goals. I trust their players are not getting the ferry back along the river after the game, though Hangeland, their tall, blond and today useless centre-half would look just the part at the head of a Viking longship. He's not the only one to disappoint in the match. Murphy the captain is anonymous, whilst Bobby Zamora, mentioned in despatches earlier this season as a possible England striker – (please!) – looks like he's returning from injury carrying a broken leg. I've rarely seen a striker challenge so weakly for balls. I'm reminded of a story that Kieran, who works for Villa, recounted and claimed as gospel. At the beginning of the season, he says, the Fulham manager was talking to each of his players and Bobby said to him, 'The thing is, boss, you're not playing me in my best position.' When asked to elaborate and say what his best position was, he replied, 'On the bench.' Bobby's not famous for his sense of humour either. But what's the betting he gets a hat-trick at the Reebok next week!

Even in defeat the crowd around me are amusing and philosophical. Roy Hodgson has become a firm favourite at the club, having rescued them from an almost impossible relegation fight and no-one is going to get on his back. At least, not yet. Plus the fact that Fulham have come back up from the depths of the fourth division over the past dozen or so years, moving out of the Cottage and playing some of their home games at Loftus Road for a while, so sitting back in their proper surroundings and entertaining the likes of Villa and Man U and Arsenal, with only distant memories of Barnet and Hartlepool on cold winter nights, perhaps the fans feel that real criticism of current performances might seem a little bit lacking in grace. Who knows!

The last light is going as I stroll back through the park and the river looks a lot less inviting. As a final little challenge, I decide to tune into the conversations of people I pass walking away from the ground. I've always had the impression that there is an amazing number of foreign languages being spoken by the fans here, and sure enough my observations are confirmed. At least 75 per cent of what I hear is foreign – Italian, Russian, Polish, Scottish and quite a few I can't recognise. Even given London's cosmopolitan make-up this seems extraordinarily high, and especially for a football crowd. Do their foreign players come from extended extended families? Does everyone receive the same warm welcome that scouts get, and has that news spread abroad? Or is it that the ground has easy access to the open seas, with no customs controller sitting at Putney Bridge? I resolve to investigate further.

Chapter 45

PORTSMOUTH v READING

22 September 1997

I was watching the most boring game in the universe at Portsmouth, supposedly doing a team report on Reading. It was cold, the seats at Portsmouth are made to accommodate seven-year-olds, it had taken three and a half hours to get here thanks to the M25 car park and the game was one where you knew there wouldn't be a goal if they doubled the width between the posts and played for the next twenty years. The crowd were so bored that they'd given up on the Mexican Wave. The referee had tried his best to enliven proceedings by giving a series of bizarre decisions, but to no avail. The spectators were so mind-numbed they couldn't even be bothered to sing about his parentage or sexual habits. I'd stopped drawing diagrams and making notes on the players, knowing I'd be writing 'Crap' against each one. I was now engaged playing games on my mobile phone, an elusive snake being infinitely more interesting than an elusive goal.

After an hour the cramp in my legs was obviously spreading to those around me. A large, red-faced and balding gentleman sitting in front of me was squirming awkwardly in his seat, his physical discomfort clearly not being overridden by the rapture of the game. He turned ninety degrees and we shared a look of agonised boredom.

'Awful. Bloody awful,' he said, attempting to prolong the time he could look away from the pitch.

'You can say that again,' I concurred. 'I've driven three hours down from London to watch this.'

'Think yourself lucky, mate,' he replied. 'I'm the bloody match sponsor!'

Chapter 46

WINTER BREAK

It's the first Saturday of February, the first Saturday of the year when I'm not at a match, not even near a match. Scotland has been shut since Boxing Day, but with the snow now receding we've finally driven north and opened up the dacha again. We motor up on a sunny afternoon; the next morning we wake up to thick snow.

I like being in the Scottish Borders: the pace of life, the scenery, the peace and quiet, all restore a sense of equilibrium. The village shop provides all the essentials for the period when driving on the icy roads is not a good idea, and the ability to sit in front of an open coal fire, with a teapot on the hearth, slippers on the feet and something interesting to watch on TV compensates for the cold outside. All that's needed to complete the idealistic picture is a pipe in my mouth and a faithful dog curled at my feet, but I forgo those for the time being.

The snow doesn't last long this time, and by Saturday the roads are passable again. Except that in football terms there's nowhere to go. Berwick, the nearest club, are playing away. I contemplate meeting up again with the Livingston crew, but they are at Forfar. I don't know where Forfar is but as I do know it's not nearer than Edinburgh I don't bother to look it up on a map. The local lads have a match against Melrose down on the village field but my desperation to see balls flying around hasn't quite plumbed those depths yet. Bolton have no need for me to travel for an hour and a half down to Newcastle and I can't make out a case why I should drive for two hours to Carlisle. And I thought Norwich was remote! Despite knowing in advance that I'd be unemployed for the day I experience mild elements of the Stockholm syndrome: I want to be suffering with others.

It gives me time for a spot of reflection after a month or so of the new regime at the Reebok. It has a kind of 'Good news, Bad news' feel about it.

Good news: I'm still employed by the club, still doing player and team reports, still getting paid, as far as I know.

Bad news: no-one from the management has bothered to make contact with me or many of the other scouts and there's no hint of any forthcoming meeting. Doesn't fill us with a sense of being appreciated, but then scouts are traditionally bottom of the pile.

Good news: Colin Harvey is still the Chief Scout and my No. 1 contact, still at the end of the telephone, still going to matches himself.

Bad news: I get the feeling that he's not really in the position he was, and that maybe he's just hanging in there. There's something about our conversations that's not the same, unless I'm imagining it. Come summer I wonder if he'll be part of a clear-out.

Good news: the club has signed a few new players in the January window.

Bad news: none of them is an out-and-out goalscorer and they haven't got rid of a few I think they should.

Good news: there appears to be a much more enthusiastic support from the crowd. No banners out and applause even at the home matches!

Bad news: Bolton's results haven't exactly taken a turn for the better: in the league, since the change, three defeats in four. (Megson's final spell: one defeat in five.)

With twenty-two matches played I work out that Bolton have completed 57.8 per cent of their games and sit precariously above the relegation zone. They have at least now managed to keep a couple of clean sheets and thanks to a victory over Sheffield United are in the fifth round of the Cup next Saturday. Look for positives, I tell myself. I have yet to form an opinion of the new manager never having met him. After the acrimonious departure from Burnley, biblical analogies are quick to be used in many newspapers. To some Owen Coyle is Moses, leading the Bolton faithful out of bondage and into the Promised Land. Just up the road, however, he is more like Judas, turning his back on his friends and taking the 30 pieces of Gartside geld. Despite his only success so far coming against his former club, many people have pointed out to me the potential irony that lies in the event of Burnley staying up and Bolton going down. Look for positives!

I make the most of the afternoon. The drains are blocked and there is sewage in the garden so I can't flush the lavatory; the car won't start and the brakes have locked during the freeze; the computer keeps turning itself off for no logical reason. So there is a lot to be optimistic about before the results come through at five o'clock! I learn from various text messages where other people are whilst I'm engaged in interesting domestics: Greg at Spurs, Kieran at Ipswich, my non-scout Orient-supporting long-suffering friend Mike watching his favourites – undefeated this decade. I'm even envious of Jack watching Histon take on Hayes and Yeading. Bolton entertain Fulham, who looked hopeless last week and who haven't won an away match for the past 11 attempts. It's the kind of game Bolton must win.

They don't win. A 0-0 draw is described on the radio as the obvious choice for the last slot on *Match of the Day* tonight, though the reporter adds that Bolton had a goal disallowed in the final minute when it looked perfectly legal, and my old mate Elmander managed to blast wide in the closing seconds when his grandad would probably have netted. I begin to wonder whether coming from Sweden engenders in him a spirit of neutrality for which his country is famous, or infamous. Perhaps he thinks that scoring goals is somehow rather unfair to one of the sides playing. I decide to judge for myself on the TV later.

Elsewhere Portsmouth, with more owners than goals this season, score a hat-trick, but all in their own net, Man City bite the dust at Hull – good for football, bad for Bolton – whilst Orient have maintained their unbeaten run with a 1-1 draw against Brighton. Mike mysteriously tells me in a text that Orient went down fighting. When I ring him for clarification he expresses the belief that they lost 2-1. Having travelled half across London, paid £22 for his seat and then seen the whole game live he has to look on teletext to see the correct result. That's what supporting Orient can do for you!

My calculations now are that Bolton have played 60.52 per cent of their league games and lie one place and one point above the relegation zone. Statto eat your heart out! I'm still looking for positives.

As a celebration of a football-free weekend Susan and I walk 300 yards in the drizzle down the village high street for dinner with friends. Insisting quietly that we leave in good time to watch the evening football, I manage to get home by 10.30 and settle down alone to await the judgements of Hansen and Co. But this, of course, is Scotland, even if only just so. No Man Utd game, no Bolton, no Hull... I'm invited instead to enjoy the highlights of St Johnstone playing Dundee whilst listening to the views of the Partick Thistle manager and the coach from Queen of the South. I'm apoplectic with excitement.

Take me back to dear old Blighty,

Put me on a train for London Town...

And Lineker.

And games.

And warmth.

And toilets.

Chapter 47

DIFFERENT CUSTOMS

Being a football scout, albeit a part-time one, doesn't impress everyone across the five continents. Whilst on a brief visit to Japan it certainly fascinates a market trader selling some kind of foul-tasting green liquid who, out of the blue, asks me if I like football, and when he learns of my interest in the game embarks on a twenty-minute conversation about Gary Lineker and Japanese teams and the next World Cup. He supposes my position with the club makes me an expert on the world-wide scene. I wish!

But then I fly to Australia and after a sleepless and uncomfortable twelve-hour overnight flight land yawning at Sydney to be greeted at immigration by one of the few unwelcoming Australians, who looks like he's also had a sleepless night. I pick up immediate vibes that this man doesn't spend too much on sending Brits Valentine cards.

'Purpose of visit?' he asks. I could be honest and tell him that I've come to explore his wonderful country but he's already got my back up and I opt not to add to his conceit.

'Football scouting,' I say. 'Came to see if anyone here can kick a ball straight.'

He says nothing but stares for ten seconds at my passport. 'That your full-time job then?' Mocking incredulity in his voice: the thought that anyone should earn a living by looking at football matches.

My tiredness turns to real irritation and a testy 'No' is the monosyllabic reply. Another pause.

'What do you do then?'

I want to hit him by now. I also want to get into the country, but it goes against the grain to tell him truthfully 'Retired' or 'Teacher'. So instead I say, 'Poet'.

I think if I'd said 'paedophile' the look on his face couldn't have been more contemptuous. He slowly shakes his head and looks briefly around to see if there is anyone he can share this with. 'A watcher of games and a writer of poems. One of the snobs of old England, are we?'

I up the ante and risk it. 'I thought the Australian definition of snobbery was getting out of the bath to go to the toilet.' As his face clouds, my next two weeks are in the balance but he can't quite find the right button to press. After another gaze at my photograph he's stamping down on the passport as though it's really my face he's hitting. I've won the Test match. For the next two weeks I'm thankful that no-one even mentions football.

Chapter 48

MILLWALL v LEEDS UNITED

25 November 2005

My Australian friend, who tried to teach English as well as his accent allowed him, had never been to a football match, not even in Australia. There was a possibility that he might get dragged to Darlington as he recently got married up there and his in-laws were among the few supporters of the club not wanted by the police, but he'd so far managed to avoid that pleasure and decided instead to accompany me one November night to watch Millwall play Leeds.

I warned him in advance that the atmosphere at the ground was likely to be hostile, given these two sets of supporters, and there was a chance that we might encounter some rough and ready moments. He shrugged it off and silently suggested that the blood which ran through the veins at Gallipoli was not going to be intimidated by Yorkshiremen and South Londoners pulling faces at each other.

He was waiting for me outside his flat at 6.30 but I assumed he'd locked himself out as he was dressed in a short-sleeved shirt and had a flimsy jacket flung over his shoulder.

When I told him that he was going to need more than that I was put in my place as a weak whingeing Pom and he assured me that 'We're a tough bunch mate, don't you worry.'

I wasn't worried. I had the heater on in the car and my thick November Nottingham Forest jacket waiting for me in the back seat. I was determined to be a warm, weak whingeing Pom.

The police did a disappointingly efficient job in separating the would-be marauders, but the Leeds coaches still ran a gauntlet of jeering, gesticulating Millwall fans who lined the entrance to show these 'dirty Northern b's' just how tough life could be along the Thames. The players, though, appeared to have agreed on a pact not to score in case one set of supporters got unduly annoyed. It was a match of very little incident and I was aware that as an introduction to the game and an incentive to become a fan this was not doing much to whet Phil's appetite. Nevertheless, the half-time tea, sandwiches and chicken-legs cheered up the evening a little. I explained that Millwall was a very welcoming club, always ready with a programme and team-sheet, good hospitality and a nice seat in the Directors' Box. True, there were a few typicals sitting twenty yards away, looking like they've just learned to walk upright that morning, but they were not the whole of the fan base. To prove my point we wandered along the concourse and met up with Pete Walsh, a long-standing and highly respected head teacher of a South London secondary school, a knowledgeable Irishman on all things football, and, with his wife, an ever-present at the New Den. Phil was duly impressed and, as brother-colonials, would have been happy to converse the night away, and maybe try to get a new teaching job. But the second half beckoned.

The game was like a sporting *Waiting for Godot* where nothing happens, twice. The standard didn't improve and neither did the temperature. Leeds came closest to a goal via a shot that hit the corner flag. Millwall were clueless, seemingly frightened of being barracked by their own fans, and spent much of the time trying to give the ball away; whether to a colleague or opponent seemed immaterial. Marvin Elliott, the player I was watching, hardly broke into a run and never played a pass that went forward or further than five yards. Phil began to shiver but not with either excitement or anticipation.

He made it through to eighty minutes before the polar ice caps set in. The Anzac spirit had to give way at some point and he indicated that he was going to get a drink in the concourse, so I accompanied him downstairs to make him feel less of a wimp. The woman behind the bar asked him where he came from, then told him that 'You lot have got the right idea.' Phil looked at her and me questioningly before she explained her philosophy, that it's a good thing to shove illegal immigrants back on a boat and push them out to sea. Another aspect of the Millwall outlook on life, we wondered. We left the bar quickly and watched the match through windows that look out onto the pitch. Phil's teeth chattered less noisily and ceased altogether on ninety minutes, but as the fourth official held up notification of three additional minutes the beer took effect and he tore himself away from the entertainment to empty his bladder.

While in the toilet Leeds score a spectacular goal. Phil says he's enjoyed the evening, but he's such a lousy liar.

Chapter 49

STUCK AT THE WITHDEAN

Whilst fans in general will use the best Anglo-Saxon monosyllables to point out an official's weaknesses, at Brighton you might detect a difference. While watching them lose a very poor game to Norwich I actually hear a voice behind me cry out, 'Referee, you and your assistants are meant to be implementing the laws of the game correctly!' I wonder at first whether this is a spoof, but I'm reassured by some locals around me that it's normal. They also tell me that another character who last season used profanities was refused a season ticket in this stand and relegated across the way to sit with the punters in the open air. 'Disgusted of Tunbridge Wells' lives on, I'm glad to see.

The Withdean is rubbish, the nearest thing to a continental stadium with only about a quarter of the ground under cover and a running track around the pitch which destroys any real atmosphere. To try to cheer it up I notice they employ more ridiculously-dressed mascots than you'd find at Disneyland. The only equivalently poor venue I've visited was the National Hockey Stadium, which housed MK Dons for a while before they took up residence in their impressive new surroundings. I bet the Brighton faithful can't wait for Falmer to be opened.

On the day I go, I'm allocated Seat 265 in Row B of Block Q entering by Gate 21. Working that out requires a bit of mental gymnastics but when I find the seat it's in the second row from the front and provides a snail's-eye view of the game. Row B is already crowded so I pass down to the first row and walk along until I find 265 where I climb over. Except that 265 is barely visible. On one side sits a mass of flesh, at least twenty stone, and on the other must be his nemesis, tipping the scales at a good twenty-four stone. Spread out, the space between them might just accommodate a broom. Both are cheery Sussex souls who gladly help me climb up and over and as I sink into the seat, with the world becoming invisible around me, I feel like I'm going back into the womb.

The conversation is all about my visit here and I wonder whether this seat is especially devoted to visiting scouts. I wonder too how many are never seen again. The two are like a bizarre double act and I suspect they practise during the week. First one asks a question – 'Who you coming to see then?' – and then the other provides the answer – 'He's coming to look at Lua Lua.' I hardly have to answer a question but I'm glad not to be doing a team report. Trying to lift my arms from my side would prove impossible. By half-time I've relaxed into a kind of warm cocoon and when friends arrive at the interval to help lift both giants out of their seats I'm rather disappointed, as well as chilled.

Hospitality at the Withdean has changed from having a nice meal provided, to elbowing your way to the tea table at half-time, though they do have instant drinking chocolate for Mormon scouts. It's a crowded lounge, even without my two large bookends, but across the way I notice you can still get a meal: there's a restaurant of sorts just behind the terrace providing a carvery six days a week and I'm intrigued to know how many takers they get on, say, a Wednesday, prepared to wander out to this place in the middle of nowhere interesting, up a cul-de-sac, through a tunnel, into the ground, somehow to sit and peer out onto a stone-built stand. If you could see across the ground at least you'd have a view of a wooded area, overlooking the pitch, and patrolled on match days presumably by volunteers from the Forestry Commission, keeping the wild boar away from the action – what little of it there is. But that's quite invisible from the Carvery.

I think also if I supported Brighton I'd find it hard to call my team 'The Seagulls'. There's just something vaguely ridiculous about the name; even 'Canaries' or 'Robins' feels better. Just. The Palace chant of 'Eagles, Eagles' has a ring to it, but – Seagulls! Squawking, screeching excrement-dropping creatures of the oceans. The club does, however, provide proper music as the teams walk out – 'Sussex by the Sea' played by a brass band, albeit a recorded one.

I wonder which was the last club and the last occasion to have a live band marching around the pitch. I wonder when and who was the last goalkeeper to play a top-class game without gloves. I wonder which club was the last to get rid of its wonderful scum-floating communal bath. I wonder how many more pointless things I can find to wonder about.

Chapter 50

ARSENAL v BLACKBURN

11 February 2008

Blackburn were making their annual visit to the Emirates and I was booked in to have an early look at them. It was the kind of game where I'm tempted to bet on the result, but at odds of 9-1 on for an Arsenal win I decided to keep my pound coin stashed away. Nevertheless I couldn't help feeling it was a foregone conclusion as a fixture.

Just as I was leaving home, I tuned into a traffic report that told me the Blackwall Tunnel had a five-mile tailback and the Rotherhithe Tunnel and Tower Bridge were closed for weekend repair works. I was irritated but not surprised, having long been convinced that Transport for London should be renamed Gridlock For London, and that anything more serious than a butterfly breaking a wing caused the organisers of the Blackwall to go into immediate meltdown. I quickly parked up and headed for Arsenal by train and tube: not one of the great train journeys of the world; travelling on public transport can be a dispiriting experience.

The stress of the journey was quelled once I took up my seat in the Directors' Box. These must be the most spacious and comfortable seats in any football ground, akin to leather armchairs, and on cold days blankets are provided to keep the nether regions warmed. Along the row where I was sitting I noticed a few regular scouting cronies, but I was taken aback a little when the three seats to my left were filled simultaneously, two with unfamiliar faces but the middle one belonging to Jack Straw.

It took a moment to fathom that the then Foreign Secretary was actually MP for Blackburn, so I assumed he had adopted his local team in order to summon up a bit of constituent backing. (No, that's far too cynical. I'm sure he's a true blue follower and has been for years.) I've always had a soft spot for Jack, a consummate politician, a man of integrity with a survivor's philosophy: I have my beliefs and principles and if you don't like them then I'll change them. From Iraq onwards, he seemed to be constantly trying to defend the indefensible. Like Blackburn were this afternoon, perhaps.

I had a brief chat to the hulk sitting between us and ascertained that he was one of six armed bodyguards who looked after Jack twenty-four hours a day. We continued our talk at half-time while his master got a drink from the bar. Apparently there was another officer waiting downstairs in the car park for the after-match getaway, but the one I was talking to was lucky enough to be an Arsenal fan, so today was a mixture of business and pleasure. The game, so far as he was concerned, was quite a pleasure as Arsenal seized control from the outset and cruised to a 2-0 lead. It was the first time, as far as I know, that I'd ever sat next to anybody tooled up with a Glock 17 automatic, or any other kind of gun. I rather hoped he didn't get too carried away with excitement in the second half.

Arsenal sat back and won the game at a canter. Blackburn looked a dispirited side, devoid of ideas and happy to get away with a moderate beating. I was tempted to point out parallels with Jack's government as we lingered after the match, allowing the crowds to disperse. He didn't seem too despondent; one of his protectors was happy; the other, apparently, couldn't stand football and preferred taekwondo. Jack seemed keen to learn about Bolton, the club not being a million miles from his own, and we talked casually about our various chances for the season.

'I suppose you're back now to watch *Match of the Day*,' I ventured. 'Re-live the agony?'

'Not today. I'm working back at Westminster for the rest of the weekend.'

I tried my luck: 'Don't suppose you could drop me off at Charing Cross on the way back?' The tone was light enough to be a joke if it needed to be. I noticed Taekwondo frown slightly at Jack, but the minister's reply surprised me:

'I think we could. Doesn't look like a security risk, does he, Ben?'

I didn't add that I was trying to be a security risk to his team, if not to him. In the lift down to the car park the bodyguard explained that he did have to search me. Judging that my notes on Rovers didn't constitute a breach of the Official Secrets Act and that the biro I was using wasn't full of lethal SMERSH liquid, I was ensconced in the back seat and we zoomed out of the ground with a motorbike escort. Did I feel important!

I jumped out at Trafalgar Square, thanking Jack for his kindness but not promising to vote for him. Suggesting that his policies were as crap as his football team seemed churlish and ungrateful. We parted on purely sporting terms.

Chapter 51

DOWN AMONG THE DEAD MEN

It's the end of February. Portsmouth, on the brink of folding, have gone into administration, the first Premiership club to do so. Crystal Palace have followed the same route. Cardiff City have had to sell land in order to avoid a winding-up order that would put them out of existence. Fans of other clubs must be looking over their shoulder. It's a worrying and potentially very sad time for English football, for the historic towns and cities that risk losing their clubs, for all true football fans, even the genuine ones down the road from Pompey at the arch-enemy Southampton. If the famous lines of John Donne apply to people, they might also be re-written to be germane for our beloved game:

No club is an island, entire of itself... any club's death diminishes us all, because we are involved in football; and therefore never send to know for whom the bell tolls; it tolls for thee.

It tolls for thee! Who will be the first of the modern era to actually succumb, and who will follow behind as many people predict?

Portsmouth were not in the spotlight at the start of the season as a club living precariously on its finances; many others seem to be equally if not more perilous. I spoke recently to a Portsmouth scout who was offered a very attractive package at the start of the season, only to be dispensed with after four months. When, if ever, will anyone take notice of the wake-up calls?

Aligned with the concern is the very real anger – righteous anger – from many, many people. Somewhere in the past twenty, thirty years this beautiful, simple, captivating game has been enslaved and prostituted in this country by greedy and often unscrupulous people. It's not happened in secret, though: not much hidden behind closed doors. What's taken place – continues to take place – is done in full view of the media, the millions of impotent and frustrated fans, and worst of all the footballing authorities, who have turned consistently blind eyes and succumbed to the lure of lucre. Football has sold its soul to money, the root of all kinds of evil, we are warned.

The people charged with supposedly protecting the game for ordinary followers have done the opposite. Out of fear, weakness, stupidity, complicity, corruption or any mixture of those attributes the game has been allowed to plumb the depths. There have been enough warnings, enough last-minute reprieves of clubs; and a mountain of mealy-mouthed words and promises from people who instead should act.

There are degrees of death in football. Portsmouth may be waiting for the sods to be laid on top of their Premiership status but at the same time Bolton are booking an appointment at the undertakers in readiness for their own demise. The Coyle record now reads one win in eight and only one point is taken from fixtures against Wigan and Blackburn, with not a goal to Bolton's credit. The downing of Portsmouth will mean effectively that there are now two, not three, positions to avoid. From my own recent observations the only other hope for not joining the long funeral procession is the fact that there are at least two other teams, Hull and Burnley, who look dire enough to compete for relegation spots, with Wolves coming up on the rails. As they stand though, all these teams have more points than Bolton.

I keep the pessimism to myself, working on the basis that a problem shared is a problem doubled, and I wouldn't want Susan to lose sleep. I also ridiculously hold on to any flicker of unrealistic hope that springs into my mind. Patients do come out of comas; the unexpected, nay miraculous, does occur, though infrequently enough to retain its magical status; tennis players survive five match points and come back to win. If only Elmander would score or go. If only Knight would see things a second before they happen instead of two seconds after. If only Bolton had bought Bentley and Modric and Odemwingie and Owen and Duff... Realism rushes in to compete with specks of light. I return to the old Israeli saying: If you want peace, prepare for war. Or more mundanely, expect the worst then when it happens you won't be surprised!

Flying in the face of logic, Colin asks me to do another team report on Fulham. When Bolton beat Spurs in the Cup replay at White Hart Lane, he says, they are going to face the Cottagers in the sixth round. After which it's only one game away from Wembley.... following in the recent footsteps of Portsmouth and Cardiff...

Buoyed by Colin's enthusiasm and the thought of walking again down Wembley Way I decide to watch the replay. It's a cold and wet Wednesday night but I'm not deterred. I've been left a couple of tickets in the Away Fans area, going as a supporter tonight rather than in a scouting capacity. The young man who accompanies me is a Spurs supporter but he's promised to sit on his hands and not look too depressed when things go awry.

Memories of yesteryear creep back when I'm queuing up for a cheese and onion pasty, which is then consumed standing against the brick wall ten yards from the toilet area. It's life in the raw, such as I've almost forgotten about. The Bolton fans who are keeping us company reflect my optimism: it's time the team did something surprising. Nobody questions why two men with obvious London twangs are here in the Wanderers end and I keep my association with the club under wraps. The Away section isn't exactly crammed so perhaps they work on the basis that bodies are bodies.

There's disappointment that Kevin Davies isn't beginning the match, nor Lee Chung-Yongh, who has been an asset in recent weeks. But at least my friend Johan isn't in the starting line-up so that's a plus. I'm wondering if he'll play in the final.

I'm unmoved by the abuse from the home fans when Spurs score their fourth goal. A wave of sympathy washes over me for the folks around who have come down from the wilds of Lancashire, not just across London, to see their team perform pathetically. It's so sad to hear them get excited about Bolton stringing three passes together and I feel that if only they could get a corner it would make their night. I don't know whether to feel depressed or reassured when I hear them berating all the usual culprits in the team that I've had suspicions about for the season. Certainly my target figures live up to expectations – falling over instead of tackling, shooting wide, not shooting at all. And to put an end to the myth that the team can't score, the keeper and the full-back pop in a couple of own goals.

It's a very, very wet night. I leave the ground totally depressed and keep my hat in my pocket as a symbol of repentance for being connected with such mediocrity. I'm glad not to be wearing my Bolton jacket: I just wouldn't have the enthusiasm to nut somebody who gave me abuse.

Chapter 52

PYRAMID SELLING

One of the advantages of being female is that there is less chance of dropping your mobile phone down the lavatory. When it happens to me at Wembley, fifty minutes before England kick off against Egypt, the one minor compensation is that it does so before the toilet is used, but it's then compounded by my biro following the phone into the watery depths of pan-land.

My natural squeamishness of all things messy – babies' nappies, vomit, dog mess on shoes – has to be overcome by higher priorities, and in a blind unthinking panic I plunge an unprotected hand down the loo to rescue the phone. The cheap biro can stay put.

The world comes to a standstill. I can wash my delving hand and get it as clean as I can; I can use my back-up pencil for notes on the game; I can wipe the phone dry with reams of toilet paper and then stick it under the hand-dryer for a double blast. But I can't get the thing to work.

I've come to Wembley to watch England again out of a sense of patriotic loyalty but this time also with a specific request. Colin has telephoned me to ask for an urgent report on two Egyptian players. One of them, Emad Moteab, featured well as a striker in the recent African Nations Cup. The other is a player called Mohammed or Mahamoud – second name uncertain, position uncertain – who 'the gaffer' has been told (by an agent, could it be?) is highly rated. It appears that someone at the Reebok is convinced that the future is built on sand and that there's a lot to be gained from plundering Egyptian treasures. I guess they've never read the stories about the curse of Tutankhamen! It s important that they get a feedback straight after the match as they are sure other clubs will be acting quickly, and Colin is going on a five-day venture to the Far East in the morning. That's why I tell him that I'll ring him as soon as the game is over.

Having been regularly advised by family and friends to seek therapy for the attachment to my mobile, I now feel bereft, distraught, adrift, when it won't respond to me. It would be bad enough under normal circumstances to lose contact with the rest of the civilised world, but to do so on a night when I have given my promise – scout's honour – that I would call with a detailed report on the observed players is too distressing to bear. My whole credibility, minuscule as it may be, is on the line here. If I fail this test, what chance is there of a future with Owen Coyle when he becomes the next Scotland manager!

While I am recovering the SIM-card and trying to reason with the handset the team-sheets arrive and things get both better and worse. Moteab is not playing, not even on the bench. That makes life easier. Mohammed, however, is in the squad. In fact he's in seven times. Why am I only a little surprised?

I weigh up my options. I could take a pin and select at random Mohamed Aboutrika or Mahmoud Fathallah or Mohamed Zidan, leaving Mahmoud El Razk, Mahmoud El Saoud, Mohamed Nageib and Mohamed Abdel Shafy to play out the rest of their days in the footballing desert. I could tell Colin that I'd been knocked down by a tram in Beckenham and missed the match because of a broken pelvis. Or I could contact Keith at Forest and ask for my job back in the morning. Only a remnant of pride and professionalism that creeps in prevents me taking any of these easy options. Instead I resolve to report on all seven.

The instant feedback problem is still unresolved. If I could access the numbers on my own phone I could find a kiosk to ring through, but I have no way of getting to them when they are stuck on a SIM-card. The Man United scout who is sitting next to me is not familiar enough for me to suggest he lends me his handset for me to remove his SIM-card and replace it with mine in the hope that it might work. Anyway, he'd then be privy to my conversation and would know that we were interested in Mohammed! The only half-satisfactory solution I can conjure is to get home and put all six of these guys (thankfully one stays on the bench) straight onto Scout 7.

The notes I take are copious and almost obscure my initial dismay at England's first-half performance, a throw-back to the bad old days. Mohammed scores for Egypt – who else – with an assist from Mohamed. But when Mahmoud comes on in the second half to replace Mahmoud England get the upper hand and knock in three goals to send most of us home happy. I applaud the England team off the pitch, noticing that Crouch has swapped shirts with Mohammed.

It takes until 2.30am to finish the reports and I go to bed wondering what Colin will be thinking at the lack of a promised phone call. Transferring the SIM-card and discovering with relief that it will work in another handset, I resolve to text him in the morning, but he gets in first, waking me from Manchester Airport whilst I'm still recovering in bed. Before I have a chance to explain about toilets he apologises profusely. 'It wasn't

Mohammed, that wasn't the name,' he says. 'It was Ahmed.'

I quickly glance at my notes and teamsheet, which for some unaccountable reason have ended up under my pillow. 'Right, Colin,' I reply sleepily and with a resigned sigh. 'Would that be Ahmed El Mohamady or Ahmed Fathy or Ahmed Hassan or Ahmed Eid? Or perhaps it's Emad Abdelnaby who just calls himself Emad for short...'

Chapter 53

VISIT

I'm in the north for a college reunion weekend and ring Colin to suggest that I might call in at the training ground on the way back on Monday. He tells me that I will be very welcome, and then arranges to be in Belgium for the day.

Alan Harper and Terry Darracott are the other full-time scouts and Colin has kindly left them behind to provide the tea and biscuits. I realise that it's like the Everton Old Boys Club, all three having spent long periods playing at Goodison. Someone, fortunately, has left my name with the security lady and it only takes five phone calls before the gates are rolled back and I'm allowed into the reception area.

It's not the first time I've been here but I'm still amazed at the money that has gone into the place. I recall a training session at Millwall's old Den back in pre-college days which consisted of one lap round the outside of the pitch and then a game of snooker under the stand. From the same era I remember too a first-aid kit that consisted of a wet sponge, a jockstrap and a packet of peppermints. The theory was that what one didn't cure one of the other two would.

Alan is happily chatting to Liz, who is happily trying to ignore him while answering phone calls and trying to arrange match tickets for me and other people for the coming week. She tells me that if Colin was around Alan would be pretending to do something useful, but while the cat's away... I explain that I haven't come to disturb people obviously engaged in an all-out fight against relegation, and Alan asks me if I take sugar in my tea.

We wander through the plush corridors to find Terry hard at work. At first he is invisible in a room full of computer screens and other paraphernalia that looks like a film set of NASA. No-one else is there and in the far corner a small area is screened off. It reminds me of the Naughty Room and sure enough, Terry is there behind the arras watching television. Disappointingly, I see that it's actually a recording of a match between Roma and Udinese, not some steamy X-rated film, and he explains that he's engaged in studying the Roma left back. I suppose it's cheaper than flying to Italy but it doesn't strike me as quite as much fun.

We chat casually for a good half-hour and I feel a bit awkward as while he is looking at me I am looking at the screen to see the aforementioned player make three clumsy tackles and get himself booked. I sincerely hope that Terry will watch this video again before bringing the Italian to the Reebok. Alan stands outside the little enclosed area and pokes his head over the screen in the old 'Wot-No-Beer?' cartoon fashion. He doesn't appear to have a lot to do today, but his good-natured humour and affability add to the pleasantness of the morning. There is a deal of banter between them, especially concerning Terry's one and only visit to Africa on which Alan refused to go. 'On compassionate grounds,' he maintains.

Terry tells me, while Alan laughs, of flying to Ghana and with Colin watching the African Nations Cup. On their very first day, as an introduction to Accra, Colin suddenly realises that he's been relieved of his mobile phone by a man who bumps into him. As quick as he used to make tackles, Terry grabs the culprit by the arm and an amateur wrestling match ensues. In an instant the police arrive, manhandle the suspect against a wall, empty his pockets to find not only Colin's phone but a couple of others too, question him about his movements, to be told that he is here to watch the match, but mysteriously without a ticket, and then proceed to rough him up in full public view. In fact, Terry adds, the guy is also walloped by passing members of the public, who seem to adopt the view that questioned by police equals guilty and guilty equals summary justice, especially as the miscreant came from the Cameroon and not Ghana. Terry feels sure that if the police hadn't prevented it the thief might well have been lynched. Colin, meanwhile, is trying to defend the poor lad's life and limb by suggesting to the police that maybe it was all a bit of a misunderstanding. Welcome to Africa.

Terry's experience of Africa has clearly made an impression on him, but it's not the encounter with the thief or the rough justice meted out that he talks about most. His strongest memories concern the kids of the country, mad keen on football, who play without proper kit, proper footballs, proper pitches, and who often come from families living a dream that one day their son will be signed on as a footballer and earn enough money to lift them out of their poverty. 'I went out as a football scout,' he says, 'but seeing these kids at first hand I came back as an ambassador. Quite a different person.' He recounts being woken one morning by shouts from the nearby beach. At seven in the morning dozens of youngsters are playing organised games of football on the sand and even in the sea. Before he's properly awake they are scoring goals. And then he tells of the taxi driver who picked him up at the airport and decided to stay with him as his driver for the whole of the stay; who invited Terry to a meal at his very basic home to meet his wife and three young children; who wrote to Terry after his return to the UK; and who, three months later, was the sole surviving parent of his three youngsters.

I look around at the technology on show here. For a while I talk to the three analysts, who have state-of-the-art systems, enabling them to see and study and dissect any moment of any game that's been videoed in any country. It makes me wonder what value there is in the match reports I and other scouts provide, given such data at their fingertips. Then I see some players lounging in the plush modern canteen after their morning exertions and being fed wholesome lunches; another going into the Ice Room – minus 40 degrees centigrade – accompanied by a resident doctor; others taking a sauna. Later I watch one of the first-team players, expensively dressed, the standard gold ear stud, drive out of the car park in his Ferrari with his personalised number plate. And Terry's stories suddenly feel like a huge lump of vomit.

Chapter 54

ORIENT v SCUNTHORPE

21 April 1998

Philip Don, the ex-World Cup and Cup Final referee who became a referees' assessor, worked in my school and frequently offered a second ticket to matches he attended. I still held a referee's qualification and sitting with him, discussing the officials' performances, gave a different take on a game. It was also nice not to have the responsibility of working. One Tuesday morning he got a late call and passed on the opportunity.

'I'm at Leyton tonight. Do you want to come along – they're your team, aren't they?'

As it happened I'd been asked by Forest to go to the match anyway to do the thirteenth report on Matt Lockwood, but as this one would say exactly the same as the previous dozen I decided that I'd ask my son if he wanted the scout seat whilst I sat and discussed the man in the middle. Orient were playing Scunthorpe in a rearranged fixture and both teams could do with the points.

'It's a 7.45 kick-off,' Philip informed me. 'I'll leave your ticket on the normal door.'

Alex and I duly arrived at 7.15 and knocked on the little door next to the club shop. It was opened by the usual unsmiling security guard, who seemed to relish his bit of match-day power, but this time before he could demand proof of identity and a sample of my DNA, Philip, waiting behind him, called out 'There he is!' and before I knew what was happening I was whisked inside and frogmarched to the Referee's Changing Room.

I was then measured up by a passing tailor and found myself clad in the black of officialdom, alongside the referee, Mark Halsey and his two linesmen.

Orient, being Orient, had forgotten to inform the fourth official of the rearranged game. Hence, they didn't have one; and in the best traditions of Jimmy Hill, I, being the nearest thing available to anyone who officially was supposed to understand the offside law, was requisitioned to put on spare top, shorts, socks and ill-fitting boots, march out with the other three to meet the captains, sponsors and mascots and have my photograph taken in the centre-circle of the hallowed pitch. Meanwhile Alex sat in the stands and phoned family members to inform them of my two forty-five-minutes of fame. Unfortunately the game was not being featured on Sky Sports.

Once the match began I was relegated to the no-man's land area between the two managers and their entourages. I was given an electric board to signal extra minutes and substitutes, but had no time to practise on it. I dared not trial it in case it inadvertently attracted the attention of a star player on the pitch who then walked off in high dudgeon. Disappointingly there was so little action on the pitch that there was a resultant lack of aggro between the two managers. I was at least hoping that I might be required to separate fighting factions and send someone to the stands.

More than that, however, what I really wanted was for Halsey to twist his ankle or one of the linesmen to begin throwing up. Just let me get hold of that flag and all sense of fair play would be going out of the window. No way would Scunthorpe score to pull back the lucky strike that had put Orient 1-0 up. I'd seen enough bizarre decisions by linesmen over the years to be happy to join their ranks in insisting that the man just coming out of his own penalty area was in fact offside and interfering with play.

Unfortunately all three officials stayed annoyingly healthy, but Orient did manage to hold out to take all the points. Halsey made a few lousy decisions but got away with it. For the first time I appreciated fully the innate and irrational hostility football officials face: all I was doing was holding up the board showing three extra minutes to be played but I was sworn at effusively by fans behind me who insisted, 'Sit down you f******* w***** ' And I'm an Orient fan!!

Alex made notes on Lockwood. Déjà vu. I was thanked by Mark Halsey and was genuinely surprised by the physical and emotional energy all three officials had expended in a relatively mediocre match. Philip Don told me he used to spend half an hour in the toilet being sick before any game he refereed, regardless of the level. I doubt if many fans ever realise the price of involvement required, just to be sworn at, insulted and berated week-in week-out.

A few years later when we are having a scout meeting in Bolton, the group has a Saturday evening meal at a local Italian restaurant. The proprietor is one Mark Halsey – I guess he never referees Bolton – and Colin Harvey has passed on the story I've previously told him. Mark visits my table during the very good meal and claims to remember the match. I express my doubts but he assures me he does. 'I had a crap game, I remember,' he says. Everyone on the table laughs. 'You've had a crap game every time I've seen you,' I reply.

My dessert turns up cold.

Chapter 55

STEVE'S STORY

'Is it you?' Bill asks, 'or do other scouts get into stupid situations too?'

I begin to wonder. Convinced that there are some people who give off sixth-sense vibes or as yet undiscovered chemistry that fouls up machines as soon as they approach, I start to question whether there are also individuals who attract mishaps and misadventures without necessarily being clumsy or accident–prone or opting to take ridiculous risks when common sense should prevail.

My friend Bob and I used to accuse each other of being jinxed when we took school journeys to various parts of the world. Invariably, trains would break down, storms would delay ferries, minibus tyres would blow, French lorry drivers would go on strike and block the ports. I can't recall a single trip that was incident-free. We vowed we'd never travel together by plane. Years on, I begin to think that perhaps Bob's accusations had more substance than mine.

Questioning Greg and John Savage, it appears that they travel week-in week-out to games with little more than traffic jams or cancelled trains to ruffle their equilibrium. But then I meet Steve Leatherbarrow, a Reading scout, whose one particular story makes me feel better.

A couple of seasons ago, he went to watch QPR play at Stamford Bridge in a Cup match. It was his first encounter with the club for a long time, and what with stories of directors walking about with guns, police raids and the like, he wondered whether he might meet people resembling members of a madhouse or exhibiting an air of complete and utter normality. He soon discovers.

Steve finds himself watching from an empty row in the Directors' Box, empty until he is joined by Bernie Ecclestone, the new joint owner of QPR. Bernie opts to sit next to Steve despite the spare seats and a conversation ensues:

'Big game for your team today.' (Muted response.) 'I suppose it must take up a lot of your time running the club.'

This time an answer. 'Doesn't take up any of my time.'

As *Match of the Day* cameras zoom in on the two isolated figures to give Steve his ten seconds of national fame, he tries again. 'Hopeful of a result today then?'

'Not really. I'm a Chelsea fan.'

Bernie then becomes more chatty and asks Steve what he is doing. Clearly overwhelmed by Steve's responses he gatecrashes him into the Directors' Suite at half-time to introduce him to his daughter, various other dignitaries and the co-owner Flavio Briatore. Whilst Bernie is present Flavio is effusive and gregarious and after another glass of champagne hints at a possible lucrative position as a QPR scout. 'Leave me your card and I'll call you,' he slurs. Steve doesn't have a card but writes his telephone number on a piece of torn-off newspaper, convinced that it will be discarded the next time Flavio puts his hand in his pocket.

To his surprise and delight he receives a call the next day from Signor Paladini, the Chairman no less, inviting him to a meeting with the manager at Loftus Road in two days' time. Steve begins to think about early retirement and just what he'll have to do to emulate the Man City scouts on their £60K a year. Unsurprisingly, he turns up promptly at the arranged time, only to find no manager and no Gianni Paladini.

An agent of one of the club's players is also expecting a meeting, but he's obviously trodden this route before and expresses no surprise at the missing personnel. The secretary manages to track down the Chairman, who is currently enjoying an espresso coffee in Richoux's restaurant opposite Harrods. He requests that the two attendants join him there and as neither has driven they both embark on a tedious journey by tube half-way across London. The agent calls it a bloody circus.

The outcome of the meeting is that Steve is requested to make a further appointment in two days at QPR's training ground. Signor Paladini insists the manager will be there and Steve's not giving up a potential windfall for the sake of another journey. Football scouts know when they're onto a winner. Usually.

Deciding to drive this time, he takes with him an impressive CV plus references from people in the game as well as examples of match and player reports that he has done. The nightmare M25 trek from Kent to Hayes is endured stoically: how much better off might he be on the return journey!

When Steve arrives he finds himself depressingly alone, apart from the Training Ground receptionist who inform him that neither Paladini nor De Canio are due at the place that day. A quick call results in a rearranged meeting for the next day. Hope springs eternal.

The enthralling Kent to Hayes run is undertaken once again with the belief that all will be well in the end. This time the manager is where he should be. Luigi de Canio, seated behind a desk as Steve is shown into his office, rises to greet him and points him to a chair. As both men sit, the Italian smiles and nods and Steve takes this as a sign for him to begin selling himself.

He outlines his wide experience in the game, produces a number of recommendations which he passes over and then shows Luigi some of the reports he's done on teams and players. The manager glances perfunctorily at them and pushes them to the side of his desk. Undeterred, Steve relates an amusing and self-effacing story of giving a player that Reading were interested in the thumbs-down on the very day that QPR signed him. Luigi doesn't appear to see the funny side. After a good seven-minute monologue Steve is relieved to see the door open and the familiar figure of the Chairman enter. More smiles, more handshakes, more explanations from Steve before Signor Paladini informs him that 'Luigi no understand a word of English. Not a word.'

A conversation in Italian then ensues and for a period Steve is totally ignored. He sits part-bemused, part-deflated, part expecting Coco the Clown to pop in next with a bucket of water to throw over everyone. The agent's words appear to be dangerously accurate. It's therefore not a massive shock when, ten minutes later, Paladini explains that, 'Steve, we know you are very important man,' (the hell you do!) 'but we not employing anybody at the moment. Not anybody.' (Early Retirement slopes out of the window.) 'But when we do, we give you a ring. You top of the list.' (Of course! Where else?)

Driving out of the car park Steve knows full well that he'll never hear from these people again and wonders why he was invited in the first place. He controls himself as Bernie Ecclestone juggles past on a monocycle but does manage to aim a custard pie at Flavio high up on stilts. The sign over the exit tells him that 'We. Are. Q.P.R. – Yes we are Q.R.P.'

Says it all.

Chapter 56

LIFE AT THE PALACE

There are times when I wonder why I bother. A weekend trip to Gillingham is followed by a Tuesday night jaunt to Crystal Palace. The last time I came here I invited Vas, my friend and barber, to join me. He managed to decline the offer and thus missed out on a stunning and instantly forgettable 0-0 draw against Sheffield Wednesday. This time he can't think of an excuse quickly enough and we duly trek down to Selhurst Park to see Palace take on Bristol City.

I prophesy it's not going to be a match full of goals. My guess is a 1-0 either way, but midway through the second half even that looks optimistic. It's my 55th game of the season and only one has been a goalless draw. This looks destined to be a replica. I should have guessed.

Everything about Palace currently exudes an air of depression. They have recently gone into administration, have subsequently been deducted points and reduced to the relegation zone, the crowd has diminished, Neil Warnock, their manager ,has left and gone west to QPR, while Paul Hart, recently abiding at QPR, has joined in the Managers'-Musical-Chairs game and arrived at Palace. Hart may be an affable kind of person but I note that with every club he's managed he has left with a record of losing more games than he's won. Is Palace going to break this trend? Judging by this particular performance, probably not.

The football they serve up is dire. Having had to sell Victor Moses to Wigan, they play two starkly average guys up front, one of whom begins the game with a bandage round his head and then plays as though it has slipped down over his eyes. The other, tall and looking the part, appears not to have studs in his boots and spends much of his time in the missionary position. As a pair of strikers they wouldn't look dangerous even with a bazooka in their hands.

Mick McCarthy is at the game and tries to appear more interested than cold. Living locally, I can only assume he's come along to reassure himself there's a team worse than Wolves at the moment. He has a choice of two here tonight. Vas talks to him at half-time and invites him along for a haircut and to meet his wife, something of a Mick fan, and he gratefully accepts. It's the best offer he's had all evening and he leaves shortly after the interval, tearing himself away from the entertainment down below presumably to go home and experience more of a buzz in combing his hair.

Palace's woes are suddenly compounded when out of the totally unexpected blue, Iwelumo fires home a scorcher. He looks as surprised as everyone else at hitting the target, having had half a dozen previous shots present more of a danger to the Met Police helicopter hovering above than the Palace keeper. The team's celebrations last at least five minutes, time which, hopefully, the referee won't add on at the end.

Of all the players on the pitch, only Nick Carle, the long-haired, tanned Australian midfielder, looks like he has any idea of how to control, keep and use the ball and he stands out clearly among the dross. Hence, with 20 minutes to go and Palace 1-0 down, the manager substitutes him to incredulous and derisory jeers of the home fans and delighted laughter of the away supporters. Managers clearly know and see things that lesser mortals can't perceive and Hart's insight is rewarded by Palace failing to get near the Bristol goal and losing the game 1-0. His record looks safe.

The icing on the evening's cake comes from other parts of the country. As we walk back to the car, chilled yet again by the icy east wind that has frozen us throughout this long winter, I listen in to my radio to hear that Orient have lost at Oldham and Bolton, having breathed again with two recent wins, have been trounced 4-0 at Sunderland, who have themselves been in freefall for two months. It all makes for an even colder evening and when Vas's new puppy greets me with growls and attempts to snap at my ankles I know just how he feels.

Chapter 57

HEARTS v HEADS

5 December 2006

The inevitable had to happen. I was working for Forest when they played Orient the following weekend. I was asked to do a team report in preparation for the game.

It was no good quoting the old line to myself that there's no room for sentiment in football. The whole irrational support for a club is based on sentiment. On the one hand I'd seen and read about lots of players who grew up supporting a club only to find themselves playing against them. I'd never yet heard of a player who refused to play or who didn't try his best. There is the folklore story, of course, about Denis Law retiring from the game after his goal for Manchester City relegated Manchester United, but I have my doubts about its veracity. At most, some players have deliberately muted their celebrations if they've scored a goal, but they have a job to do and they do it.

On the other hand, scouting is not quite the same as playing: less money and longer attachments for a start. I once met a scout at Southend who worked for one of the Bristol clubs but was actually an Orient supporter – a rare enough occurrence. He'd told his club that he'd never do a team report on Orient, such was his loyalty. When I agreed to assess them, therefore, it wasn't without some misgivings.

Orient played Bradford City in an absolutely dire game. The visitors were poor but still ran out winners by 2-1. It had been a while since I'd seen Orient and they looked like a team in disarray: weak at the back, a non-existent midfield and a strike-force that couldn't score in a harem. No wonder they were low in the league. Forest, by comparison, were currently riding high and when I sent Keith the findings it was in anticipation of a real hammering awaiting the Os at the City Ground come Saturday. An unlikely draw would be the only result to satisfy both my personal and professional involvement.

Orient didn't manage a draw. Instead they won 4-1. Martin Ling, their manager, sent me a sarcastic text which simply said, 'Cheers Les.' I didn't tell Keith this; in fact I didn't talk to him for a week. If I'd been him and he was me, would I believe that he hadn't stitched us up and let his heart rule his head?

We never mentioned it again.

Chapter 58

EXTREMES

An extraordinary night: a game to stick in the memory. And of all places: Crystal Palace.

Because of them going into administration Colin wants yet another update on any players who might be in the shop window. As Moses, their only real star, is now wandering through the Wigan wilderness, I could tell him without another visit that apart possibly from Nick Carle no-one is going to break into a Premiership team. Tonight they play Wolves in an FA Cup replay and I can only hope that the game is not another typical dour affair that is so often the case here. Having held Wolves at Molineux I can't see them getting a lot from the replay, apart from much-needed gate receipts. I take with me a young Palace fan who rarely gets to see his team, hoping that his disappointment won't scar him for life or turn his affections elsewhere.

Actually watching a game is some antidote to the ordure that's surrounded football over the past few weeks. The sorry saga of John Terry's infidelities has provided another episode in the ongoing national soap opera, dragging the sport once more through the midden, with the familiar cast of solemn-faced sinner, heartbroken partner and a troupe of so-called friends who emerge from the woodwork to enlighten us all with their two-penny worth of inside information. Expressions of moral indignation, views on the need to set an example and to wear an England arm-band with pride, have all really been submerged beneath the prevailing mood of prurient amusement. The derisive jeers that have greeted Terry's recent appearances at away matches have sprung from being entertained rather than offended. Fans would, I'm sure, happily ignore their hero's sexual misdemeanours as long as he scored on the pitch as well as in bed. Moreover, suspicions that Terry's unsuccessful bid to keep his private life out of the media glare has been prompted less out of concern for his marriage than to ensure his sponsorship deals are not affected seem only to illustrate what football has become.

They don't seem to go in for that sort of thing much at Selhurst Park. What I witness here tonight reflects the extremes of British football. The newspaper I've brought depicts the very worst face of the game with its pampered millionaire superstars and savage financial depredations. Pitted against that, the very best: a ground bubbling with red and blue balloons, a cauldron of deafening sound, a body of loyal fans expressing defiance in the face of circumstances that at the very least bemuse them. Palace is not a club where, I imagine, too many of its players have second homes in Florida. Its training facilities are not phenomenal. Its crowd are decently sized and well-behaved. Yet somehow it has managed to land itself a £30 million debt. Why should loyal fans not feel a sense of bewilderment and fury at such mismanagement? I'm surprised they are able to contain their anger, but tonight it seems the focus is entirely about what happens on the pitch.

A short while ago when I came here, Keith from Forest sat and suffered next to me watching a bevy of players who just weren't very good. On that occasion he cited one individual in particular as being 'the worst player in the Championship': Palace's full-back

Danny Butterfield. Keith's verdict might have been a little harsh at the time, but possibly only a little. As an ageing journeyman defender he struggled to head, pass, tackle or cover very effectively, which didn't leave many positives to his game.

With Moses' exodus Butterfield has, incredibly, been pressed into service as a striker. Is the logic behind this that he can't do worse up front than at the back? As I take my seat I wonder what Keith would say.

What Danny B has done in his life so far, or will do in the future, it's a relative certainty that no seven minutes has, or ever will, emulate seven minutes of his life tonight. In slightly less than that space of time he scores not one, not two, but three times to send Wolves to the dogs and secure a lucrative home tie against Aston Villa with a half-million pound payday that might – just might – be the difference between the club's survival and extinction. Among the squat and squashed stamping grounds of this south London district, this is what passes for a fairy-tale.

You could get long odds on the chances of Danny Butterfield leading the England line when they take on opponents in South Africa come summer. And I doubt – though I don't know – that he'll drive home tonight in a Porsche with personalised number plates. Though the headlines tomorrow may bring him to the public attention he's not a mega-star, nor likely to become one. But out there for a few precious minutes stood one very real personality. He underlined Palace's authority. The world seems to be his friend. His enthusiasm was infectious and embraced all, from the policeman on the perimeter to the referee and enemy in the middle. He enjoyed himself as much as a shiny-faced youth tobogganing down some slope on a tin tray. As he wheeled away in Spitfire fashion having just completed his hat-trick – an expression of combined ecstasy and amazement on his face – a man sitting in front of my young companion turned around with boyish delight and told him that he would remember this moment for the rest of his life.

I will too.

Chapter 59

SHOOTS OF SPRING

Things in football are rarely grey. Everyone who is balanced knows that grey exists, but for many involved in football the choice is usually between black and white. That's why teams and players are either fantastic or complete rubbish. That's why weekends are either spent in the doldrums or on a high. It doesn't take newspapers to encourage these extremes, but of course they do their bit with the old hero to zero, rags to riches to rags paths trodden regularly. And it's strange the way that often all the teams you like (or work for) do well on a particular day or do badly on another. I've noticed with astonishment how the fortunes of Bolton and Orient seem to be intertwined, just in order to affect my weekend mood entirely.

For the first time in several months I see a convertible car with its hood down. The temperature has risen to double figures and the sun is visible with blue stuff surrounding it. The winter has been possibly the coldest I can remember, and along with the rest of the country I'm longing for a bit of warmth. Even before I drive across to Brentford there is a touch of pathetic fallacy in the air, though when I mention this to my neighbour he looks at me blankly. 'Just pathetic,' he replies.

Brentford is not on the agenda as one of the pinnacles of the day's entertainment, but two players there have come to Colin's attention and I'm asked to suss them out. Jack, who sees this lot regularly, tells me that with at least one of them I'm wasting my time. Before I venture across I drop in at Spurs for an early kick-off to watch them see off Blackburn 3-1. I never like to leave early but at least I see some goals before comparing the standard of play down two divisions. With an extra-quick zoom across town I arrive at Griffin Park in time to see the last knockings on TV of the game I've just left. Standing by the screen is Paul Ince whose MK Dons team are the opponents for the day. We share a few words about the match but are then interrupted by a tall ginger-haired man in a horrible flowery shirt who holds out a hand expectantly. 'Incey, good to see you.' Ince obliges by shaking hands. 'Long time no see. How you doing?'

'Sorry, but I can't quite place you. Have we met before?'

Ginger's laugh is so rattly I wonder if I should call for an ambulance. 'Remember when you played for West Ham over at QPR and you came sliding in to win a corner off the defender. I was the one who threw the ball back to you!'

As chance has it I find myself sitting right behind Ginger in the stand. As chance has it the ball is headed out of play and up into our area. By chance or by some form of magnetism nobody but Ginger manages to catch it and return it to the waiting full-back, who, no doubt, will be lined up for a chance meeting some years down the line. But it all adds to the feeling of joie-de-vivre that the sun has brought. Even the game, though not quite up to the standard of the earlier match in terms of skill and vision, produces enjoyment.

The Brentford keeper, on loan from Arsenal and highly rated, drops an easy cross and gives away the first goal. Brentford equalise. One of my target players then gives away a penalty which the keeper fails to save. Brentford equalise. In the 91st minute their keeper drops another cross and gives away the third goal. The away fans are delirious until in the 93rd minute Brentford equalise. Three-three seems fitting for an early spring day and it only gets better. Bizarre results come in from elsewhere. Chesterfield lose 5-0 at home but at Burton the score is 5-6. More importantly, Orient achieve their first win in seven and Bolton, having been trounced by Sunderland, hit Wigan for four, their best score of the season. Unbelievably, two of the names on the score sheet belong to Elmander and Muamba. Has spring really arrived?

Chapter 60

CROATIA ZAGREB v MAN UTD

22 September 1999

Perhaps more in hope than expectation Stoke City were looking to strengthen their side's promotion push with the influx of some foreign players. I confess to having my doubts when they targeted a couple of lads who were performing for Croatia Zagreb. Mario Cvitanovic and Tomislav Rukavina were not exactly household names, probably not even in their own households, but no doubt someone around the Potteries had seen or heard or been told about them and I was asked to take a look.

I jumped at the chance to watch them as I was firstly invited to Old Trafford and then a month later travelled to Zagreb. In the first leg, a lacklustre 0-0 which was an advert for how boring European ties could be, both players did little to attract attention, being concerned with plying their midfield skills more in defence than anything remotely attacking. There was more interest in the bare-chested Croats behind the goal, who at first seemed to be competing with Newcastle fans in a 'who can look the biggest muppets' competition, but I was quickly informed that this was more than a macho thing. Their shirtless display of solidarity was because they refused to recognise the new name of their team, Croatia Zagreb.

It appeared that they had had to suffer three name changes in nine years and they were less than thrilled with the end result. An equivalent would have been changing United's name without any consultation and suddenly calling them 'England Manchester'. So these fans, who made a journey of two-thousand miles for this game, did two things. Firstly they boycotted any merchandise bearing the 'Croatia' name and instead sported hand-made scarves with their original name of Dinamo Zagreb. Secondly, though they crossed countries and seas to offer their support, they stayed away from home games.

When I made the journey for the return game I saw hordes of these lean, shaven-headed, angry young men in the city of Zagreb, many outside the stadium. But not inside it. They had stated that they would not attend until their original name had been reinstated and they seemed to be scoring points. The crowd at the last home game in the Croatian first division had numbered a mere one thousand, swallowed up inside the Maksimir Stadium. I was wholly on their side and found enough who spoke English to engage in sympathetic discussion before I went in, though I politely declined the offer to wear a home-made scarf, just in case there were Mancunians sitting close by.

For the visit of such a prestigious team it looked like the Zagreb middle-classes had turned out to try to compensate for the lack of crowd, but I couldn't work out whether a huge banner that was unfurled stating 'Red Devils welcome to the Blue Hell' was meant to frighten or encourage the United team. The Croatian President, Tudjman, arrived and took up office three rows in front of me. His government was bankrolling Zagreb and building a 65,000-seater stadium. Not that there was any hint of bias towards one team in the country! His popularity apparently waxed and waned with the performance of the national side and the country's leading team.

It was not his day. United took control of the game from the start and popped in goals just before and just after half-time. My two stars didn't shine and I was amazed that anyone had seen something in them to warrant this journey. Much more significant was the veteran Prosinecki, who came on and looked a class above the rest, but after an hour the locals' attention was switched to the score flashes from the game between Graz and Marseille. When it became clear that Graz had won and Zagreb's European involvement was no more they vented their anger at President Tudjman and his cronies by singing a song which sounded like 'Tudjman, Tudjman, buy us Giggs.' That, or they want some cigs.

Rather than join in the jolly song the President decided to make an early exit, in true scout fashion, no doubt to avoid the traffic, and he missed the team's one delight when Prosinecki popped in a consolation. It was no more than a token though, and back at the hotel two eloquent, informed and intelligent Croat barmen discussed the result with me, asserting that until Croatian teams could keep hold of more home-grown talent, like Bilic, Boban and Stimac, they were never going to challenge seriously.

Given the political, economic and social instability in the former Yugoslavia republics, that day looked as likely as Zagreb's Bad Blue Boys wearing their Croatia Zagreb tops to home games.

Chapter 61

WISE WORDS

Ernie Tippett joins me at Chelsea to watch them take on Villa. Ernie and I between us share responsibility for all the league teams in the South-East, from Peterborough down to Portsmouth, Norwich in the east to Reading west of London. He is a recently qualified London cabby, and I have to smile when he phones me to stay he's stuck in traffic in Park Lane so will I save him a team-sheet. As it happens he makes it in time, but by tube, not taxi.

Bolton play Villa in a week and Chelsea in a fortnight, so two team reports are necessary. I'm explaining this to Kevin, the local Man Utd scout, and I moan a bit about the fact that we only get £20 for doing a match report. At around four to five hours' work that's not even up to the minimum wage! Several years ago I got double that at West Brom, but maybe the further north you go the tighter money becomes. I'm then astonished when Kevin tells me that United pay nothing for a team report, and that there have been occasions when he's been sent alone to do a report on both teams – a quite impossible task. He further explains that there's a United economy drive with notices at the club offices saying 'Is it really necessary to photocopy?' That kind of belt-tightening should quickly make an impression on the club's £700 million debt.

We sit just behind a frail and aged Richard Attenborough, who is lifted into and out of his seat, and just in front of Sven, who is as charming and friendly as ever and, rumour has it, is just about to take over the reins of the Ivory Coast national team. I ask him if I can use a photo of him in my proposed book and rather than handing me a business card he gives me his mobile number. I'm sure I once saw Dickie Attenborough in a film that was set in Africa and I wonder if I should advise Sven to get some low-down from him before flying off. A cool and unflappable Swede in the midst of a hot and steamy East African country doesn't at first appear like a marriage made in heaven, but then modern football has all kinds of anomalies.

Kevin shows me an article from the morning paper quoting Fabrice Muamba saying that he's playing the best football of his career under the new manager. He actually managed to score a goal – his first for Bolton and the first for 56 games – a couple of matches ago and continues by saying that there's such a confidence in the side they feel capable of beating anybody on their day. Is this Muamba revealing rejuvenation at the Reebok, or is he trying to earn a few brownie points by singing the praises of Owen Coyle? A team capable of beating anybody? Kevin smiles at the assertion and, as Bolton have Villa and Chelsea lined up and entertain United at the Reebok for a 5.15 kick-off today, he suggests Muamba's words will prove to be either prophetic or idiotic.

In recent weeks both Chelsea and Villa have had wobbles, dropping points unexpectedly whilst still maintaining their elevated position in the league. Today's game is a preview of the Cup semi-final in a couple of weeks and I'm sure it will be a tight contest Villa have only conceded 25 goals in 28 matches – an average of one every 108 minutes – and I haven't seen any team score against Chelsea in my last four visits here. I anticipate a single goal either way will win the game. Ernie goes for a 1-1. Kevin thinks it might actually be goalless.

Chelsea score after 15 minutes. There goes Kevin's prediction. Fifteen minutes later Villa equalise. There goes my prediction. On the stroke of half-time Lampard slots home a penalty. Goodbye Ernie.

Martin O'Neill, renowned for his wise and effective half-time team talks, tactically reorganises his trailing Villa side so as to keep the game tight and his team in the hunt in the second half. As a result, Chelsea win 7-1. Good tactics, Martin! Good predictions, lads! Two hours later United thump Bolton 4-0. Good call, Fabrice! I begin to wonder whether we shouldn't all swap jobs.

Chapter 62

JUST WHEN YOU THOUGHT...

We live on the lip of tragedy. In football, as in life.

The minute you breathe a sigh of relief, lower your guard, relax into an armchair of contentment, you risk the telephone call that tells you your brother has been arrested, the Dear John letter that informs you the woman you love has gone off you, the doctor's report that says the mole in your neck needs to be checked out urgently.

And invariably the bullets come unexpectedly, the very moment you're not prepared for them. I've tried working on the theory that what you anticipate rarely happens, so I try to brace myself for bad news every time the phone rings, or for every unrecognisable envelope that I open, or every twinge and ache that I encounter anywhere on my body. But it's all so exhausting. 'In headaches and in worry, vague life leaks away,' said Auden. So I give up. And get caught out.

All season I've told people that both Bolton and Orient are relegation fodder. There's hardly been a voice in agreement. 'Got too many good players'; 'Much better than other teams'; 'Far too strong to go down.' Whether I really believe that demotion is likely or whether I'm playing the silly personal game of 'expect the worst', I'm not sure. Except that somewhere around late February I begin to chide myself for unwarranted pessimism, for lack of faith in good people, for being depressing and grumpy and negative. Orient have lost only one in nine, have held Leeds at home and been the first team all season to win at table-topping

Charlton. Bolton have won three games out of four and are creeping up the ladder to the rung marked 'comfortable'. I begin to look forward to Saturdays.

Foolishness! You would think that years of unremitting disappointment would inure you against false hope, but once again it's like falling in love: you know you shouldn't do it, but higher (or lower) powers prevail. By mid-April the tables are literally turned and both teams are back in the mire. Orient have followed Bolton's example and sacked their manager. I text through to Gary Megson asking him if he fancies the position. As if! His reply is remarkably docile, declining the chance and pointing out that now, having won only once in thirteen attempts, Orient are looking enthusiastic for next season in League Two. I wonder what has happened to Gary's spirit of adventure, the challenge of a hopeless cause. Bolton have lost four out of five games without scoring a goal and face away games at Chelsea and Spurs as two of their remaining fixtures. The pundits are still confidently predicting the demise of Burnley and Hull and this is the most solid thread of hope that I can find to grasp. These, though, are the same commentators who earlier in the season were confident that both teams would be fine, so you wouldn't risk your house on their expertise. (They probably had shares in Northern Rock a few years ago.) In anticipation of the inevitable, therefore, I begin to work out the possible opposition next year in The Championship and League Two. 'Be prepared' is a good old scout motto.

Chapter 63

E-MAIL

An e-mail arrives unexpectedly from Italy. Paulo Verzeletti is an Italian guy who, a few years back, spent a month at my house during one summer holiday receiving English lessons from me and another teacher. A month is a long time not to get round to discussing football with an Italian and I learned from him of his avid support for Brescia, his local team. More surprisingly, and quite shockingly, he casually informed me that he was part of a semi-official gang who regularly went to away matches and spent every other Sunday taking part in hooligan activities.

To meet Paulo you would find it hard to believe this. He is intelligent, polite and well-educated and when I taught him was at university studying business management with a view to entering his father's cutlery firm. But stirring up strife under the umbrella of football supporting seems to be an almost acknowledged and accepted weekend pastime in Italy, only occasionally warranting press coverage when someone dies.

I begin to decipher his message – what a marvellous job we did for his language skills! – which tells me that he now has an important position in the football club – he doesn't say what – and the manager and chairman of Brescia are personal friends of his father. Not that nepotism exists in any way throughout Italy! Then comes the crunch:

'Les you is still Premiership scout yes no? I tell my dad he tell the boss and he tell the manager because we own three scout and not none of them can go to Africa south because one is having a baby and one doesn't get on good with black people and one is going to prison for drugs. Les we ask you can go to World Cup for us because we want getting back into Serie A. We pay all and give you bonus. I tell my club you important scout for Boston Wonderers and you do fantastic job learning me English. So you can please e-mail with RVSP. Thanks Les, I love you. Ciao. Paulo.'

When I show the e-mail to my wife there is an anticipated degree of concern that falls over her face. I have previously warned her of an outside chance of a trip to the finals, but there has been no hint from Bolton of me or anyone else going out; hence the possibility has been pushed back to the realms of highly unlikely. This opportunity comes out of the blue and with it come all the original doubts and fears which are now expressed audibly. We all know that the country is not the most stable or crime-free place in the world, that several people we've met have left for good over the past ten years because life is intolerable, that Italian reliability and organisation don't come top of the charts. Then there are a few commitments already made for the June and July period, a few schools who would be expecting me to run courses for their bright kids, another birthday spent out of the country. Inexorably the negatives pile up. I think it over and e-mail back. Yes, I'll go.

Chapter 64

HUNGARY

24–27 May 2008

Hungarian football, in the annals of English history, has always merited a place of regard and regret. The black and white footage that gets a periodic dusting down shows their national team trouncing England 6-3 at Wembley in the 1950s with Ferenc Puskas and Co. deftly waltzing round leaden-footed English defenders like ballerinas among deep-sea divers. Not only was Hungary the first foreign side to win on English soil, it heralded the unpalatable realisation that the founders of the game were no longer its masters, home or away. We had been found out – and have spent the best part of half a century trying to regain the initiative.

Being asked to go to Hungary, therefore, had a particular attraction. It was going to be a four-day visit and I'd never ventured behind the former Iron Curtain before, but above all I was hoping that some of the old footballing magic lived on. My brief was to look at one player in particular but also to note anybody else of interest whilst I was there.

In England scouts are often chatted up by agents who go to matches. I'd like a pound for every fantastic player who has been recommended by some of the agents I've come to know. They are rarely flavour of the month among managers and chief scouts but the two who looked after me for my stay in Budapest were well thought of by the hierarchy at Bolton.

Viktor Kovedski and Tibor Pataky didn't exude ingratiating smoothness. They were actually attached

246

to MTK Hungaria, the team that was on the threshold of winning the top division title, and they had connections with a number of English clubs, Bolton among them, though exactly what the set-up was I couldn't quite work out.

I took in five games in the four days there, including a full international, played at the Ferenc Puskas Stadium, which gave me a small chill of delight, an Under-19 international and a couple of other matches, until the highlight of the trip, which was to see MTK and their main striker, who had come to the attention of people at Bolton. It wasn't altogether straightforward though: why would I ever expect it to be? MTK were playing another Budapest-based side called Rakospalotai and the expected win for MTK would deliver them the championship. Rakospalotai, however, didn't play in Budapest: their ground seemingly was unsuitable. For some unaccountable Hungarian reason they played their home games in the town of Sopron, a mere 120 miles north-west on the border of Austria. It appeared that their home support had taken a bit of a dip since relocating, which isn't very surprising. As though that in itself was not sufficient disincentive for a massive following, this vital and supposedly prestigious game, which was to be televised nationally, kicked off at 5pm on a Monday afternoon. I didn't even try to understand why. Magyar logic seems as impenetrable as their language.

It was not until 3pm that Viktor and Tibor picked me up from my hotel. Leaving only two hours to drive 120 miles seemed to be a bit risky but I relied on these guys knowing what they were doing. After they got stuck in traffic and then become lost in a one-way system I began to doubt they did know what they were doing. We arrived at the ground at 4.55pm and I appeared to be the only one who was remotely perturbed.

On the two-hour journey to the match I learned a lot about the country since its break from Communist rule, about football and in particular about MTK. The second richest man in Hungary, whose name I couldn't pronounce even with practice, had poured billions of forints into the club, which in pre-war days had been the number one football team in the country. There had always been a strong Jewish influence in MTK, leading to anti-Semitism even up to the present time, whilst in 1950 the secret police took over the running of the club, renaming it 'Textiles SE'. Almost as imaginative and evocative as 'Airbus UK' or 'Vauxhall Motors'. However, despite the suffocating hand of state intervention – or perhaps because of it – I'm told they were the first team to experiment with 4-4-2 and the deep-lying centre forward that proved the undoing of England at Wembley. So I looked forward to a tactical treat.

Parking immediately outside the main office we were escorted straight in, down a corridor, through an office, down another corridor and then into a tunnel. We turned the corner and suddenly joined the back of the two lines of players making their entrance into the arena. As though we belonged, we walked out behind them to appear on Hungarian national television and I was disappointed that out of the whole population of TV watchers currently tuned in, the certainty was that not one of them would recognise me. I therefore resisted waving as cameras zoomed in upon us but my other three colleagues smiled and gave it their all as one arm of the media accompanied us on our walk around the edge of the pitch to gain our open-air seats on the far side. I couldn't help imagining being able to gate-crash like this at Chelsea or Old Trafford at the start of a title-decider. I vowed to try it some day.

The game was poor, the prospective striker even poorer and there were only about three thousand people there to watch it. I was feeling awkward that after four days of excellent hospitality from my Hungarian hosts I wouldn't be recommending anyone I'd seen to Bolton, but the truth is that the standard of play in matches on the trip was nothing like Premiership or even Championship level. After a goalless first half MTK knocked three past a fairly hapless defence and subsequently lifted the trophy, much to the delight of Mr Unpronounceable, who was probably watching the first tangible return on his investment. Despite my boyhood wonder of the Magic Magyars taking a dent, I still managed to give it a go when it came to the post-match celebrations: Hungarian hugs all round, a pleasing lack of kisses and champagne flowing over in plastic cups. MTK's benefactor was so pleased that he offered me a trip back to Budapest. When I told him that I already had a lift he insisted that he'd get me back a lot quicker, so not wishing to seem ungrateful I didn't argue, and told Viktor of the change of plans. An hour later we made our way to the far end of the car park where I was strapped in for the journey back to the capital. Expecting a BMW, a Merc, even a Rolls, I was even more delighted to be flying high on my first ever ride in a private helicopter. I mentioned my flying experience in the hope that I might be invited to co-fly the machine but the pilot knew when he was onto a good thing. 45 minutes flies by and I'm back in time for dinner.

Chapter 65

CHALK AND CHEESECAKE

On a chilly, windy April evening it's a bit like old times at Leyton Stadium. The visiting Norwich fans, come to cheer on their top-of-the-table side, have filled the whole of one stand. East Londoners have turned up to sit in the remaining three-quarters and with much noise and a marked absence of mutually hostile chanting from one set of supporters to the other, it's reminiscent of past times. You could almost imagine that it would be safe to integrate rather than segregate the fans here, but maybe that's wishful thinking.

I've come to run a rule again over Wes Hoolahan and at the same time see how Grant Holt, whom I first saw at Rochdale, lukewarmly recommended to Forest, where he did nothing, then plied his trade unspectacularly at Shrewsbury, is now knocking in goals for fun and is one of the leading scorers in League One. I don't warrant many plaudits for spotting hidden talent here, but then it was five years ago that he first shone at Rochdale.

A day before the match I'm invited to the board room by Steve Dawson, an Orient director. An old Norfolk friend travels up from Basingstoke to accompany me, though I warn him I don't want any gloating when his team slot home their fifth goal. I ring Bolton and ask them to cancel our original tickets, which they do, but in typical Orient fashion I discover when we arrive that they've cancelled Steve Dawson's as well. Peter, my friend, looks crestfallen and hungry, having left Basingstoke the previous night, and by the time I produce the text from Steve, still on my mobile, and new tickets are printed, we have barely ten minutes to gobble down the roast beef and pecan pie that's on offer.

When the team-sheets come round neither Hoolahan nor Holt are in the squad. Good news for Orient, who lie just above the relegation zone by virtue of goal difference. Quite good news for me as I don't have to submit further reports and can get to bed earlier. I'm fairly confident that no-one in the Orient side will be of interest to Bolton. Or anyone else.

It turns out to be one of those memorable nights that justify this insane attraction to the game of soccer. Orient not only score the opening goal, but when they concede an equaliser and look to be on the verge of collapse, they score again. Their new manager, making his home debut, is animated on the touchline and it seems to infuse his players, who don't give the league leaders an inch. Remarkably they hold onto the lead for the whole of the second half.

I'm basking unusually in an after-match glow of victory whilst consuming a coffee and unhealthy cake when the Norwich lady chairman comes and stands beside me. Embarrassed by eating a jam sponge that is clearly not out of her recipe book, I slip it onto an adjacent table, though Delia pretends not to see. Instead, having identified me as an Orient supporter, she expresses her congratulations on the performance and victory in fulsome and generous terms, wishing me and the club the very best for the remainder of the season. I venture to mention my connection with Bolton and suggest that there's still a possibility we might be playing Norwich in next year's Championship. Like everyone else she insists that our players are too good for relegation, though when I suggest she could sign Elmander in exchange for one of her recipes she smiles and politely declines the offer. I've seen Delia on TV programmes galore but in the flesh she impresses as a very nice lady.

I'm then struck by the various differences in character of people who become football chairmen. Taking the slowest lift in the world down to the exit, we are joined by Barry Hearn who has been, I believe, a godsend for the Orient over the past dozen years. He's not, however, renowned for creating soufflés and I detect that he clearly has a bee in his bonnet about Portsmouth and their forthcoming appearance in the cup final. In un-Delia-like terms he is expressing an opinion that they are a bunch of cheats and should be kicked out and without trying to follow his argument I remark that at least the fans have something to cheer about. He doesn't buy it and says they are to blame. I warm to the argument and tell him he's talking a load of cobblers. He responds by telling me I'm talking a load of bollocks. I figure that as he's the owner of the club he's probably entitled to out-insult me, so I don't threaten him with a lawsuit or the promise to never darken the turnstiles again. My assertion, however, that a lot of chairmen are in the game merely for asset-stripping goes down like a lead balloon and I gauge it timely that the lift doors open before I dig any deeper into the hole. But it's not a night for acrimony. After a victory against the leaders even an argument with Barry Hearn can end in smiles. Icing on the cake.

Chapter 66

ASH SUNDAY

Football scouting has the ability to take you into situations beyond the realms of just the game. For my last match report of the season I'm off to Portsmouth to watch them take on Villa. A defiant and peculiar feeling exists around the club and its fans at this moment in time. Already relegated, still uncertain about its future, yet in the cup final for the second time in three years, there is a gallows humour about the place, epitomised by the chant of '1-0 to the Championship' when Pompey take an early lead.

As chance may have it I'm also on an ash-cloud mercy mission to rescue weary travellers returning from the continent. By pure coincidence I'm with my son Alex a day earlier when he gets a call from a mutual friend who, with his extended family of eight, is making his way up to Cherbourg by any means possible, all planes being grounded, to get a ferry across to Portsmouth. Does Alex have any suggestions how they might get back to London at midnight on Sunday? What are the odds of finding someone who, as I do, has access to a minibus, who just happens to be in Portsmouth anyway and who doesn't have to get up and go to work the next morning?

The match finishes about six and I'm fortunate that I can hang around in the Jimmy Dickinson Lounge for a good hour and a half before having a slap-up dinner in McDonald's. It gives me an opportunity to speak briefly to the Portsmouth manager, Avram Grant, who doesn't give me any tips as to how to win next week's

253

game. He then discovers that an attractive young lady is anxious to converse with him and for some reason opts to sit with her rather than me. I get into conversation with another tea-drinker who is not rushing home and learn that he is Cliff Portwood, an ex-Portsmouth player from the early sixties. He recounts his free-scoring days as a winger at Fratton Park before being transferred to Durban, somewhat of a step. Contracted there for two years he played and at the same time became a celebrated pop star, eventually moving to Australia to host his own TV show before someone discovered that he was actually in the country illegally. Only a personal visit by the Aussie Prime Minister paved the way for his presence to be maintained, and he went on to make a World Cup record, singing alongside the likes of Bobby Moore, Gordon Banks and Geoff Hurst. Like so many other ex-players he can rattle off story after story, but unlike most of them he can't decide if he's an ex-footballer or an ex-pop star. If Iceland hadn't exploded I'd have never heard the tale.

Down at the docks there is a stream of weary travellers staggering through the arrivals lounge. Everyone seems to have a story. One group comprises a youth football team whose logo indicates they come from Inverness and a motto that states 'The sky is our limit'. Just so, lads. It's only a mere 600 miles back home if they can make it and I hope they haven't got a midweek fixture. Two Albanian taxi drivers are keen to know how much I'm charging for operating a minibus and when I tell them it's a free service they don't believe me. They boast about the killing they are making thanks to the erupting volcano. I'm not impressed. Clearly it's an ill dust-filled wind that blows nobody any good. Most people arriving seem philosophical and just pleased to be back on English soil, though one tattooed character sporting a vest and beer belly seems to want to give his story to the world. 'Know what it must have felt like now in the war,' he boasts. 'Dunkirk an' all that.' Except you weren't being shelled by German artillery, you hadn't just marched hundreds of miles, you didn't have to risk your life queuing on beaches or wading into the sea and your boat wasn't bombed and targeted by Stukas. Yes mate, just like Dunkirk!

(I later learn that David Lee, another Bolton scout, has at the same time been making his way from the south of France up to Paris. Finding that there were no Eurostar seats available he managed to mingle into the middle of a school group and was ushered through the gates with them onto a train. Still ticketless and prepared to risk being thrown off in mid-undersea-channel, he is then confronted by a returning individual who possesses a spare first-class ticket but wants to sit with his mates in second-class. Would David please take the ticket? You couldn't make it up!)

It's the middle of the night when we make it home and I'm past the wall of tiredness. In fact I wonder about driving back down to the coast to pick up some more arrivals before they are fleeced by opportunist taxi drivers, but common sense kicks in. Instead, at four in the morning, I open the computer and plot the downfall of Portsmouth FC in next week's fixture against Bolton. Once the dust settles there are still points to play for and relegation to be avoided.

Chapter 67

CROUCH END ROVERS

4 January 2000

Whilst working for Southampton I was asked by John Mortimore to travel across to North London and look at a 14-year-old lad playing in a Sunday morning team. It was an unusual request and John seemed a bit embarrassed about it. I learned that the chairman, Rupert Lowe, had been talking to a lady in circumstances that remained unclear, who had told him that her son was an excellent player. Assuring her that the wheels would be put in motion, he passed the info on to John who in turn passed it on to me. We both knew the outcome, but the chairman is the chairman.

John provided me with as many details as he possessed and my first step was to telephone the manager of the lad's team and get as much background as I could. It wasn't a fruitful call. I was answered by the manager's wife who told me, in a somewhat blasé manner, that her husband was in hospital having just taken an overdose. I hoped it was nothing to do with managing the team but I didn't venture to ask her. After I'd expressed my sympathy she said that it was a regular event but explained further that her husband, assuming he recovered, would not be managing the team any more. It was being taken over by a Greek restaurant owner and very helpfully she provided both his name and telephone number.

I trust that Chrysostomos Demetrius Papadopoulos doesn't name restaurants after himself unless they have a big frontage and he knows a cheap signwriter.

I was answered again by a woman, who told me that her husband didn't take phone calls owing to the fact that he was partially deaf. This task developed another layer of unreality. Acting as go-between she told her husband, who was by her side, presumably cooking the moussaka and beef stifado for the evening's menu, the details and purpose of my call, whereupon I was invited to breakfast the following Sunday morning prior to going to watch the match in a park near Crouch End.

Chrys, as he became, was nothing if not hospitable. I arrived at his place at 8am, was ushered into the empty restaurant and seated with him and his wife amidst forty empty tables and then provided with a breakfast of halloumi, olives and Greek garlic sausage served by a waiter who either acted as a night watchman or was a live-in servant abiding somewhere down in the cellars. Most of our conversation was directed through Mrs P, who interpreted through a mixture of slow deliberate English, sign language and smatterings of Greek. When she visited the toilet, as she did three times during the meal, Chrys ventured out on his own with results that were not wholly productive.

'How long you have worked for Southend?'

'Southampton. Only about eight months actually. I worked for Stockport before.'

'Is he! When did he tell you that?'

'Sorry, who?'

'Yes I know. I feel the same.'

Mrs P couldn't come back quickly enough but when she did the discussion took another bizarre turn. Chrys couldn't tell me anything about the lad I'd come to see. In fact he couldn't tell me anything at all about the team as today would be his first game in charge. The previous manager, it seemed, was a very good customer and had passed on the baton before trying to pass on himself. But Chrys regarded this as the first rung on the ladder towards achieving his goal of becoming a full-time football manager. He had a cousin in Cyprus who apparently helped with the Under-16 Nicosia District side so with such connections the mountain would clearly be easy to climb once he got going. The other thing was he would like to know what percentage he might get if this lad was signed by Southend (!) and became one of their players.

I knew already that I should down another cup of Byzantine coffee and get clean away from this madness, but the scenario had the fascination of watching a car accident and I duly accompanied Chrys to his first pre-match get-together.

It got no better. 'We gonna go out and kill them. You hit them hard. Then you kick the ball into their goal, that will show them. You score goals and you kick the ball away if it gets near to our own goal.' Keep it simple, Chrys. Shankly would be proud of you.

'What system are we playing, coach?' asked one of the team.

'That's right,' Chrys replied, 'and you do the same in the second half.'

I duly watched the lad who had brought me to these parts. He scored an own goal after three minutes, gave away a penalty after ten and got booked five minutes later. He was a tall and impressive lad and his jean-suited mum who was cheering from the touchline was even more impressive – maybe Rupert's not such a Rupert after all – but he was not going to make it big in a million years. Sorry mum.

After 25 minutes the team went 4-0 down. Without any warning Chrys marched up to me, spat out the word 'Scaa'da', presented me with his clipboard, on which I saw only one word – 'Difense' – picked up his bags, walked to the car park and drove off. The team, I learned later, never saw him again. I hung around until half-time and then made my own exit, leaving behind the spectacle of a group of young faces eagerly listening to an animated team-talk being delivered by a good-looking woman in tight jeans. I did wonder for a moment whether I was leaving prematurely.

Chapter 68

LAST HAMMERINGS

It's the final weekend of the league season and there's not a lot to do. Colin tells me to go where I fancy so I spend Saturday afternoon at home, listening to Leeds getting promoted and Grimsby dropping out of the Football League after 91 years.

Against all my pessimistic forecasts both Bolton and Orient have stayed up, creeping rather than sprinting over the finishing lines and thereby presumably justifying the changes in managers. It's as clear as can be that new blood will be needed in both camps.

I eye up the Sunday fixtures, consider going to Chelsea to watch them win the Premiership, Arsenal to see them play Fulham reserves, or to West Ham who entertain Manchester City. As both sons are going to Upton Park I join them. Just for fun.

Fun is the predominant emotion, at least on the surface. A fortnight ago I watched West Ham play some of the worst football of the season and then secure their top-flight status by beating Wigan 3-2. City have just lost fourth spot to Spurs and so neither side is out to rupture a tendon and the good humour of the crowd senses it. As the home fans strike up their traditional anthem it's amusing to watch the wives of some of their foreign players vainly attempt to join in. I wonder how 'forever blowing bubbles' sounds in Czech or Portuguese.

The new porn-broker owners glide smoothly into their seats, not having enamoured themselves to either fans or players by their mouthy pronouncements on the team and the manager. It's not the West Ham way of doing things, I'm told. And Barry Fry, treating himself and his wife to a day away from Peterborough, graces the Directors' Box wearing a tasteless striped suit and looking more of a spiv than ever. It's all good fun.

The contest is not top-drawer fare. West Ham play the same wingless game that they have played all season but manage to take the lead. A few minutes later City equalise and from then on there's a gentleman's agreement that anything other than a draw would be a bit unsporting on such a day. Strikers are able to get up and smile when they miss good scoring opportunities, perhaps deflecting attention away from their own lack of ability. Both sets of defenders look less than competent but it's reassuring to note that with one club scores of millions in debt and the other bankrolled by King Midas there's little visible difference in the bodies that sport claret shirts and those in sky blue.

One event above all others makes the day memorable and worthwhile. There are 34,989 people in the stadium, of which about 32,000 must be Hammers fans. But at the mention of Carlos Tevez, and his introduction into the game as a City sub, the whole ground unites in rapturous applause and cheering. Tevez gets more acclaim from the West Ham faithful than any of their own players, and I can't recall any other occasion when an opponent was given such a greeting. (I somehow think that Craig Bellamy might not have received quite the same reception had he been in the City squad.) As Tevez comes on it becomes more extraordinary. I'm wondering what the reaction will be if Carlos scores a goal, but as he touches the ball for the first time, he's booed. There is a clear understanding among the fans here of just where the demarcation lines lie. The fun goes on, and at the end, with the crowd singing 'We love Tevez more than you' he dons a claret shirt and milks the adulation for all it's worth.

The end of any long-lasting event has the ability to produce elements of poignancy, and last games of the season are never any different. Teams struggling and succeeding against relegation produce, I believe, a greater concerted swell of emotion than those who go up or win things. There seems to be much more of a feeling of all being in it together, rather than just watching your favourites do it for you. A lot of people believe that West Ham and other teams around them have survived only because Hull and Burnley have been so poor. I'd concur and include Bolton in that group. The collective sigh around Upton Park is tinged, however, with disquiet. Their popular manager, Zola, is likely to be removed. Some of their players will surely be sold to offset debts – and some need to be. Earlier in the season there was talk of West Ham providing another England trio, the spine for the World Cup of Green in goal, Upson at centre-half and Cole as centre-forward. Green OK. But Upson! Cole! Heaven help us!

Money from the sex trade may dig West Ham out of a hole but it doesn't supply scouts with hospitality. It's therefore thanks to the tannoy that results come in from elsewhere. Bolton finish with a home win; Burnley stick two fingers up as they exit the Premiership, knocking four past Spurs having been 2-0 down. Whilst Chelsea do it with a fabulous 8-0 hammering of Wigan to take their goal tally to 103. Unlike the recent election, there's winning, and there's winning in style.

A week later I decline a chance to attend the Cup Final when a ticket becomes available. Unsure of what prompts this decision, I don't tell anyone for fear of being sectioned. It's not that I have other pressing engagements: I'm on my own for the week so there's not even the glamour of waltzing round Waitrose to tempt me out of the house. Nor is it that I'm sated with football after seeing 67 matches: I've still got South Africa to come. And neither can I put it down to visiting Aldershot at 6pm for their play-off match against Rotherham: they've refused a ticket request.

It gets worse. At 2.45 I settle in front of the box, turn to BBC to find that they're showing an old film and so resignedly switch to ITV to be greeted by adverts. When they return to Wembley some young sweetly-dressed singer performs 'Abide With Me' with a lot of style and a dearth of feeling, then gives it her all for the National Anthem, which can be sung by eight of the assembled players whose country it is. The cameras manage to focus on three of them who surprisingly seem to know the words.

What is it about ITV that they just can't get it right? I've not come across a footballing viewer who doesn't think that the BBC are streets ahead every time. It's not only the annoying interruptions for commercials. For some reason their commentators and their pundits just seem amateurish by comparison, not to mention the intrusive, insensitive and clearly unwelcome enthusiasts who thrust microphones under the noses of players and managers at full-time to ask fatuous questions that even politicians would struggle to answer. What did you feel when you missed the penalty? What does this victory mean to the club? Will you be looking for a new job or more money next season?

I give it fifteen minutes before I go outside to plant runner beans, realising that there is a reason for my apparent indifference. It's the very opposite of indifference. I'm not a Portsmouth fan but I don't want to be present at the final moments of their relegated season to see the end of an era, their last lingering hopes of something extinguished, as I'm convinced they will be. There's enough sadness in the world for me to bathe in; I choose not to go out of my way to seek more.

The bean plants don't necessarily understand this logic when I explain it to them but at least they don't ask questions or try to analyse my mood. As a concession to sanity I resolve to watch the final five minutes. My hope is that against every intelligent forecast and prediction Portsmouth have somehow scraped a win and I'm the idiot who chose to garden whilst the momentous events were unfolding. Alternatively, if Chelsea are going to win then I would like them to break new records and score another seven or eight to make it memorable and to establish their inalienable right to do the double.

It's the worst of all possible scores. A single goal scored by the biggest egotist in the Premiership, just after Boateng takes the worst ever penalty in Wembley history. Does life have to be this cruel? As a character in a film once said, 'I can take the despair. It's the hope I can't stand'. The Chelsea celebrations are understandably callous and their ridiculous dance looks pathetic from my bias-based armchair.

The gloom is lifted a little with scenes from the Scottish final, for once not contested by either of the big two. Dundee United triumph for only the second time in their history, whilst little Ross County emulate the Highland Clearances and bring to Hampden 20,000 supporters, four times the population of Dingwall where they play. No-one there looks in despair. I tell myself to snap out of it.

Then I see that Millwall fans have caused trouble in their play-off match at Huddersfield. What a surprise.

I head for the courgettes.

Chapter 69

FOND FAREWELLS

On a balmy May evening, following the hottest day of the year so far, England sign off with a 3-1 victory over Mexico. The next time they perform for a home crowd the World Cup will have come and gone and the country's footballing exploits, successful or otherwise, will have passed into history.

Wembley is sold out for the occasion and the atmosphere alone makes it worth being there. Save for a section of visiting supporters the whole ground is bathed in red and white from free tee-shirts left on the seats, forming the biggest St George's cross in history: in fact the biggest flag ever seen. There is a tangible sense of patriotism around the place: the healthy and admirable type, not the jingoistic Englishman-abroad edition that too often has been portrayed by imbeciles over the years. The visible presence of soldiers, sailors and airmen, some recently returned from active service, adds to the sense of national pride. It's ironic and poignant that being engaged in a war, albeit far away, adds to a sense of oneness when combined with sporting occasions like this. As if to enhance this, a quick shot of David Beckham is seen during the National Anthem, having just returned from a visit to troops in Afghanistan.

The Wembley crowd invariably impresses. There always seems to be a sense of excitement, of passion, of good humour, even of decorum, as though the ground itself conveys a moral tone to things. Often people are coming here for a once-in-a-lifetime visit for their team to take part in a play-off or an FA Cup final or semi, a momentous occasion, but even for England matches, when the team doesn't perform well, there is a lack of the venom that you might see at other grounds. I recall the stoicism and balanced views expressed in the orderly tube train queues after the disastrous defeat by Croatia a few years back; the general feeling that we got what we deserved and good luck to the Croats.

It makes me wonder, seeing the euphoria here before the game, just what it would be like if we were once again hosting the World Cup finals; how unimaginable the scene would be were England once more to win it. Tonight's game is a friendly, with nothing riding on it except for players to impress the manager and to try to book their seat to South Africa. Yet the 88,000 plus who have turned up give no indication that it's not important: there is enough enthusiasm to overlook the fact that many players on display are not first choices and will not be travelling. It's still an England match.

Mexico play the football and England score the goals. The contrast in styles is fascinating if not reassuring. The visitors manage to retain the ball with skill and confidence that exposes England's failure to do the same thing. Isn't this one of the side's constant besetting weaknesses that has cost us dearly in the past? Thanks to the long neck of Crouch two goals come from set pieces but they are the only times England really threaten. In contrast, Mexico are unlucky not to score but manage deservedly to pull one back before half-time.

During the interval there is an impromptu meeting of a number of scouts attending the game. We are congregated just in front of the press gallery and as we discuss our views I'm sure I can detect Patrick Barclay and his *Times* counterpart leaning forward to pick up some titbits. I'll check his column tomorrow.

The debate inevitably centres around the England squad and their chances of any success in the forthcoming tournament. There is a surprising amount of unanimity and I make some mental notes for future reference to see how spot on or wide of the mark our combined wisdom will prove. Top of the agreed list is the feeling that, unless there is a rabbit in the hat somewhere, our players are not going to bring back the trophy. Tonight's first-half performance, even if it is without some bigger names, adds weight to this opinion.

On the back of the team sheet, in my own private shorthand, I jot down for posterity our generally agreed observations:

GOALKEEPER: Green as No. 1, especially as his first-half display here tonight has kept England in the game – but he's not great on crosses. James can be brilliant and calamitous. Hart is inexperienced.

CONCLUSION: We haven't got a top-class keeper which is essential for any World Cup winners.

DEFENCE: No cover for Ashley Cole if he doesn't play. Leighton Baines looks out of his depth. Johnson on the right is good going forward but not great getting back. King is normally solid in the middle but can he play regularly? Terry has definitely gone off the boil since his naughtiness and Ferdinand still makes gaffes and doesn't inspire us as a captain. Upson and Dawson as stoppers? Oh, please!

CONCLUSION: We don't have a solid defence.

MIDFIELD: Why do Gerrard and Lampard rarely perform for England like they do for their clubs? Walcott's speed is dynamic but he still hasn't learned to use the final ball. Lennon might be a better bet but hasn't proved himself consistently. Milner, Johnson, Huddlestone – contributors to a static midfield. And in a static midfield, when you want someone to get hold of the game by its neck, who do you need? Not Michael Carrick, who camps regularly in no-man's land and who, as one scout asserted, 'breaks wind more often than he breaks sweat'. Room for Joe Cole to do the unexpected, or the untested Scott Parker who might make things happen? Unlikely.

CONCLUSION: We have an undynamic midfield.

STRIKERS: In this match every time Rooney goes to ground there is a collective holding of breath. But did he peak two months ago when he couldn't stop scoring? Is too much expected of him? Crouch, by common consent, does best coming off the bench but his goalscoring record cannot be faulted. Yet he and Rooney don't combine well in open play. Defoe can be anonymous too often, Heskey has all the qualities of a top-notch striker except that he doesn't score goals, and maybe we are down to the emerging Darren Bent, though his miss from three yards which Redknapp ridiculed last season sticks accusingly in the mind.

CONCLUSION: We're not strong up front.

That leaves the manager, who is undoubtedly a good guy, though his deification will certainly not persist after July if England under-achieve. And we probably have some of the best first-aid equipment in the magic sponge bag, so we should be all right.

Perhaps our scepticism is sensible. Four years ago I recall our team going off to claims that we had the new generation of wonder-players, world-beaters, the best squad since 1966. What inspires on paper doesn't always translate onto grass.

The second half of the match sees Glen Johnson produce a third goal, waves of Mexican attacks repelled, authentic Mexican waves from a semi-bored crowd and affectionate valedictory waves from players and supporters at the end of the game. If goodwill, enthusiasm and encouragement can win us games then we're home and dry. Just don't forget the white rabbit, lads!

Chapter 70

THE ITALIAN DISCONNECTION

Three weeks before I'm due to fly to South Africa I get a phone-call:

'Hello Les, it's Paulo.'

'Hello Paulo, how are you?'

'I'm very OK Les, but I have some information to tell you. Les, I am not working for Brescia no more. I'm going to becoming manager of my father's company.'

He pauses. I wait. He carries on pausing. Eventually I say, 'So?'

'So Les, it's not needed now for you to do reports on World Cup.'

All my xenophobic anti-Italian anti-any Johnnie Foreigners with their first-class degrees in Unreliability feelings swell up like a tsunami, but before they erupt into a controlled and very English barrage of invective, balm is outpoured. 'But Les, don't worry. I know you have cancelled your diary to go so the club will still pay for all. You still go if you want go, but not necessary for reports.' My love for the Latin race returns instantly but I have to verify exactly this bizarre arrangement so that it will stand up if need be in an international court.

It's as straightforward as any Italian arrangement can be. I have flights, accommodation and match tickets booked by a club who don't want me to do anything, but clearly now no 'bonus' as was originally suggested. It seems fair enough, though flying 5,631 miles to be a neutral spectator feels like an indulgence too far. So I call Colin and suggest to him that perhaps

Bolton can foot the bill for some extra games in return for me sending in reports on any players I see from lesser teams whilst I'm there.

His response is lukewarm. Is he loosening ties with Bolton or does he know something that I don't? Bolton are not sending anyone to the World Cup and I can't understand the reticence. Like a hooker offering a free service I phone Bobby Hope at West Brom and Keith at Forest. Their responses are the same. No reps from their clubs are going out: they've decided it's too risky. Ray Haughan at Liverpool sends me a text when I offer him a deal: 'Sorry Les, I'm lying on a beach in the Philippines wondering where it all went wrong.' My reply consists of only one word.

A close friend tries to keep things in perspective, adding to a lack of reassurance by several hundredweight:

'Where are you based?'

'Johannesburg.'

'Worst place of all, security-wise.'

'It is? I thought it was places like Soweto you were meant to avoid.'

'Soweto is in Johannesburg!'

I fail to win the geography prize. My friend suggests I fail to win the intelligence prize. When I assert that growing up in an East London ruled by teddy boys and the Kray brothers can't be less risky than 21st-century Jo'burg, he looks at me pityingly and offers only one piece of advice: 'Make sure your travel insurance covers repatriation of your body.'

Chapter 71

BRINGING IT ON

Watching England's opening game on my next-door neighbour's television is a mixture of déjà-vu-ad-nauseam-ad-infinitum. I've lost count of the number of times Andrew and I have sat together, sipping wine, munching peanuts, in unwarranted expectation of an England performance, only for me to creep away two hours later like a scolded dog. We should both know better, yet it's the old irresistible, unintelligent, inexplicable pull over which we have as little control as a pin drawn towards a powerful magnet. When my wife asks me why we do it, why there is always such hype and hope and subsequent misery, I have no answer.

There is a group of us present comprising different sexes and generations. I can't decide whether I'd prefer to watch in company or in splendid isolation. I guess it all depends on the outcome: good to laugh with the world; best to cry alone. I'm grateful that an American friend has declined our offer and is watching elsewhere; the Special Relationship might just come under a bit of a strain if things don't work out.

As he always is, Alex, my son, is nervous and naively optimistic. (Every year he predicts that West Ham will win the Cup). This evening his forecast is that we'll easily beat the Yanks – 'Look at their team!' I've learned to tolerate and ignore such hopes but I find it more difficult to swallow the pundits' fortune-telling, with Kevin Keegan predicting a 4-1 victory, Jurgen Klinsmann confident that England will go all the way. Thank goodness for Adrian Chiles, who doubts if we'll even score a goal in the competition. Having seen all these players in the flesh during this last season, both at club and country level, I remain unconvinced that we can live with the likes of Messi and Tevez, Torres and Fabiano, and I have a feeling we'll get no more than a draw from tonight's game.

Concerned at the risk of boring the assembled gathering, I hold back from expounding once again my belief in the fundamentals of team play, though they remain as strong as ever. Under successive England managers I've maintained to any unfortunate passing listener the view that whether you're a Sunday morning pub team performing on what remains of Hackney Marshes or a side challenging for the Premiership title, playing together regularly is an absolute must. It's surely not a discovery on a par with gravity to realise that when you work alongside players for game after game, you learn to anticipate their decisions, you read situations, you gel together much more successfully than by giving each other a hug and a squeeze before the kick-off. And yet it seems years, decades, since we had anything resembling a stable England eleven, even a stable pattern of play. It worries me, therefore, to learn that Capello has kept his team selection inside his own head until getting on the coach to travel to the ground; that only then do the players know who is and who isn't starting. And to add to doubts is the realisation that right up until the final friendly kick-about he was still experimenting with formations. Tonight's selection apparently has been made to take account of and counter the Americans' strengths in midfield. The Americans' strengths! America!!

Naturally if and when it all comes good the psychology will shut me and my like up for a long time. And after four minutes it's spot on. Alex is already celebrating a wide margin of victory; Keegan is after a pay-rise. Gerrard has captained the side for less than three-hundred seconds before giving them a lead. ITV surpass themselves by missing the goal and showing a Hyundai car advert instead. This is what we've been waiting for.

Except of course, it's not. Scoring the first goal four minutes from the start is not as good as scoring it four minutes from the end, and it doesn't take long before warning signs begin to emerge. Our defence loses out to four crosses, all of which are headed wide but could have gone in. Milner is replaced after half an hour. Nothing much is happening up front, our midfield is not retaining the ball and the Americans are creating more openings than we are. It still takes a keeping error of monumental proportions, though, to give them parity. Perhaps Green was distracted by a passing Hyundai. Perhaps he felt like auditioning for the Tin Man in *The Wizard of Oz*. Alex seems more worried about the flak he himself will get for it being a West Ham player who cocks up than for the fact that England might not win this game. He's sure that the second half will be different.

Once more I refrain from the role of elder statesman but as the game flops towards an uncommendable draw many of the weaknesses that I've seen throughout the season become prominent. Heskey, for all his good link play, fails to convert an excellent one-on-one; Terry's distribution is poor; King isn't fit enough to play the second half; Carragher is done for pace and almost concedes a winning goal; Alex finally admits it's embarrassing. By full-time he is relying on the fact that Algeria and Slovenia, the other two in the group, are much poorer sides. (Where have I heard that before this season?) Capello states that apart from the keeping mistake he thought the team played well. Strange: Italians don't normally like to be in a very small minority.

If history repeats itself we should be able to rest assured. No-one can recall England playing well in their opening game, and even going back into the annals of 1966 I remember a disappointing goalless game against Uruguay that kicked off the tournament. If, however, history doesn't repeat itself; if the unthinkable happens and we fail to trounce the two minnows; if, once more, the past twelve months have seen our team flatter to deceive, then there's a chance I might be coming back on the same plane as my esteemed fellow-countrymen, joined no doubt by Keegan, Klinsmann and the rest of the Clairvoyant Club.

Chapter 72

POT OF GOLD...

'Welcome to South Africa' is blazoned across a wall in the airport terminal. Close by is the additional information of this being 'The Rainbow Country'. As I disembark after a fourteen-hour journey I'm certainly surrounded by all the colours of the rainbow. There are people sporting shirts and hats and flags from all five continents, some quite incongruously. A group of Turkish men are covered in German badges; two Scandinavian-looking blondes are carrying a banner supporting Ghana; a middle-aged man clad in a suit and tie that wouldn't look out of place in Whitehall has a yellow and green bobble-hat on his head – Brazil or South Africa, I can't make out. All here to help take home the little pot of gold at the end of the rainbow.

I've chosen to stay with a friend of my daughter who is working in Johannesburg rather than book in at my allocated hotel. Tom has been here for six months in some kind of journalistic capacity that I can't quite understand. That's par for the course as far as Tom's concerned. In the dozen or so years I've known him since his teenage times he's embarked on a number of bizarre adventures that make my existence feel totally staid. A combination of Tom and Africa strikes me as a potent mixture.

During a brief stop-over in Nairobi I pick up a newspaper that shows the French team huddled together under blankets and a headline that announces: '-10.3˚'. Great! After seeing off the longest winter in the UK since the earth cooled I feel cheated by packing jumpers and gloves for a trip to Africa. Tom suggests I bring a sleeping bag as he might not have enough blankets for me to survive the nights. June 21st, he reminds me, might be the longest day in England but it's the shortest south of the equator.

For some illogical reason Tom, who was raised in South London, became a Luton Town fan at an early age and we travelled together to watch them a few times prior to them sinking out of the league. Before any club had noticed him Tom brought to my attention the performance of a young centre-half, Curtis Davies. Having watched him and passed a recommendation on to my masters at West Brom, he was duly signed by them for £3 million, though not until two years later. Still, proof that Tom has an eye for talent.

For this tournament he has managed to acquire a number of tickets and intends to accompany me to games. The heavy hand of FIFA, however, has not made life easy and I learn that Tom has had to spend eight hours in a bank to prove payment for tickets that FIFA lost. They gain more glory with some nonsensical parking arrangements at the Soccer City stadium, and even before arriving here I've noticed how much prominence is given to those four letters at every opportunity. This is no longer The World Cup, it's The FIFA World Cup. Every training bib from every team, every fourth official, steward and stretcher-bearer has a FIFA reminder on the back, every playback on TV or screens tells the universe that it is FIFA who are running the show. Passable, I think, if you're doing an exemplary job; not too good if you're messing up.

Driving is not one of the skills that Tom has acquired (for which we are truly thankful), so five hours after landing I embark with him by taxi to pick up his boss, a bubbly blonde young Spanish lady called Raquel, whose friend is going to take us to the match. En route Raquel phones to say that her friend has just decided not to drive – no reason offered – so we are now semi-stuffed. Tom asks the taxi driver, who we learn is called Cyprus, if he can take us all the way. There then follows ten minutes in which Tom makes constant phone calls in Spanish whilst distractedly telling Cyprus the wrong way to go, and Cyprus makes phone calls on his mobile in IsiZulu whilst holding his taxi intercom and steering with his knees. Africa. Tom. Health and Safety eat your heart out.

There is a moment when I'm walking the final two kilometres to the stadium (which is as near as the taxi can take us) when I wonder if I shouldn't be watching this at home with family and friends and cheese and Chardonnay. We have no idea how we are getting back after the game. Public transport is a non-starter and our taxi driver has refused to rendezvous despite a lavish offer. (FIFA have apparently advised that they should double their normal fares). Instead he tells us about a petrol station two kilometres further on where taxis will be waiting when the game finishes. And do we believe him!

There is a moment, therefore. But a moment only. If the Soccer City stadium looks impressive from the outside, styled on a calabash, a traditional African bowl but looking to me more like a huge chocolate space-ship, it's phenomenal once inside. 84,485 vibrant, colourful, noisy, unsegregated, happy, beer-drinking bodies provide one of the unforgettable impressions of life, akin to seeing St Mark's Square in Venice for the first time or jumping underneath a speeding catamaran to win a 50p bet. Surrounding me are men and women, boys and girls, from Argentina, Australia, Italy, Japan, Oswaldtwistle, not to mention South Africa and, of course, the followers of the two teams, Brazil and the Ivory Coast. The blaring vuvuzelas which have attracted so much criticism from the TV people seem totally appropriate and I learn they are part of traditional Soweto support, blown long before Sky started laying cables. I'm slightly glad, though, that the old boy sitting behind me seems to have emphysema and can only produce a noise in my ear like a cow passing wind. I'm impressed further by every single one of them falling silent during the two national anthems.

The game is fun too. Ivory Coast have obviously caught some of Sven's natural, boyish enthusiasm and their coach encourages them to go at the Brazilians with confidence and cheek, pinning them back in their own half. Their left back, Tiene, looks interesting, along with their lively No. 9 Tioté, who puts himself about. It brings into relief the insipid, lifeless performance of England in their last match against Algeria and I think about beginning a 'Bring Back Sven' campaign.

Quality tells. For all their pressure the Africans can't cut it in front of goal. Brazil can, expose my left back and take a 3-0 lead before Drogba nods in a consolation, much to the delight of everyone in the stadium except the Brazilian defence. There's still time for a punch-up on the field, which seems out of place in a good-tempered match. A Brazilian player rolls over nine times like he's going downhill after an innocuous challenge; an Ivory Coast defender is struck by a mortar off the ball and then tells the referee that Kaka elbowed him; the referee doesn't see it but clearly judges that the African player is an honest, upright individual so sends Kaka off. The game finishes with hugs and a total lack of recrimination all round. Everywhere I look there are smiles.

The journey back could be a dampener. We ask three police officers where the taxi rank is: none has any idea. We then wander aimlessly like shell-shocked sheep for anyone else to ask in a sea of swarming bodies when suddenly a lady I've been sitting next to spots me among 84,484 other people and asks if we need a lift. It feels like half a miracle. We're almost too grateful to accept. But we do, and two kilometres later we pile into her husband's Land Rover that's equipped for a safari and are dropped home at midnight.

A text is waiting from Alex, indignant that Kaka didn't touch the Ivorian, calling them cheats. What does he know from the other side of the world!

Chapter 73

HOLA!

I watch the Spain–Honduras match accompanied by fourteen Spaniards. Tom, who has worked in Spain, is dressed in a red matador outfit, attracting endless photo requests on his way to, and inside, the stadium. I swap my ticket so I can be seated next to him in the front row of an upper tier, convinced that he will be picked up by TV cameras and beamed across the world. As a back-up attraction I put on my Bolton tie, then text a few people back in England to watch out for us.

Spain are so superior that a final score of 2-0 is a disappointment. There is no-one in the Honduras side who merits a mention, even though Wilson Palacios performs better for them than he usually does for Spurs. Spain's build-up play is impressive – Tom believes they are the best team in the tournament – but their final ball in is sub-standard. Even when it finds Torres in a good scoring position he fluffs all the chances and is subbed before the end. For a striker I'd rate equal best in the Premiership he's having a bad spell, or perhaps a torrid time.

From a scouting point of view the game is a waste of time. Any player who is half-decent has already been picked up by one of the main European teams, so there's no point in suggesting that Bolton have another look at Fabregas or Xabi Alonso. It's a pleasure, though, to watch the attractive football Spain serve up, even if they don't finish well. Arsenal have, for the past few years, been the club most likely to produce this kind of play in the Premiership. On their day I think they are still the best team to watch, and so far in this competition Spain run a close second behind my predicted winners, Argentina, for playing the game with a smile on their faces. It's ironic though that among the freak results so far Spain have lost to Switzerland and could still go out of the competition at the first hurdle.

Why does the England national team not play with this style? I can only conclude that it's because the kind of football we see in our home-grown leagues each week engenders a different approach, one much less concerned with technique and more with directness. It's what English fans seem to like and few I know would swap it for the sort of games seen regularly in Italy, for instance. So do we exchange the beauty for the blood and thunder? How would the national side play if Arsène Wenger became their coach? When Keith Burt watched a recent England Under-21 training session he was astounded at the lack of imagination. 'We train them better at Forest,' he says. 'About eighty per cent of the time is spent on telling them what to do when they lose possession. No wonder we can never keep the ball.' Keith's opinion is that our national coaching scheme is still organised by men with long white beards.

Tom is bullish after the game: a win is a win. His Spanish friends are much more critical of their side, despite the victory. Raquel has clearly acquired a few good old Anglo-Saxon adjectives to convey her opinion. As the invectives are spewed out like poisoned paella I dread to think what vocabulary she might shower on us if she followed England.

Chapter 74

BAFANA BAFANA

Disappointingly, South Africa's fixture against France is being played at Bloemfontein, four hours from Jo'burg, a trip just too far for one day when I don't have a car. With time on my hands I embark on a tour of Soweto and see, like I've seen in other countries, the real meaning of poverty. It comes as a surprise to learn that the area houses – not quite the word – seven million people and stretches over a vast landscape

Spending time in the Apartheid Museum is both informative and moving, though I could easily spend ten not two hours there. Many of the images remind me of sanctions, boycotts, protests and demonstrations in the UK and all over the world that were regularly on our TV screens back in the bad old days. South African cricket and rugby were exiled; no-one had ever heard of them having a football team. Suggesting South Africa for a World Cup venue would have been laughable.

The next best place to watch the hosts take on France is in a bar, squeezed in among a mass of home supporters. It's one of those occasions where glory or despair rests only partially in your own hands. South Africa have to beat France whilst at the same time Uruguay have to overcome Mexico for Bafana Bafana to go through. But there has to be an unlikely combined margin of five goals. Calculators sit next to beer glasses.

I'd love to be part of the celebrations if South Africa can pull it off, but another large chunk of emotion wants to see the French team beaten because they are the French. There is nothing intrinsically anti-Gallic in this, despite the knowledge that the French don't like us, tend to surrender when a motorbike backfires and are better at cooking and sex than the English. Some of my best friends eat snails. The nub of hostility results from the way they cheated their way into the finals via the infamous Henry handball trick. I can imagine at this very moment in time that thousands of pubs and bars in Ireland are as crammed as this one, each containing locals and leprechauns just dying to see the French humiliated as a small compensation for their own unfair dismissal of some months past.

They don't have to wait long. By half-time the South African dream is alive and kicking. Kicking well in fact. France have conceded two goals, had a man sent off and are in complete disarray. Uruguay are one up against Mexico and need to score again whilst South Africa have to pop in another couple themselves.

There could hardly be a greater contrast between the vibrancy in the bar and the body language of the French team as they dejectedly troop off at the break. I'm almost tempted to feel sorry for them but manage with just a little effort to resist. We learn from the TV that the team is being sent back to France on second-class plane tickets, such is their disgrace. Will there be old women with knitting needles awaiting their return? Nicolas Anelka, the ex-Bolton striker, has already been despatched and exiled for a bust-up with the coach, giving the press more ammunition about him being an arrogant, big-headed and totally self-centred player, though when Gary Meson managed him at Bolton for a few months he held a completely opposite opinion of the man and was desperately sorry to see him leave. Player revolts and threatened strikes have made this a very unhappy tournament for the French. So 'Allez les

Bleus', a bit sooner than expected. 'On récolte ce qu'on seme,' as they say.

Almost always it's a sad sad story when dreams are wrecked, but on this afternoon in this bar it's a bit of an exception. Try as they may the home team cannot gouge out another goal and in their efforts to find one they allow the French to score. Uruguay seem happy to sit on their solitary goal and the writing is on the wall well before the final whistle blows.

Yet despite the silence that greets the French goal, the game finishes with the crowd in the stadium, and in this and presumably every other bar in the country, cheering on their favourites to knock in one final, glorious valedictory goal. They don't do it, but it really doesn't matter. Their unfancied heroes are still heroes for having done so well.

It's something else that grabs me. I'm sorry for the disappointment of those around me, pleased at seeing the French go out, but above all I think how amazing it all is to actually be here. The bar is crammed with black, white, mixed-race people cheering on their multi-coloured national side as one in a way that would have been inconceivable a mere twenty years ago. My morning tour throws this miracle into stark relief. I'm not naive enough to think this country is devoid of enormous problems, and it hasn't taken the World Cup to achieve this seeming harmony, but every South African I've spoken to has raved about it coming here. Perhaps for a few weeks it has highlighted to people like me just how incredible this transition has been.

Chapter 75

GERMANY THROUGH AND THROUGH

After another frantic journey across Johannesburg we arrive at the Soccer City stadium ten minutes after Germany kick off against Ghana. I've decided, following England's fantastic 1-0 win over Slovenia, to blow the England vuvuzela that I've bought and wear my England shirt. It's not exactly that belief and confidence have been flooding back but it's now not quite as embarrassing to be seen in it as it was following the Algeria game.

I'm aware of being hugely outnumbered by German supporters, but they in turn are outnumbered by those supporting Ghana, including, it seems, everyone from any African country and me. Not only would it be fun to see Germany go out, but if they happened to win it would mean they play England in the next game, and we all know that we only beat them in finals.

The Germans don't look that good, but true to form their organisation, efficiency and determination help them to grind out a single-goal victory, thanks to an excellent strike from their excellent striker Ozil. Would that Rooney could rediscover form like this. As it happens, both victor and vanquished have cause to celebrate at full-time as due to an Aussie victory elsewhere Ghana go through to the next round, the sole torchbearers now for the African continent. And who should be starring for them, having recently changed nationalities, missed a penalty at Wembley, fouled Michael Ballack and put him out of the World Cup and been ostracised by his own brother as a result, but my old scouting target of Kevin-Prince Boateng. It's a small world.

What is it about the Germans that regularly brings them success? In this World Cup they have impressed in their opening game, then against all the odds lost when playing Serbia, uniquely missing a penalty in the process, and now they get through with the smallest of margins in a way that you knew they would. They haven't exited from the group stages since 1934. How far do tradition and national characteristics influence a football team's performance?

So far in this competition the French have shown themselves to be temperamental and lacking in stomach; the Brazilians have been criticised for playing football that is unattractive and lacking in style, despite it helping them to win; the English have started badly as they always do; some African countries have played with flashes of brilliance and disastrous lack of discipline. All things that we've seen before or that come as no surprise. After the opening games my money is still on Argentina to take the cup. The quality of some of their players shines through a lot of the dross that we've seen so far. More than that though: the despised Maradona, never one of my top hundred favourite people, appears to have established with his players something akin to a love affair. He may cut a ridiculous figure, may have taken to drink and drugs like a cat to milk, may come across at press conferences as a nutter, but as he hugs and kisses his players I wonder if there isn't something of his bizarre personality that rubs off on the team. They seem to be the ones enjoying themselves most at the moment and they can't all be drunk or on drugs. Time will tell if it's all superficial.

Germany Through and Through

Though German people in general are not famed for their exuberance, many of their followers join in the post-match celebrations outside the stadium, not quite matching the chants and dances of the Ghanaians but putting on a decent show. None of them appears bothered about my England shirt – no sly digs, no warnings of things to come, no comment on England's showing so far. Is that because already they think it's all over?

Chapter 76

SIDESHOW

Mishaps now become monotonous on the way to matches and for the third time in four games Tom's organisational skills come a cropper. With plenty of time to make a 4pm kick-off we leave late and Tabo, Tom's driver, zooms in and out of traffic, in his own words, 'like a maniac', until he's stopped by the police, who threaten to cut up his licence on the spot. Pleading and whimpering succeeds in just about redeeming the situation but we then have to find a parking space with time running out.

There are four passengers in the car. The two Spaniards have decided to dress up as Mario and Luigi, Italian characters from some computer game that everyone except me knows about. Tom has chosen to don a suit and wig and arrive as a slimmed-down version of Pavarotti. How he loves dressing up! I can't quite get into the spirit of all this and simply go as a boring Englishman, shorts, braces and a knotted handkerchief on my head.

There is nowhere to park. I attempt to flash my Bolton pass at a few police officers and convince them that we are FIFA officials. They don't even bother to look at the pass. It does occur to me that two blokes dressed as Gameboy images, a dead opera singer and a 1930s seaside icon might not give a totally convincing impression of being FIFA reps.

With time running out we encounter yet another policeman, who clearly indicates he might help us for a certain return favour. We're momentarily flummoxed, wanting to see the game but being shocked by such brazen corruption. It's Tabo who makes the decision: perhaps he's more used to this than we are. He hands over the equivalent of £15, telling the officer that that is all we have in cash. We are let through a barrier but not directed to a parking bay. Bribing a policeman leaves the first sour taste in my mouth since arriving here, and a further young Metro Police officer who looks and acts and talks to us as though she's mentally unbalanced does nothing to rectify the feeling or enhance my admiration for South African police.

We make it late to the game but are in time to see Slovakia go a goal up against Italy. The diminutive Stoch seems to be running the show and a number of Italians who are sitting around me bemoan their team's performance. One puts the blame on Lippi, their coach, for selecting a team with an average age of seventy.

For reigning world champions they do indeed look mediocre. Ball control, speed and work rate are all poorer than their opponents and thanks to amateurish defending they concede a second goal shortly after the interval.

I'm expecting some real hostility towards their team from the fans around me, but it doesn't happen. They are certainly not cheering the Slovakians but they are still laughing. Am I imagining it or is there some feel-good factor that is permeating right through this competition?

When Italy pull a goal back they are on their feet cheering.

When they appear to equalise they become hysterical.

When Howard Webb disallows the equaliser they continue to shout.

When Slovakia pinch a third they barely react.

When Italy score with a minute left they go wild with manic enthusiasm.

And when the final whistle goes the atmosphere hardly changes.

Italy are the first team I see go out of the competition and based on every football experience I've had I don't anticipate the reaction of their supporters. Long after the match finishes they are happy to hang around, mixing and having photographs taken with Slovakian jubilants, waving Mexicans in big hats, a group clad in swimming trunks and tops calling themselves the 'Italian Diving Team 1990' (they turn out to be Australians and I don't understand the date). And Tom, Mario and Luigi, who yet again become a target for dozens of photo calls from dozens of nationalities. I feel slightly second-rate at being anonymous, dressed in what other people must assume is my normal outfit. Getting embroiled in this carnival, I can only hope that if and when England make their exit our fans are likewise caught up in the atmosphere and can go home with grins on their faces, albeit resigned ones.

It takes an hour afterwards to relocate our car but who cares? The celebratory mood has extended to the surrounding streets and we are accompanied all the way back by fans enjoying themselves and wanting more pictures. Tom sums it up aptly when he says that for all the national hysteria about winning and losing, the football feels just like a sideshow.

Chapter 77

A WING AND A PRAYER

As the group stages come to a conclusion I apply for, and am granted, a short extension to my marital exeat pass so as to watch the Americans play Ghana and England take on Germany. For a couple of days in bars and pubs around Johannesburg there is frantic activity, with England fans who have over-optimistically assumed their team would be group leaders so bought tickets for the Rustenburg match, now trying to sell them to needy Yanks and then looking to buy replacements for the England game at Bloemfontein.

Whilst having a meal in a pretentious mock-European covered complex called Monte Casino, housing bars, restaurants and inevitably casinos, I'm caught up in a conversation with a middle-aged couple carrying an England scarf and a Cameroon vuvuzela. One unusual feature is that the man is wearing a dog-collar and I soon discover that he's an Anglican priest, was once nearly chaplain of Scunthorpe United and now works in a church on the outskirts of Johannesburg. His wife comes from Chad but as they don't have a team in the World Cup she's supporting Cameroon as her nearest country.

The man is a football enthusiast and his wife has clearly caught the infection. They seem fascinated to talk to a scout from England and together they ply me with a million pieces of advice and information about different African players I should be spotting, who is going to win the Cup and exactly how England ought to be approaching games. Not every comment is a pearl of wisdom. He tells me that England can beat anybody on their day so long as they score more goals; that Gerrard is the captain of England and it's one of the reasons he's the captain; that 4-5-1 was an English invention that started in Portugal. I'd love to hear one of his sermons! His wife joins in with a comment on Robert Green's howler, asserting that the most vulnerable area for a goalkeeper is between his legs.

Clearly a man of faith, his faith has been somewhat misplaced. Like others, he had bargained on England playing a Saturday game in Rustenburg as leaders, not runners-up, of their section. Like others he now has to get to Bloemfontein on Sunday afternoon if he wants to see them play the Germans. But he's agreed to take a morning service on Sunday and is now desperately working out a way to make the match. Neither he nor his wife drive and she never uses the railway, having once been caught up in a train crash. Flying is the only option but this is proving problematic.

They are both cheerful and confident that the difficulty will be overcome. 'God has solved bigger problems than this,' he tells me. I ask him if God can solve the problem of England's defensive inadequacies. He's not too sure about that one, which disappoints me, and we continue to discuss the various approaches England might take to beat their next opponents.

Just before we depart the man's mobile rings. A smile of satisfaction, though not surprise, spreads across his face as he says, 'Thank you, that's very kind of you. Thank you.' His wife smiles and waits. 'Problem solved my dear. Mr Hartington has offered to fly us there in his Cessna. He's going to have tea with his sister whilst we watch the match.'

A Wing and a Prayer

'Coming in on a wing and a prayer' was an expression first used by a World War Two pilot returning in his disabled plane. It seems to have worked too for the vicar. I wonder if England have anything else to hold on to?

Chapter 78

...AT THE RAINBOW'S END

My season, which began at Leyton Stadium watching the Newcastle Horror Show as their defence conceded six goals, ends eleven months and two days later, 5,000 miles away, witnessing an England performance that makes even Newcastle look good.

I arrive at the match with no gut feelings about the outcome. There is conflict and rivalry spanning a century between the two countries and the two teams, but of what importance is that when twenty-two bodies battle it out on a new day? Pundits on the TV assert that man-for-man England look a stronger squad; that whilst they have started poorly and seem to be improving, Germany have gone backwards since their opening thrashing of Australia. The trouble with pundits is that they always claim to be wise after the event. Analyses are a lot more worthwhile than predictions. Bring on the Man from Mansfield.

England fans around the stadium express confidence, but I wonder if it's more in hope than expectation. I haven't seen the vicar but I trust he's on his knees and not queuing for a burger. Many point out that we have actually managed to beat Germany since 1966, and not only the 5-1 rout that brought us most happiness. They have a young and relatively inexperienced side; we have players who have regularly trodden the big stages. It's all about the present and not the past. I tell myself this over and over again but the images of missed penalties and goalkeeping blunders won't be banished easily.

Before the match starts I am invited to share an authentic German bratwurst with a group of opposition supporters who seem uncharacteristically nervous. So far in this World Cup I've not met many supporters who don't think that their team is rubbish. Except the Argentineans! And maybe for good reasons. The atmosphere here reflects the same bonhomie as elsewhere, at least at the start of the match. It's a 3pm kick-off. England are in red, the Germans in white. And the last time we had that combination...

By 4.30pm history has been recorded, infamy is etched into World Cup annals and England are on the way to being dumped out of the tournament. In spite of the anger I feel about the goal that wasn't, a goal that could well have resulted in a different outcome, there is a kind of ironic symmetry that is certainly not lost on the German supporters around me. Looking at them, there are few who would remember 1966, many who were not even born. But they all know about the turning point in that game, about the Russian linesman who robbed them of glory. Would that we had a Russian linesman at this game, or even a Uruguayan with half-decent eyesight. What 40,000 people in the stadium can see, what the man next to me holding a white stick can see, the linesman and referee, both well-placed, fail to spot.

I'm in a quandary. Never having been an advocate of technology I now cannot defend its absence. When I hear that many countries, including England, voted for its inclusion, and that FIFA and in particular Sepp Blatter, who is at the match, blocked the idea, an unrighteous anger surfaces inside me. At times like this it's good to have someone to blame.

By the end of the game, however, there is no avoiding the stark reality that England have been awful. I'm glad in a way not to have lost by a single goal: that would have given the injustice a jagged edge. But our heaviest World Cup finals defeat is harder to swallow than it ought to be. All that has happened is that warning signs, spotted and commented on weeks and months ago, have turned into a fully-fledged disaster, killing off any hopes or expectations that football would do its regular thing of throwing up surprises and making the pessimists and doom-predictors look like a bunch of defeatists.

The inquests and recriminations begin before the final whistle blows. They will go on long into the future and millions of words will be written and discussed about them. Seeing the German goals fly in and knowing the game is up revives the feelings of past exits. It resembles to me the moment when you are told you haven't got the job you've been interviewed for after weeks of preparation. The man sitting next to me likens it to seeing the woman you love marry someone else. Finality. A kindly South African lady gives us both a hug and reminds us that no-one has been killed.

The disappointment has several tentacles but none bigger than Wayne's waning. If I'd been sent to look at Rooney from a scouting point of view he'd have got an emphatic thumbs down in this match, as well as the previous three. No England performance has been as lacklustre, a shard of the player he was two months ago. Touch, control, passing, shooting – there wasn't a positive to his game. He didn't even get booked out of spilling frustration. The questions abound. Has he been fully fit? Has the weight of expectation lain too heavily on him? Has the manager played him in his most effective role? Is he a happy boy?

Someone near me points out that the most successful international managers are also fluent in their adopted languages. Wenger and Mourinho are examples; even Ferguson can make himself understood in English. Listening to Capello being interviewed can be a painful process. Not only does he require a translator on hand, but his answers are often embarrassingly stock and off the point. How successfully then does he communicate with players needing a half-time dressing-down or an arm round the shoulder to encourage? I struggle to envisage him in the changing room, sending out his team with the cry ringing in their ears of 'Get stuck in. Give it all you've got. Bleed for your country!'

There is some small solace in the fact that not a single English fan is arrested for yobbish behaviour. It would be nice to think that the thugs have been eliminated as well as the team. Though this is a smaller stadium the good vibes that I've experienced elsewhere have continued here and I'm impressed by the realistic and philosophical reaction of the England fans. But it's not much compensation for the ultimate disappointment.

For many years now I have been convinced that I could make a better job of being Prime Minister than the incumbent, or Archbishop of Canterbury, and, of course, the England football manager. I still await the call. But given that I'm in a large company of people who know how to pick and run the team better than Capello, one thing to me stands out above all others as inexplicable: the £6-million-a-year question that could feature on a logic paper for nine-year-olds.

Your team is two goals behind with 25 minutes to play. They aren't creating a lot and don't look threatening. On the bench you have a choice of two strikers. One who has a reputation for not scoring goals, who has notched up no more than five for his club all season, two for England in the past seven years and who has already in this tournament missed a one-on-one that might have taken England to the top of their group. The other happens to be the most prolific goalscorer for England that they have at the moment, netting eighteen times in thirty-five games, many as sub, and who has had about twenty minutes on the pitch in the four games so far. It's a do-or-die situation, score or go out. Which one do you choose?

Perhaps one day I will discover the reason behind the decision that leaves Crouch a spectator on the bench and brings on Heskey to be little more than a spectator on the field. I think we might be entitled as observers and fans to require a manager being paid so much to get the big calls right. That one wasn't.

I leave South Africa with a mixture of feelings, pleased to have made it here, to have been part of the festivities, regretful that my team will be following me home in a day or so. Contrary to the numerous dire warnings I've avoided being robbed or kidnapped or killed and I haven't frozen to death at night. Many South Africans have expressed their desire to paint a different impression of their country to the one that was so often described to me. But I'm aware too that there's another side to the coin.

As chance would have it I fly back seated next to Michel, a French film director, who informs me that he works part-time as a scout for Paris St Germain. There is an immediate empathy established, both having suffered at the hands of our national teams, but we avoid dwelling on the negatives and talk generally about our roles with the clubs who employ us.

We exchange snapshots of the past season. He tells me about sitting behind the King of Lesotho and being offered some chocolate toffees by his bodyguards. I recount seeing Mick Jagger with Bill Clinton, cheering on the USA as though he were a natural son of Uncle Sam and then the very next day supporting his home country like a true follower of St George. Neither game produced much satisfaction.

Both of us have enjoyed taking guests to games. I talk about inviting to Chelsea to see his first ever soccer match a Canadian friend who then adopted himself as the club's talisman, claimed a share in their Double success and initiated the Hamilton, Ontario, branch of the Blues' Supporters Club. Current membership: one; of an American evangelist who was keen to go to some matches, despite my qualms about his reaction to some of the language which wasn't exactly biblical, and chanting that didn't emanate from *Ancient & Modern*. I need not have worried, discovering on our trips that he spent a year in Britain a decade ago and was on the books at Stockport County as a highly gifted player. Amen!

Michel tops this by telling me he is acquainted with famous French stars and has taken Brigitte Bardot to a game recently. No, unfortunately he doesn't know Keira Knightley! 'But I'm ready for a rest now,' he says. 'I don't want to see any more football for a while. I need the battery to be recharged.' I feel the same. With England's exit the World Cup that I leave behind is now of passing interest rather than of vital importance. I may or may not watch more games on the box, may switch allegiances to Wimbledon and cricket, Strauss and Andy Murray. 'In fact', he adds, 'I might give it up completely.' The depth of his malaise surprises me.

'Why?' I ask.

A Gallic shrug responds. A minute later he adds, 'Maybe I cannot be bothered. Can you? Can you be bothered to start again in another month?'

Can I be bothered? I think hard for a few seconds. Can I be bothered? Another season of being paid to watch football matches. Of getting Directors' Box seats at Arsenal, Chelsea, Tottenham, with hospitality thrown in. Meeting managers and coaches and players and scouts. Maybe the occasional expenses-paid foreign trip added to the shopping basket. Can I be bothered? I think hard. I nod in response.

'Well,' I respond resignedly, 'someone's got to do it.'

Other books from SportsBooks

The Boys from the Black Country
Mark Gold
The author looks at the history of his club, Wolverhampton Wanderers, and his town with an affectionate and humorous eye. From Victorian times to the razzmatazz of the Premier League, *The Boys from the Black Country* tells the story of the club from the viewpoint of a fan and historian. This is football history with a difference. Alongside an original account of all the club's highs and lows Mark Gold brings a comic touch to parts of Wolves' glorious (and not so glorious) past. Where else could you find Geoffrey Boycott and Henry Blofeld commentating on the team's first FA Cup appearance in 1893, or discover what sort of terrace chant Wolves supporter Sir Edward Elgar might compose were he alive today.
9781899 96 3
£7.99
Paperback

Stan Anderson – captain of the north
Stan Anderson is the only man to have captained the north east's three big clubs – Sunderland, Newcastle and Middlesbrough. Indeed only three players have played for all three. Stan was also a member of the England squad for the 1962 World Cup in Chile and he remembers the great players he played alongside such as Duncan Edwards and Bobby Charlton. His stories of

financial double dealing by Sunderland shows just how players were treated as serfs in the 1950s and '60s. Written with Mark Metcalf.
9781899807 98 7
£17.99
Hardback

The Teams of Sunderland AFC
Paul Days and Brian Leng
The authors, both long-time Sunderland supporters who have contributed to many books over the years, have collected together as many of Sunderland AFC team photographs as they could find. The first is from 1884–85 and the latest from 2010. This is a true labour of love and a great historical record.
9781899807 97 0
£25.00
Hardback

The FA Cup 50 Years On
Mark Metcalf
When Wolverhampton Wanderers beat Blackburn Rovers 3-0 in the 1960 FA Cup final, the competition was king. Players preferred an FA Cup winners medal to topping the League. Mark Metcalf spoke to players and fans involved in the final to paint a picture of the FA Cup that year and the final in particular.
9781899807 91 8
£7.99
Paperback

William Garbutt – The Father of Italian Football
Paul Edgerton
In Italy managers are called 'mister' and the habit goes

back to William Garbutt, who, unable to play any more following injury at the age of 29, went from Blackburn Rovers to coach Genoa. He also coached Roma, Napoli, AC Milan and Athletic Bilbao during a career which also saw him help coach the Italian national team. When he died his obituary was carried in most Italian papers but his passing was ignored in England.
9781899807 82 6
£7.99
Paperback

A Develyshe Pastime
Graham Hughes
The modern game of football is thought to have its origins in 12th century England. Certainly once the Victorians began organising it in the latter half of the 19th century it spread around the world in various forms. American and Canadian football, Rugby League and Union, Aussies Rules and Gaelic football all have their roots in the rough games played between villages in mediaeval England. Graham Hughes traces the paths the various disciplines took and profiles the men who turned them into major sports.
9781899807 79 6
£17.99
Hardback

Chapped Legs and Punctured Balls
Paul Cooper lived for football like most other 1960s kids and this is his account, both hilarious and nostalgic, of the things that went with the game in those more innocent times – the clothes and shoes kids wore, the balls they played with, from the very rare leather case ball with its occasionally crippling lace to the stone that was used in the playground if nothing else was

available.
9781899807 77 2
£5.99
Paperback

Passport to Football
Stuart Fuller, author of four books of travel guides to football and a well-known blogger on football related matters, brings together his experiences on watching football in far-flung places too numerous to mention here, although they do include Moscow, Macedonia, Klagenfurt, Budapest, and Kazakhstan. Stuart brings an experienced and humorous eye to the business of watching the beautiful game, noting for example that in a game between Istanbul BBS and Rizaspor an off-side goal was allowed to stand because the linesman was arguing with the bench of the team against which he had just given a free-kick!
9781899807 83 3
£14.99
Paperback

Tales from the Gwladys Street
Fans have been having a rough time of it in recent years. Clubs have hiked their admission prices while TV demands have resulted in odd kick-off times which often mean difficult journeys. But still they flock to football matches. David Cregeen and Jonathan Mumford tells the story of one club, Everton, through the mouths of their fans and players. The resulting stories show how obsessive football fans can be and how they seek humour in every situation. The stories are from Evertonians but the type of experiences recalled are not unique to one club.

9781899807 89 5
£12.99
Paperback

Finn McCool's Football Club
Stephen Rea was a typical ex-pat in the US. The former Belfast journalist needed somewhere to watch and play football (or soccer as they insist on calling it over there). He found Finn McCool's Irish bar where a diverse collection of nationalities made up the regulars and the football team. They even began to get serious, joining a league. But then Hurricane Katrina struck. Rea's book is both a wry look at an obsession with football and an account of what happened to some of those who suffered one of the US's worst disasters, with an official death toll of 1,100. Many of the team and pub regulars were among those affected by the tragedy.
9781899807 86 4
£8.99
Paperback

Modern Football is Rubbish
Nick Davidson and Shaun Hunt are going through a midlife crisis as far as football is concerned. Now they've reached early middle-age they are wondering what has happened to the beautiful game. Where have all the muddy pitches gone they wonder? They wallow in nostalgia for 3pm Saturday kick-offs and cup upsets and they rant against inflated egos, spiralling salaries and satellite TV. And they wonder about men in tights and gloves.
9781899807 71 0
£6.88

Paperback
Charlie Hurley – The Greatest Centre Half the World has ever seen
Mark Metcalf
Charlie Hurley was not only a great player, he was one of the characters who illuminated football in the 1950s and '60s. He tells of clashes with another footballing great, Jim Baxter, his disputes with the board at Reading when he became a manager and the uncompromising attitude of players and managers during his playing days. Born in Cork, but raised in Essex from the age of seven months, Charlie started his playing career with Millwall before joining Sunderland in 1957. He was to make 400 appearances before leaving for Bolton Wanderers in 1969.
9781899807 69 7
Price £17.99
Hardback

The World at their Feet – Northern Ireland in Sweden
Ronnie Hanna
The story of Northern Ireland's first trip to the World Cup finals when, despite being the smallest country, they reached the quarter-finals. Able to pick only 17 players instead of the 22 they were allowed by FIFA, Northern Ireland were eventually beaten by France.
9781899807 74 1
Price £7.99
Paperback

Memories of George Best
Chris Hilton & Ian Cole
Malcolm Brodie, of the *Belfast Telegraph* who covered George Best throughout his brilliant and ill-starred career,

called this 'the best Best book ever'. The authors talked to many of the Manchester United star's contemporaries to find out the true story of the wayward genius.
9781899807 57 4
Price £14.99
Paperback

From Sheffield with Love
Brendan Murphy
Published to celebrate the 150th anniversary of Sheffield FC, the world's oldest football club. The book charts the rise of organised football in Sheffield and Nottingham, the two oldest centres of the game.
9781899807 56 7
Price £8.99
Paperback

The Irish Uprising
Andy Dawson
The story of Roy Keane's dramatic first season at Sunderland, which ended with promotion to the Premier League.
9781899807 60 4
Price £10.99
Paperback

Accrington Stanley – the club that wouldn't die
Phil Whalley
Fan and writer Phil Whalley charts the comeback of Accrington Stanley the club which resigned from the Football League in the early '60s. After going bust they re-formed in 1968 and began an astonishing climb back to the League.
1899807 47 0
Price £16.99
Hardback

The Victory Tests – England v Australia 1945
Mark Rowe

The five Tests between England and the Australian Services fulfilled the public appetite for sport following the end of the war in Europe. It gave the men who played in them the chance to indulge in harmless fun for once. The result was a 2-2 draw played in sportsmanship and with a sense of camaraderie missing from the modern game. Mark Rowe uncovered the full extent of legendary Australian all-rounder Keith Miller's war record – not what is has grown to be – and spoke to the surviving players in a lovingly crafted book.

9781899807 80 2
£17.99
Hardback

The Rebel Tours – Cricket's Crisis of Conscience
Peter May

The title says it all. After the d'Oliveira affair cut official ties between South Africa and England, the leading players organised tours of the Republic under the slogan that sport and politics should not mix.

The reaction of the English establishment shows in the cover. Mike Gatting, David Graveney and John Emburey face the press and although they were all banned from the international game all three were welcomed back into the establishment with a rapidity that disturbed some obserrvers. Peter May talked to the people involved on both sides of the fence.

9781899807 80 2
£17.99
Hardback